Keepin' It Hushed

AFRICAN AMERICAN LIFE SERIES

*A complete listing of the books in this series
can be found online at wsupress.wayne.edu*

SERIES EDITOR

Melba Joyce Boyd
Department of Africana Studies, Wayne State University

VORRIS L. NUNLEY

THE BARBERSHOP

Keepin' It

AND AFRICAN AMERICAN

Hushed

HUSH HARBOR RHETORIC

 Wayne State University Press • Detroit

15 14 13 12 11   5 4 3 2 1

LIBRARY OF CONGRESS CATALOGING-IN-PUBLICATION DATA
Nunley, Vorris.
Keepin' it hushed : barbershops and African American hush harbor rhetoric / Vorris L. Nunley.
p. cm. — (African American life series)
Includes bibliographical references and index.
ISBN 978-0-8143-3348-8 (pbk. : alk. paper)
1. African Americans—Languages. 2. American literature—African American authors—
History and criticism. 3. English language—United States—Rhetoric. 4. Popular culture—
United States. 5. Barbershops—United States. 6. African Americans in literature.
7. African Americans—Communication. 8. Black English—United States. 9. Literacy—
United States. I. Title.
PE3102.N42N86 2010
895.6'09—dc22
2010033646

Designed and typeset by Sharp Des!gns, Inc.
Composed in Meta Serif

Contents

Acknowledgments

THIS PROJECT COULD NOT HAVE BEEN COMPLETED WITHOUT THE COMMITMENT, faith, endurance, and belief of many folks. I would like to mention a few. I thank my mother, Doris J. Nunley (who had she been fortunate enough to be born in another era, could have obtained a Ph.D. well before me), and father, Lafayette E. Nunley, whose hard work, sacrifice, sense of decency, commitment to justice, love, endurance, and courage were models for my own achievement. My brother Phenoyd. Your depth of character, strength, faith, and vision are an inspiration. Aunt Edna, you were there when I needed you. Cathy Lyons, your practical wisdom, intelligence, commitment to the well-being of others, and your sense of self remind me of the best of what human beings can be. Beverly Silverstein, your faith in my ability never wavered, your understanding and support lifted me, and your care made all the difference. Thank you. Cheryl Glenn, your verbal, material, and scholarly support was invaluable. Jon Olson, you are a class act. It is people like you—few indeed—that remind me that race does not have to diminish personal and human relations. Joyce Wilusz, thank you for your effort, kindness, and patience.

Howard and Cedric, your friendship, support, and lack of ego helped me get through. Kristin, your friendship, support, and kindness made all the difference. Deborah Atwater, you made my project, not your ego, your focus. Your presence was invaluable. Tiffany and Michelle, your reading of the manuscript improved it immensely. Traise, your reading of the manuscript and discussions of what to expect improved the book and made the unexpected more tolerable. Thank you. Bernard W. Bell, your insights were invaluable. You were there for me when it counted. Elaine Richardson, Dr. E., you have always treated me as though you could learn from me, as well as instruct me. You did not domesticate your cultural impulses to be more acceptable to others. I admire you for both qualities. Jodi, your generosity and care made all the difference. Dylan, Setsu, and Tammy, you treated me like family and helped me ward off insanity.

Keith Gilyard, your advice and mentorship on the professional and personal levels have been invaluable. You went beyond the call of duty to nurture this project through. You are a model for how an African American male can be scholarly, intelligent, reflective, and still be Black—Black as a verb and as a noun.

Finally, Joyce Johnson, your faith in me exceeded my own, your vision for me was broader than my own, and you saw in me what I did not see in myself. Your commitment and spirit infuse me. Your friendship has made me both a more complex and better human being.

There is nothing like a Negro barbershop for hearing
what Negroes really believe.

RALPH ELLISON, interview

Coupling rhetoric to epistemology is a significant
gesture in my work because rhetoric itself is a serious
philosophical subject that involves not only the
transmission, but also the generation of knowledge.

MICHAEL LEFF, in James Berlin's *Rhetoric and Reality*

Overture/Head

We Wear the Mask and the Bit

We wear the mask that grins and lies,
It hides our cheeks, and shades our eyes,—
This debt we pay to human guile

PAUL LAURENCE DUNBAR, "We Wear the Mask"

ONE HUNDRED AND FOURTEEN YEARS AFTER THE PUBLISHING OF DUNBAR'S poem, Blacks still speak differently in front of White folks and others in the public sphere: Black folks still wear the mask. The mask does more than grin and lie. It domesticates, disciplines, and commodifies African American rhetorics and African American subjectivities: the mask does not come free. The cost: African American rhetorics and their affiliated epistemes (knowledges), politics, and subjectivities are hollowed out for more acceptable public consumption.

Fortunately, some African American rhetoricians are different. They make it plain. They embrace African American *parrhesia* (*Speaking frankly. Speaking truth to power.*), increasing American rhetorical sovereignty; they refuse the bit and the mask; speak candidly in front of both hush harbor and more public sphere audiences. In short, they speak their minds in front of White folks.

Muhammad Ali was different. *Keepin' It Hushed* is a genealogy about rhetorics, knowledges, and spaces, a critical tradition where Black folks can be themselves, assert their subjectivities, and cast their rhetorical buckets down where they are and hope to be.

Ironically, for all of the theoretically astute, socially constructed, celebration of post-structural, postcolonial, antifoundationlist, antiessentalist, post-racial optimism contextualizing the aftermath of the election of President Barack Obama, the mask and the bit remain: Black folks mostly still avoid speaking frankly in front of Whites or in the public sphere—particularly about race and Black anger—which is still understood to be hegemonically White, heteronormative, male, and *dangerous.* The public sphere for African Americans remains what Saydia Hartman refers to as *scenes of subjection,* geographies of terror and self-making where African American rhetorics (or knowledges) and worldviews informing African American life and culture are trivialized or marginalized.[1] As such, these knowledges continue to be, in their most substantive forms, relegated to hidden African American spaces, thereby bracketing these knowledges out of democratic deliberation. In short, *Keepin' It Hushed* is a spatial and rhetorical genealogy; it is about the spaces where such talk has occurred during and since the Middle Passage and the enslavement of the minds so often kept to themselves; and it is about the spatiality where, since the early twentieth century, Black men could be philosophers and fools, thoughtful and ignorant, progressive and sexist, but mostly where they could be everything that being human allows: the spatiality referred to as the *barbershop.*

Keepin' It Hushed excavates, theorizes, and reclaims a residual and emergent genealogy/tradition of African American rhetoric and knowledges frequently alluded to but *rarely named,* theorized, or taken into account in the public sphere or in public spaces because of the danger of its hidden transcripts containing Black perspectives. This is a tradition/genealogy of danger in both its secular or sacred manifestations, reaching back into the mists of African American life and culture, back into both the Middle Passage and the Enslavement; yet, remaining so relevant to the current zeitgeist that a Black man from an Ivy League school could not be elected president without addressing its words, its force, its *nommo* (the material and symbolic power of the spoken word): African American hush harbor rhetoric (AAHHR).

To not know this rhetoric is to not know Black people, their subjectivities, their perspectives. Ralph Ellison's *Invisible Man* illuminates the significance of these secular and sacred rhetorics on the lower frequencies to the Marxist, Brother Jack:

> Ask your wife to take you around to the gin mills and the barber shops and the juke joints and the churches, Brother. Yes, and the beauty parlors on Saturdays when they're frying hair. A whole unrecorded history is spoken then, Brother. You wouldn't believe it but it's true. Tell her to take you to stand in the areaway of a cheap tenement at night and listen to what is said. Put her out on the corner, let her tell you what's being put down.[2]

As *Keepin' It Hushed* will illustrate, AAHHR remains a powerful aspect of African American rhetoric containing and conveying African American epistemes and rationalities central to African American life and culture and to what Black folks are puttin' down. Away from the discipling gaze of whiteness. This rhetoric emerges from camouflaged spaces and places. Spatialities, rhetorics, and knowledges so intertwined into an ontology of what it means to be Black that the man who was to become the first Black president was married in and nurtured in its womb for over two decades. Enslaved and free African Americans referred to these spatialities as *hush harbors.*

As I discuss in the last chapter, public sphere rationalities, discourse, and rhetoric often require a *public podium–auction block rhetoric* that decenters the distinctive tropes, knowledges, and perspectives of hush harbor rhetoric typically deployed in front of primarily Black audiences in hush harbors. Like smooth jazz, public podium–auction block rhetoric requires the smoothing out of Black noise, dissonance, angularity, and improvisation tethered to African American memories, experiences, and knowledges smoothed and flattened into a more palatable brew of domesticated, tolerant, consumer-friendly Blackness. Is the aforementioned understanding limited to so-called militant, angry Black radicals mired in the 1960s, fossilized in the amber of an atavistic identity politics? No. From David Walker and Maria W. Stewart,

Frederick Douglass and Dr. Martin Luther King Jr., to Ralph Ellison, John Oliver Killens, Toni Morrison, bell hooks, Kara Walker, Chris Rock, Gwendolyn Brooks, Cornel West, Melissa Harris-Lacewell, and the animated series *The Boondocks* (2005–present); from poetry to novels, from Negro spirituals to hip-hop, from literature to urban pulp novels; all either refer to, write from and about, or are inspired by these Black rhetorics and spatialities. All are informed by an awareness of not only how Blackness and Black knowledges are tethered, not sutured, to such African American spatialities and rhetorics, but also of how rhetorical *kairos* (opportune moment)—which always involves material-rhetorical spatiality—influences the donning or the removing of the hush harbor mask.

Yet, as ubiquitous, pervasive, and important as these Black spatialities and rhetorics are to African American culture, politics, knowledge, and life, African American hush harbors (AAHHs) and what I referred to earlier as AAHHR have not only been *overlooked* and undertheorized as a tradition of African American rhetoric, but, as I will use Barbara Christian, Michelle Wallace, Kenneth Burke, Judith Butler, and James Berlin and others to illustrate, have also not been *connected to rhetoric and the manufacturing of ontology and knowledge.* Not recognized as a singularity that exists based on its own assumptions, investments, and orientations about the nature and/or practices informing theory, reality, and the manufacturing of knowledge, African American culture, and the AAHHRs affiliated with it, is reduced to mere difference and otherness, to identity and culture. As with queer, womanist, feminist, and other so-called ethnic or cultural rhetorics that are often alluded to but are rarely taken into account as theoretically substantive outside of concerns with identity and culture, AAHHR is rendered almost irrelevant to the production and manufacture of knowledge. In short, as Aristotle's notion of what circulates as both culturally tethered (Greek/Athenian) and as an essential rhetorical nomenclature, African American *improvisation* remains tethered to African Americans and African American culture with little or no migration into the general rhetorical nomenclature.

Precluding such migrations into the nomenclature and theory of both the rhetorical and the philosophical creates the conditions of possibility for the disavowal of African American knowledge from expertise and knowledge in the public sphere, aiding and abetting the exclusion of AAHHR knowledges anchored in African American culture from the realm of reasonable debate. As such, African American *political rationalities*—a term I explain later in the chapter—that expand what is sayable and intelligible are trivialized and ignored, narrowing and domesticating what circulates and counts as democracy.

Through an interdisciplinary method traversing critical theory, philosophy, cultural studies, and rhetoric, as well as culling insights from literature, religion, history, popular culture, and other fields and disciplines, *Keepin' It Hushed* attempts to rectify the aforementioned scholarly, theoretical, and cultural exclusions and disavowals.

In the movie *Barbershop* (2002)—the barbershop is a primary hush harbor in African American culture and the focus of this study—the philosopher-barber Eddie adroitly and pithily taps into the hush harbor reservoir of African American rhetoric and episteme informed by the quotidian of Black life, culture, and rhetoric to which I refer: "Now I probably would not say this in front of white folks, but in front of ya'll I am going to speak my mind."

And that is exactly what Muhammad Ali did.

After winning the heavyweight championship of the world, and then proclaiming himself to be both a Black Muslim and a believer in Islam, Ali had this to say about himself at a news conference: "I am America. I am the part you won't recognize. But get used to me. Black, confident, cocky; my name, not yours; my religion, not yours; my goals, my own; get used to me."[3] Through such a proclamation, Ali attempted to resculpt and transgress the national political rationality around Blackness and masculinity that would construct him and his performance of an undomesticated and unforgivable Blackness locating him both outside of and within the excess of what it meant to be American. Ali resisted staying in his place.

Unlike too many African American athletes and entertainers, Ali's rhetoric was more than puffery, more than posturing. Beyond mere trash talk, Ali's discourse—its tone, content, wit, and form—reflected the bold, brassy, and fearless talk and rationalities I often heard in Black spaces such as the pool hall, the church, and the barbershop. Such talk privileges protean Black worldviews and knowledges that challenge the political rationalities that buttress White comfort in the public sphere to which African American public podium–auction block rhetoric often attends. By African American podium–auction block rhetoric I refer to rhetoric by African Americans while taking into account Black/African American worldviews, epistemes (knowledges), tropes and commonplaces intended to identify with and persuade primarily African American audiences; podium–auction block rhetoric by African American rhetors privileges more mainstream American (read: White), worldviews, epistemes, and tropes that are hegemonic, and therefore offer a more comforting, domesticated, consumable, and marketable Blackness that is more rhetorically and politically legible and acceptable. I will return to African American hush harbor and African American public podium–auction block rhetoric comparisons later in this chapter in my discussion of *The Boondocks* and when I address President Barack Obama's "Race Speech" in the final chapter.

My primary interest in hush harbors and AAHHR is not merely as sites of difference, ethnography, anthropology, or sociology—though some, unfortunately, will reduce this project to these registers because they cannot think of African American culture outside of the aforementioned categories, as normative nomenclature—I am interested in hush harbor and AAHHR as sites of an African American rhetorical tradition and of knowledge generation. My project then is one of both theory and of recovery. Therefore, I understand *Keepin' It Hushed* as a serious philosophical project that couples rhetoric to epistemology and that resists a reduction of rhetoric or Blackness to mere decoration, otherness, or excess. Such an understanding of rhetoric and AAHHR is necessary because of a normalized resistance to and misunderstanding of rhetoric that is over twenty-five hundred years old. It is tenable to think of rhetoric and African American culture as sites of philosophy and of knowledge because, as Michael Leff notes in James Berlin's discussion of the new rhetoric, "coupling rhetoric to epistemology is a significant gesture in my work because rhetoric itself is a serious philosophical subject that involves not only the transmission, but also the generation, of knowledge."[4] Such a project has wider implications in an epoch of photoshopped, airbrushed, media-mediated images of reality, where the boundaries between news as journalism, advocacy, and consumer product blurs, and where an imagined postideological and postrhetorical society is in fact constituted on ideological-spatial-rhetorical terrain. Understanding rhetoric, then as more than eloquence and deceptive speech seems critical.

Keepin' It Hushed as an epistemological enterprise, resists the kinds of epistemic violence that jettisons African American life, culture, and knowledge from the palace of the subject into the dungeon of the object, from the mansions of the theoretical to the caves of difference, and from the sanctuary of relevance into the cellar of identity politics by ignoring African American suppositions about the construction of reality and meaning. AAHHR takes African American suppositions about the construction of reality and meaning to be normative—for most African Americans.

Rather than providing an ethnography of a particular barbershop, *Keepin' It Hushed* opts to illuminate the pervasiveness of AAHHR hidden transcripts in African American life and culture through the use of literary, poetic, theatrical, filmic, animated, and public texts. I have chosen these texts because they traverse generations and genres. And while my chosen texts are hardly comprehensive—such a project would take volumes and is not the goal of *Keepin' It Hushed*—they do suggest how the residual and emergent traditions that construct Black culture wade through the waters of Black rhetoric, space, and knowledge by way of AAHHR.

This introduction, "Overture/Head: We Wear the Mask and the Bit," connects AAHHR to rationalities informing what is and is not sayable by African Americans in the public sphere and how African Americans continue to struggle with how to make the hidden transcripts of AAHHR publicly viable. The hush harbor angle of the Senator Barack Obama–Rev. Jeremiah Wright debate that has been overlooked is discussed in chapter 8, which will illuminate the continuing struggle. Chapter 1, "Beyond Difference: Mapping and Theorizing Hush Harbor Spatiality, Rhetoric, and Knowledge," provides a cartography of various iterations of hush harbors, and how they can be thought of within the context of residual and emergent traditions. It then addresses how racialized space can and must be theorized beyond some connection to skin, bodies, and the occupation of a space. Understanding space as inherently ideological will be key in this regard. Chapter 2, "Hush Harbors: Spatiality, Race, and Not-So-Public Spheres," serves as a productive bridge from ideology of space to public sphere theory and its application/

misapplication to Black civil society and hush harbors. Chapter 3, "Wingin' It: Barbershops and the Work of *Nommo* in the Novel," connects AAHHR to nommo and attempts to define nommo more specifically than has heretofore been the case. "Poetic Hush Harbors: Barbershops as Black Paideias," chapter 4, shifts from the literature of the previous chapter to poetry to further illustrate the ubiquity of the hush harbor trope in African American culture, and to examine barbershops as pedagogical sites. Chapter 5, "Barbers and Customers as Philosophers in Memoir and Drama," makes the case for barbers and their customers as philosophers by using Barbara Christian, Antonio Gramsci, and Aristotle.

Chapter 6, "Commodifying Neoliberal Blackness: Faux Hush Harbor Rhetoric in *Barbershop*," posits that the first *Barbershop* movie that was ostensibly about a hush harbor and AAHHR rhetoric was precisely not a hush harbor movie because its commodified, neoliberal version of AAHHR was oriented toward making non–African Americans comfortable, thereby producing a more consumable Blackness. For rhetoricians interested in pedagogy, chapter 7, "Hush Harbor Pedagogy: Pathos-Driven Hearing and Pedagogy," offers a hush harbor pedagogy. Chapter 8, "A Question of Ethics? Hush Harbor Rhetoric and Rationalities in a Neoliberal Age," concludes *Keepin' It Hushed* by posing the question "Should AAHHR be imported into the public sphere?" and then gathers together this project's concern with AAHHR, neoliberalism, and communal hope through what I think to be a distinctive analysis of then Senator Obama's and Rev. Jeremiah Wright's hush harbor–oriented speeches.

Normally, at this point, the genre of the "scholarly" text requires me to delve directly into the primary subject at hand—by shifting to chapter 1. For now, however, I want to defer the shift and make explicit my rationale for what for some may seem a long or unnecessary theoretical/conceptual framing. Frankly, if rhetoric and American life and culture, were, in my view, taken seriously as sites of episteme, of knowledge creation, then the conceptual concerns of *Keepin' It Hushed* could be addressed within five or six written pages—but such is not the case. Sometimes it is as though Patricia Hill Collins and Geneva Smitherman never wrote books that seriously considered African American language, life, and culture as epistemic. Therefore, for those who are not fellow travelers, and for those who are open to different ways of theorizing

African American rhetoric, I want to clarify at the outset my three primary investments in the kind of work I would like *Keepin' It Hushed* to accomplish.

First, I want to illuminate the method and terrain upon which I argue that AAHHR produces knowledge(s). I am not trawling for consent; rather, I am clearing the epistemic waters by linking the manufacture of knowledge to rhetoric, rhetoric to philosophy, and philosophy to both to make the terrain for my claim for AAHHR as epistemic more tenable. Second, I want rhetoric and knowledge to be understood as both producing neoliberal, social, and political rationalities and being constituted by them. Such a gesture situates knowledge into the realm of not only a usable past but also into an understanding of its persuasive effects in society—certainly the realm of rhetoric. Such a shift sculpts a space to understand AAHHR both as producing knowledges and as a primary ground for manufacturing Black or African American *subjectivities.* Finally, including *The Boondocks* makes more palpable the *continuing* relevance of AAHHR for a neo-soul, hip-hop, spoken-word generation. Linking *Keepin' It Hushed,* Muhammad Ali, and AAHHR to rationalities and neoliberalism offers subtextual depth and texture as the reader tackles particular chapters; that is, beneath the vernacular banter is a biopolitics that does not merely resist (which depends too much on the power and subjectivities it opposes) but, more importantly, produces distinctive subjectivities.

Such a linkage is of vital importance to *Keepin' It Hushed,* which argues that rhetoric in general and AAHHR in particular are epistemic, not merely style or ornamentation, but manufacture, transfer, and convey knowledge: rhetoric and *Keepin' It Hushed* then are philosophical pursuits. To understand rhetoric in this manner challenges Platonic notions of truth and its nature. Instead, *Keepin' It Hushed* embraces Aristotle's concept of *phronesis* (practical wisdom), providing a useful bridge between *Keepin' It Hushed*'s concern with both the conceptualization and the practice of theory by and for scholars, and its deployment and use in the mundane but significant domain of the everyday. Therefore, whereas philosophy as conventionally deployed admirably attempts—and fails in my view—to mimic the methodology, logic effects, and certainty of the natural sciences, too often relegating itself to the realm of abstract spaces and scholarly places, rhetoric uses (or should use) the insights of its wayward sibling to address the probable and the possible—the domain of most human practice—knowledge and effects to remain in the world to sculpt it. And rhetoric, if properly understood, illuminates what is probable and possible through taking into account, as much as possible, all the elements impacting the rhetorical situation, such as asymmetrical power relations, space, and gender that any useful notion of practical wisdom must consider. Phronesis then is key to *Keepin' It Hushed*'s methodology of rhetorical theory and practice. As a result, the danger posed by AAHHR exceeds the domesticating tendencies of liberal humanist advocacy for tolerance and civility.

By *rationalities*, I do not refer to the rational or its plural, not do I imply some mind/body split. Instead, rationalities are the very terrain—not the background or horizon—upon and through which subjectivity, meaning, experience, and being both construct and are constructed. While political theorist Wendy Brown's notion of political rationality provides the critical edge informing my understanding of political rationalities and my linkage of them to neoliberalism, particularly in chapter 8, Henry Giroux's definition of rationality in "Critical Theory and Rationality in Citizenship Education" is worth quoting at length: "By rationality, I mean a specific set of assumptions and social practices that mediate how an individual or group relates to the wider society. Underlying any one mode of rationality is a set of interests that define and qualify how one reflects on the world. This is an important epistemological point."[5] AAHHR knowledges and standpoints can be at odds with dominant rationalities in the public sphere and public spaces. Take note of how Giroux's explanation can be read to penetrate ideology to the very hermeneutical ground upon which ideology is constructed. He makes explicit that his is an "epistemological point."

As a rationality, AAHHR should be understood as a field of intelligibility—or, more provocatively, *Blackness as a field of intelligibility*. And as *Keepin' It Hushed* illustrates in chapter 8 in its discussion of the Reverend Wright's speeches and President Obama's response to them, and illuminates in a variety of other ways, African American rationalities can run counter to the normalized (re: nation-state, White, male, heteronormative), civil, decorous rationalities of more public spheres. Giroux goes further and in doing so provides clues to where *Keepin' It Hushed* comes down on the ethics of whether hush harbor rhetoric should be purposely entered in the public sphere: "The knowledge, beliefs, expectations, and biases that define a given rationality both condition and are conditioned by the experiences into which we enter. Of crucial importance is the notion that such experiences only become meaningful within a mode of rationality that confers intelligibility on them." Giroux's definition then makes evident what I will later posit in terms of ontology—that the very terrain of meaning, experiences, and what it means to be a human being gains traction through a network of rhetorics and rationalities. And if the trajectory of my argument is tenable, then to theorize and discuss AAHHR is to theorize and discuss Black knowledge, Black life, Black lives, and Black ontology. Muhammad Ali's hush harbor rationality attempts to inject a Black mode of being into the world. Changing his name, addressing race and racism frankly and in public, and his stance against the Vietnam War cut against the grain of dominant political rationalities. Arguably, the dominant rationality of our time is neoliberalism and, in what follows, I illustrate how, as a political rationality, neoliberalism suppresses AAHHR, providing American and African American culture with fewer Muhammad Alis and more Michael Jordans and Robert Johnsons.

Wendy Brown in "American Nightmare: Neoliberalism, Neoconservatism, and De-Democratization" describes how "a political rationality governs the sayable, the intelligible, and the truth criteria of these domains."[6] She explains how a rationality functions as a normative organizing logic that is both pervasive yet invisible as it circulates as neutral, nonideological, and hegemonic precisely owing to its normativity. A political rationality understood within the context of a nation-state—a nation-state whose formation provides an additional texture enabling a rationality to circulate as being invested in both the common good and the good of the common—as when a federal, state, or local government camouflages the interest of a special interest group with the discourse of "we" or the communal good. Brown goes on to explain that a political rationality is a "specific form of normative political reason organizing the political sphere, governance practices, and citizenship."[7] Significantly, Margo Huxley productively links the concept of rationalities to the political, to spatiality, to governmentality, and to *subjectivity*. She explains how space and environment are bound up in rationalities of government and, more significantly in relation to the primary concern of *Keepin' It Hushed,* how subjectivity is "fostered through the catalytic qualities of space, place, and environments,"[8] a fostering vital to an understanding of AAHHs and hush harbor rhetorics not just as geographies of difference and/or resistance, but as biopolitical sites of the manufacture of African American ontologies and knowledges. Here, I mean biopolitical in the sense as theorized by Michael Hardt and Antonio Negri, whereas they read *biopower*—what I associate with the public sphere and its official institutions—as "the power over life" "that functions through the government of populations, managing their health, reproductive capacities and so forth," they understand the *biopolitical* as "the power of life to resist and determine an alternative production of subjectivity."[9] Therefore, when I refer to the public sphere as being dangerous to AAHH subjectivities, I am referring to the biopower register of the public sphere; AAHHR embodies the African American refusal of biopower for the more democratically agile biopolitical.

Understanding the public sphere and the Whiteness associated with it as material and discursive strands of biopower, as mediated political rationalities, recasts the exclusion or reconfiguring of AAHHR from the public sphere. In its effects, if not through intent, marginalizing AAHHR and knowledges shifts from the merely incidental to a political project structuring nation-state, institutional, and personal interactions. This is a sphere constructed by a matrix of rhetoric and practices that manufactures, mobilizes, and monitors truth, that indicates who can utter truth and where truth can be uttered. While individual intention matters, rationalities mediate intentionality, operating on the level of power, categories, and framing. Framing what it means to be a citizen, an ideal citizen, an American citizen, and even who or what fits the category; framing who gets to speak as a citizen and how, and what behaviors, rhetorics, knowledges, and identities are deemed legitimate, acceptable, normative, and natural within the American imaginary as citizenship. And of course any conception of American citizenship is associated with a broader concern with democracy. So if we think about AAHHR and its articulation through *The Boondocks,* Kanye West, and Harry Belafonte, the intensity of the responses to their rhetorics are recast. Differing opinion is not the primary issue, anger is not the issue; the struggle over *truth,* to whom it belongs, and where and how it is be uttered is the issue, as is what bodies are conferred such rights. Therefore, hush harbor rationalities that enter into the public sphere interject into that sphere forms of intelligibility that alter the terrain of meaning necessary for a messy, but vibrant, democracy. *Keepin' It Hushed* views the entrance of hush harbor rationalities into the public sphere as vital. It is about who gets heard as a legitimate representative citizen in the public sphere of the American imaginary, and how one must speak to achieve authority in that imaginary, in that sphere. President Obama's and Kanye West's racial critiques are deemed dangerous precisely because they challenge the hegemony of the dominant rationality that is so normalized that it is both invisible and not seen as political. Instead, normative rationalities circulate under the masquerade of the civil, the decorous, and the reasonable.

Hush harbor knowledges do more than challenge White, mainstream, and American knowledge on the political or social register; they challenge on the level of ontology and subjectivity on the very notion of what it is to be fully human. So the *parrhesiatic* elements of Rev. Jeremiah Wright's hush harbor rhetoric are demonized because, as Brown writes about political rationality in the context of neoliberalism rationalities, "Certainly, neo-liberalism comprises these effects, but as a political rationality, it also involves a specific and consequential organization of the social, the subject, and the state."[10] Both Michel Foucault and Cornel West argue for the centrality of plain speaking to a vital democracy. Yet, African American *nommo* and *parrhesia* (frankness) are excluded from a normative political rationality that depends upon the exclusion of AAHHR and knowledge for its normativity.

When nommo does travel into the public sphere, it retains traces of African American epistemologies and exigencies. And the subjects that depend upon the dominant normativity not only for their sense of what makes a viable American nation-state but also for how they identify themselves in relation to the national imaginary, nation-state, as American, as citizen-subjects, and as White, also depend upon the exclusion of hush harbor subjectivities. So while Black bodies increasingly populate the public sphere, as the presence of President Obama makes clear, that presence is contingent upon, as I argue more in depth in chapter 8, the exclusion of AAHH subjectivities and knowledges that might scrape the skin of the normative political rationality in such a manner as to make Whites uncomfortable from the sore of Black political rationalities.

In terms of neoliberalism, what makes me tend to shout, and what makes Kanye West offer some of the most accessible, stinging critiques of neoliberalism and its effects, is how neoliberalism organizes the social, the subject, and the state around one primary logic: that of the market. This is more than a simple critique of greed, the quest for profit, or an analysis of a late stage of capitalism. Neoliberalism, arguably our era's most pervasive secular religion, is a project that endeavors to do more than merely influence the behavior of subjects, the state, and its institutions. It strives to make market logic the primary, natural logic through which the economic, social, religious, public, and personal spheres operate. Market logic privileges choice, the atomistic individual, and the privatization of the social contract. It reduces the human and human social relations to the market ethos—commodities and products for exchange, where the notion of citizenship slowly shifts from that of the political citizen to that of consumer citizen: you are what you buy.

When Kanye West raps about a "single Black female addicted to retail" in "When It All Falls Down" (2004) and goes on to say about himself, "Man I promise, I'm so self conscious, I cannot go to the mall without at least one of my watches,"[11] he is reflecting and resisting a neoliberal ethos. An ethos that reduces his life to the terrain of market exchange. A neoliberal ethos inadvertently smuggled into the Black biopolitical when any critique of an African American who is making some money or getting a little shine is warded of with "don't playa hate" and "don't hate the playa, hate the game." When President George W. Bush after 9/11 encourages Americans to go shopping, the market logic of neoliberalism becomes increasingly normative. In such a context, AAHHRs and knowledges that are not easily consumable or commodified—that do not comfort Whites and others because of how such knowledges fray the carpet of the dominant rationality—are trivialized, distorted, or dismissed.

Ali then brought into public African American iterations what James C. Scott refers to as hidden transcripts, hermeneutics of Blackness, African American rationalities. These rationalities often flow on the lower frequencies of African American culture outside of officially sanctioned sites of knowledge and pedagogy.[12] These rationalities resist the neoliberal tendency to reduce Blackness to an easily consumable commodity. Ali's rhetoric embraced the emancipatory freedom and rhetorical sovereignty of African American discourse delivered during card games, at picnics, at liquor stores, on corners, and on the front porch of my grandfather's farm. Ali would bravely drop the mask that lied, grinned, and made Whites and African Americans invested in mainstream notions of decorum and civility comfortable.

Certainly cable television, the Internet, the blogosphere, and social networking have in many ways reconfigured and fragmented the mainstream public sphere. And Blackness, Black bodies, Black faces, and Black culture seemingly permeate the dominant mainstream American public sphere. All of this suggests a promised land of new potentialities as the frontier of public sphere rhizomatically expands to and is constituted by numerous micropublics that would by sheer numbers cause the hegemony of any primary public sphere to wither. Yet, if scholars take African American life and culture seriously, any optimism about the radical openness of the hegemonic public sphere must be must be tempered. As with the quest for literacy, the speaking of Black truths into the public sphere by Black bodies risks intimidation, violence, and social and physical death. It is historically, presently, and persistently dangerous. *Historically:* In 1837, Maria W. Stewart, the first women to speak publicly to a mixed-gender and mixed-raced audience, was run out of Boston in part because she dared assert African American episteme (knowledge), subjectivities, and experience into the public sphere. *Persistently:* Decades later, in 2006, Kanye West was roundly criticized and lost several commercial endorsements when, in the aftermath of Hurricane Katrina, he nervously uttered on national television that President "George Bush doesn't care about Black people!"—a perspective that was de rigueur in Black spaces and places in front of Black audiences.[13] Harry Belafonte, a singer and activist of international renown, a close friend of Coretta King and Dr. Martin Luther King Jr., was disinvited from Coretta Scott King's funeral after referring to President Bush as "the greatest terrorist in the world."[14] *Presently:* President-elect Barack Obama resisted calls for him to distance himself from African American hush harbor (AAHH) and from the AAHHR of Rev. Jeremiah Wright.

The aforementioned critiques are often leveled at the United States and at White folks but in primarily Black spaces in front of primarily African American audiences. My point here is not that Rev. Wright and the hush harbor rhetoric and knowledge he draws from represent the correct Black perspective or the authentic Black perspective. Nor is it only to emphasize how African Americans often to speak less assertively, less boldly, less frankly in front of White and mainstream audiences. Instead, it is to, as they say in the church, "make it plain": African American public rhetoric and speech are often cleansed of the tone and registers of African American knowledge, memory, and the funkiness of African American existence because, as bell hooks notes, "their presence changes the direction and shape of our words."[15] Democracy, as such, becomes more procedural than substantive—Black discontent relegated to the personal, to the private. The acceptance of African Americans in hegemonic, mainstream culture, their comfort, their reputations, their jobs, their safety, and, too often, their very lives often depend on not transgressing or disrupting the biopower of White comfort constructed through political and social rationalities anchored in mainstream, commonsense understandings of society and race. This claim may seem odd and hyperbolic given the centrality of the spectacle of Blackness in the popular American imagination: from Kongo Square in the nineteenth century and the Fisk Jubilee Singers to sports, hip-hop culture, Black Entertainment Television, and BlackPlanet. com; from Oprah Winfrey to the president of the United States. Black folks occupy and circulate the entire topography of the visual and aural landscape.

However, as Richard Iton illustrates in his excellent *In Search of the Black Fantastic,* the ambiguous inside-outside discourse mediating the African American presence in America popular culture "has often been experienced asymmetrically: as political disenfranchisement on the one hand and over-employment in the areas of popular culture on the other."[16] So, the visibility and prevalence of African American life and culture in the public realm are not necessarily congruent with substantial political inclusion, nor do they challenge dominant rationalities beyond pleas for tolerance and inclusion. Further, the very inclusion of certain kinds of Blackness is contingent upon the exclusion of substantial aspects of African American rhetorics, knowledges, and experiences. Knowledges and experiences are monitored, disciplined, and jettisoned if too disruptive. Therefore, when the visage of Blackness seems to saturate cable, social networking, the Internet, and network television, increased African American participation in the public sphere may actually mask exclusion from the political-social sphere and an adherence to the racial order of things.

As of this writing, an important study out of Cornell University and published in the *Archives of Pediatrics and Adolescent Medicine* reveals that *90 percent* of African American children will be on food stamps at some point in their lives. "Food stamps," according to Thomas A. Hirschl, Cornell professor of development sociology, "are important indicators of poverty and risk of food insecurity."[17] A more anecdotal, but in my view a more telling, example of how critically important it is to disarticulate representational access from an intervention in the racial order of things, is the perceived inability of a Black presidential candidate to talk about race proactively in the public sphere instead of as a response to a racialized antagonism if he wanted to be elected to office; and the number of African Americans who, with seemingly little critical reflection, not only supported but also encouraged a mask that grins and lies, and avoids the issue of race. What these two examples illustrate is that the public sphere remains a key spatiality in the maintenance of the interlocking ethnic, gender, heteronormative, and racial order of things. Black people, Black thought, and therefore a kind of Blackness must be kept in its racial space/place when they/it seep(s) beyond the racial compound and the rhetorical camp allowed for it. Blackness that exceeds these racial-spatial and rhetorical boundaries must be reterritorialized into a material and rhetorical compound that continues to function in the dominant interest. To push the racial-spatial, rhetorical trope further, ontology, being writ large, and racial ontology, Black being, in particular as they relate to the body, are inherently rhetorical and spatial in the American context.

Judith Butler's theorizing about ontology, the body, and precariousness of life in *Frames of War* is useful and worth quoting at length because it links ontology to politics, hermeneutics, and language, or what I would conceptualize as rhetoric as a terrain of intelligibility or being as rhetorical:

To refer to "ontology" in this regard is not to lay claim to a description of fundamental structures of being that are distinct from any and all social and political organization. On the contrary, none of these terms exist outside

of their political organization and interpretation. The "being" of the body
to which this ontology refers is one that is always given over to others, to
norms, to social and political organizations that have developed historically
in order to maximize precariousness for some and minimize precariousness
for others.[18]

Using Butler to tether ontology and being to rhetoric and ideology is not
to deny the corporeality of the body and the physiology and biology necessary
to life. Instead, it is to make legible that being is more than merely existing,
and that ontology and meaning and what we think of as human are not self-
evident. These concepts—including the body—gain gravitas and meaning
through norms, discourse, culture, politics, and the persuasive rhetorics that
legitimate them all. Everything is not rhetoric, and rhetoric is not everything.
Nevertheless, ontology and being are constructed partly through rhetorics/
knowledges; therefore, being and what is human are struggled for again and
again and again. As such, life is more precarious for some than for others.
African American ontology, rhetoric, and knowledge practices have always
been and continue to be haunted by the terror of precariousness. AAHHR has
always been a field of intelligibility of African American being and humanity.
For Black folks, it argues I am/we are fully human on our terms, based on
our experiences, on our meanings with and against the grains of countless
other I's and we's. The shoving of AAHHR and knowledges to the edges of
intelligibility, to the fringes of the sayable, under the guise of practicality,
while useful, inadvertently relegates those rhetorics and subjects who bear
witness to African American precariousness, political and social rationalities,
and possibilities to the hinterlands of the trivial under the guise of postracial,
postideological, tolerant winds of change. *Keepin' It Hushed,* then, is precisely
about a rhetorical tradition/genealogy of overlooked and undertheorized
Black spatialities, political rationalities, and Black talk, where the shape of
Black words and Black knowledges are sculpted primarily by other African
Americans. These rhetorics emerge from African American communicative
spheres—what enslaved Africans and African Americans referred to as hush
harbors, Black lifeworlds where a distinctive political rationality has been
and continues to be privileged; where the unsaid in the public sphere gets

said; where the unhearable gets heard; and where the filtering of American and African American culture and life occurs through African American hermeneutics.

African American life and culture has pivoted and continues to pivot on and through spatiality and place, on White and public geographies of terror and scenes of subjections, and in Black, hidden geographies self-making in spatial scenes forging Black subjectivities.[19] To wit: The Middle Passage. Slave ships. Slave pens. Auction blocks. Plantations. Minstrel stages. Field Negroes. House niggas. Prisons. The South. The North. Urban cores. Suburbs. The hood. Academia. Indian reservations. Internment camps. Black women's clubs. Ghettos. Gay-and-lesbian–circuit clubs. All remain significant scenes of subjection and of possibilities as thresholds for the ongoing construction of American identity. And if, as Saydia Hartman suggests, these spaces, these scenes, are racialized, then race and ethnicity remain central to the American nation-state project and to American and African American identities

Space and place, then, are so significant in American/African American life, culture, and the social-political construction of race that Darrell Wayne Fields, architecture professor and critic at Harvard University, suggests that Blackness and race as material and discursive practices are the *architectonic* of space.[20] In another variation on the theme of Blackness and space, Hortense Spillers, in "Mama's Baby, Papa's Maybe," disrupts the spatiotemporality of Blackness, female, and gender. In short, despite and because of the flow of people, capital, and ideas, the racial order of Blackness continues to be refracted through a *spatial* order of Blackness. And as geographer David Harvey argues in *Cosmopolitanism and the Geographics of Freedom,* in a postmodern, increasing global world, due to uneven, neoliberal, asymmetrical economic and spatial development, space and place become both less and more important. Geographer Ruthie Gilmore illuminates the spatial-racial order of race, Blackness, and their intersection with racism: "Racism is the state-sanctioned and or extralegal production and exploitation of group-differentiated vulnerabilities to premature death, in distinct yet densely interconnected political geographies."[21] The public sphere is a primary node, a switching station, and a political geography through which the flow of people, capital, ideals, and isms are circulated, negotiated, and justified. Social disorientation, humiliation, and sometimes social and physical death haunt interlinked informal and state-sanctioned sites and political geographies. Even African American academics, politicians, and entertainers cannot escape the threat of either the scenes of subjections or of racialized public and quasi-public spheres. If the aforementioned seems strident, consider the following from cultural critic Michele Wallace in *Dark Designs and Visual Culture:*

> Black intellectuals, cultural critics—whatever you want to call them—are still not free to speak their minds anywhere except in their living rooms. The secret of conquering the so-called public sphere, which is just another name for the white-dominated marketplace of ideas, continues to be having something critical to say about Blacks. This isn't to say that Black intellectuals aren't doing something useful and necessary for Black culture in their criticisms. But often, it is at the risk of their intentions being seen as careerist and self-aggrandizing rather than philanthropic and salutary.[22]

While some might take issue with her characterization of the limitations and possibilities of Black intellectual discourse—that too often African American intellectuals or pundits are confined to opining about racial issues gives credence to her take on the limitations of Black expertise—what interests me here is her racialization of the hegemonic public sphere as White (and as male and heteronormative), as constructed on a normalized foundation of White privilege and a marketplace ethos, and most importantly, that in the supposed rhetorical free zone of academia, even African America's best and brightest domesticate their rhetorics, their knowledges, and therefore themselves.

In the fervor of post–civil rights, post-Black, post-soul, postracial discourse, Wallace's critique might be trivialized by some as a remnant of a bygone era, a critique irrelevant in a new globalized, glocalized, cosmopolitanized, youth-oriented, text-messaging, hip-hopped world. Yet, even the hip-hop sensibilities of the popular *The Boondocks* series alludes to the danger of speaking Black truths to White audiences.

The Boondocks, a sassy, animated, hip-hop satire resuscitates the notion of the-more-thangs-change-the-more-they-stay-the-same for Black folks speaking African American truths to White folks. The series is a spin-off of the once nationally syndicated comic strip that is currently on hiatus so that the writer and illustrator of the strip, Aaron McGruder, can produce and work on the series. *The Boondocks* seems to fearlessly interject into the public sphere discussions of race, class, caste, and gender that I often hear in AAHH spaces and places. *The Boondocks* is important to mention because it allows me to resist the easy dismissal of *Keepin' It Hushed* by those who make a fetish of "the new" to argue that the hip-hop generation of Black folks can speak as freely to White audiences, as well as to Black. *The Boondocks* argues differently.

In its very first episode, in its very first sequence, *The Boondocks* addresses African American rhetoric, Whiteness and its hegemony in the public sphere, epistemology, and the danger of speaking African American truths to White folks. The sequence opens as the camera slowly pushes in from a wide shot of a pristine, tree-lined suburb toward a genteel, upper-crust, well-heeled, predominantly White garden party. A voice-over of the lead character, Huey, a preteen Black male intones, "I am not a prophet. But sometimes I have prophetic dreams. Like the one where I was at a garden party." After mounting a stage and reaching the podium, Huey gently taps the microphone to get the attention of the murmuring partygoers: "Excuse me everyone. I have an announcement to make." Everyone turns toward the stage. "Jesus was Black, Ronald Reagan was the devil, and the government is lying about 9/11."

A riot ensues. Tables are overturned. Glass shatters. Men and women throw chairs and punches. A woman screams, "Noooooooo! It can't be true!" Music in a minor key adds a solemn, ominous tone. The music stops. A crash edit rips us into another scene where Huey is in bed. There's a close-up of his head. Then we hear and see a slap. "Ow!" yells Huey. His grandfather's face looms over him:

"Hmmm, hmmm! You having that dream where you make White people riot, weren't ya."

"But I was telling the truth," responds Huey.

"How many time have I told you, you bet not dream about telling White folks the truth. You understand me. Shoot! Making White people riot. You better learn how to lie like me. I'm getting ready to find me a White man and lie to him right now."

Like the grandfather who tells the Invisible Man to stick his head into the lion's mouth and yes 'em and no 'em to death, Huey's grandfather hands down African American epistemology and counterknowledge about the danger of and resistance to African American knowledges and the standpoints therein. In addition, the sequence illustrates how even the current generation continues to wrestle with the danger of speaking truth to power, privilege, and Whiteness and, despite the garden party of high Black visibility in the public sphere, the party comes at the expense of Black truths, Black knowledges, and African American rhetorical sovereignty.

As the aforementioned makes clear, the hiding and camouflaging of these African American transcripts is more than about the important struggle over the manufacturing of truth, it is about ontology, about tactics of survival when facing premature social and physical death. Muhammad Ali's self-assertion, Michelle Wallace's analysis, and *The Boondocks* satire all coalesce around the frank expressions of African American subjectivities often hidden from public view. All ward off the ontological diminishment and domesticated political rationalities too often required in the public sphere. *Keepin' It Hushed*'s interdisciplinary method, deploying theories of rhetoric and critical geography, and deploying literature, poetry, film, theater, philosophy, and popular culture, is necessary to take into account the pervasiveness and the various iterations of these hidden transcripts throughout African American life as manifested through African American expressive culture. These various forms make visible why, in the words of columnist Ralph Wiley in *Why Black People Tend to Shout*, "Black people tend to shout" because of a public sphere that too often requires a bit in the mouth of and a mask over the face of African American rhetors.

Keepin' It Hushed and AAHHR participate in a rhetorical tradition that—like the West African symbol of the Sankofa bird, which peers both backward and forward as it flies—remembers why in the past, the present, and the foreseeable future, Black people tend to shout . . . and speak in hush harbors.

1.

Beyond Difference

Mapping and Theorizing Hush Harbor Spatiality Rhetoric and Knowledge

KEEPIN' IT HUSHED IS BROADLY CONCERNED WITH BRINGING INTO THEORETICAL purview and scholarly consideration a continually evolving tradition of risky speech, hidden transcripts, and productive and subjugated knowledges by and for African Americans I refer to as African American hush harbor rhetoric (AAHHR). As alluded to earlier, I borrow the term *hush harbor* from enslaved African and African Americans. They used the term and others such as *hush arbor* and *bush arbor* to refer to geographies such as the slave quarters, woods, and praise houses where Black folks could speak frankly in Black spaces in front of Black audiences. In these hush harbor spaces, Black rhetors and speakers were free to engage in and deploy otherwise heavily monitored practices, knowledges, and rhetorics disallowed in the public sphere under the disciplining gaze of Whites and Whiteness. In informal, unofficial meeting places such as cane breaks, woods, praise houses, funeral parlors, jook joints, the Chitlin' Circuit, and their contemporary manifestations in beauty shops and barbershops, hush harbor geographies were/are quasi-public or hidden spaces where Blackness on parallel, alternative, and lower frequencies circulates. In these spaces, enslaved Africans and African Americans can come in from the wilderness of the racially mediated public sphere.

Hush harbors were necessary to the maintenance, circulation, and affirmation of African American knowledge; refuges that warded off Black social death. By *social death,* I refer to disciplinary, normalizing surveillance requiring radicalized, gendered, classed, and queered subjects to domesticate, trivialize, or ignore knowledges, performances, and other practices and beliefs by these subjects grounded in specific ontological orientations to increase the likelihood of individual social and economic access and acceptance. Hush harbors were necessary because, as Melba Boyd points out, "Slaves could be beaten, even killed for having a spelling book, for trying to read as such rebellious rhetorical space was linked to intellectual freedom and by extension, ultimately physical freedom."[1]

A distinctive, new ethnicity—now referred to as *African American*—and a distinctive new ethos—*Blackness*—emerged in significant part from within a crucible of a traumatic, contact zone of social death, creative survival, and cultural syncretism in a disciplinary spatiality sutured to the Middle Passage and that is the spatial ancestor to the hush harbor: the slave ship. Marcus Rediker in *The Slave Ship: A Human History* (2007), the most comprehensive history to date of the slave ship as a crucible of ontological erasure and as a disciplinary chamber, discusses how Africans from various places and ethnicities formed common bounds through signals and other methods of communication to create an unimagined community of survival and hope. Though a scene of subjection, the foregoing suggests the productive possibilities emerging from the slave ship that Africans in America carried with them into a "promised land" of darkness. African American subjects in hush harbors fended off some of that darkness through the quest for literacy.

Charity Bowery, a slave from North Carolina, alludes to both the hush harbor and the quest for literacy: "I have seen the Negroes up in the country going away under large oaks, and in secret places, sitting in the woods with spelling books."[2] Negroes went away not only because, as Boyd noted, the attempt to become literate could cost them their lives but also because the exchange of otherwise suppressed African American individual and/or communal subjectivities challenged hegemony. As *Keepin' It Hushed* makes clear, not only do hush harbors still exist, but also, as tropes, hush harbor spaces and rhetorics continue to emit rhetorical force within African American culture. These Black spaces for good, and sometimes ill, are repositories of African American knowledge, life and culture, style, politics, and *being* that remain important to African Americans. Once again I have linked AAHHR reference to *being*. However, instead of linking *being* to hush harbor rhetoric, here I link *being* to space because, as geographers Henri Lefebvre and Doreen Massey note, "*[S]pace*, this is what ensures the survival of *being*" and "Space connotes Being."[3]

African American Hush Harbors and Hush Harbor Rhetoric

Given their secretive function and the danger associated with attending hush harbor meetings, it is not surprising that hush harbor locations were not extensively written about while they were being used nor has a comprehensive history been constructed. Nevertheless, their existence and importance can be cobbled together from a variety of sources. Lawrence Levine, Ira Berlin, and others provide a useful genealogy in this regard.

Lawrence Levine's germinal text on African American cultural history and practice, *Black Culture and Black Consciousness,* posits that a serious consideration of Black culture, history, and thought cannot occur without revealing the existence and tactical import of hush harbors as sites where "slaves broke the prescription against unsupervised or unauthorized meetings by holding their services in secret, well hidden areas."[4] Take note of how the earlier documented quote by Charity Bowery describes the kind of meeting to which Levine refers. In *Remembering Slavery: African Americans Talk about Their Personal Experiences of Slavery and Emancipation,* minister and ex-slave W. B. Allen alludes to the implicit subversive potential and the threat of the transgressive rhetoric of those who dared attend clandestine hush harbor meetings to temporarily escape the presence of Whites: "My father was once attending a prayer meeting in a house that had only one door. The slaves had turned a large pot down in the center of the floor to hold the sounds of their voices within. But, despite their precaution, the patrollers found them and broke in. Of course, every Nigger present was in for a severe whipping."⁵ Hush harbors and AAHHR were heavily scrutinized because of the danger of resistance, rebellion, and the retention of African culture within hidden transcripts.

James C. Scott defines *hidden transcripts* as "non-hegemonic, subversive discourse generated by subordinate groups and concealed from certain dominant others."⁶ The turning over of a pot is a West African practice: an African retention. Slaves believed that a pot turned upside down would capture all sound, ensuring that slave patrols, other Whites, or Black informants would not hear them. Whether the turned-over pot actually captured the sound of the voices of the enslaved is not my concern. Rather, it is that the practice is evidence not only of African retentions but also of the continual struggle of the enslaved to assert their own humanity on their own terms to resist social death.

The aforementioned point about the valuing and privileging of African American knowledges and subjectivities is important for two reasons. First, while bodies marked as Black and their historical and personal experiences are tethered to any conceptualization of hush harbors or of AAHHR, *Keepin' It Hushed* desutures a necessary connection between Black spaces, Black rhetorics, and Black bodies. *Keepin' It Hushed* attempts to avoid the epidermalization of African American rhetoric and knowledge. This is to say, because a particular spatiality is totally or primarily inhabited by bodies that are phenotypically Black, this does not mean it is a hush harbor or that the rhetorics emerging from that space is AAHHR. Further, because the spatiality is put to African American uses, and/or the rhetor is Black, does not make that space a hush harbor nor that of its rhetoric. For example, African American fraternities and sororities where Black rhetors speak in front of primarily Black audiences in Black spatialities are not necessarily hush harbors. More provocatively, I would argue that most African American fraternal or sorority spatialities are not hush harbors. This is not to imply that African American fraternities and sororities are less Black, politically irrelevant, or primarily Eurocentric. Rather, given their understanding of themselves as Greek organizations, their histories and functions as a conduit to mainstream power and acceptance for Black middle-class political and social formations, and their well-known history of mirroring some of the practices of White sororities and fraternity practices as satirized by John Oliver Killens and written about by Lawrence Otis Graham in *Our Kind of People,* Black sororities and fraternities occupy intersecting but distinct Black rhetorical geographies and histories. AAHHR and hush harbor spaces privilege African American knowledges, worldviews, and rhetorical forms, not just Black bodies. This is not necessarily the case with African American sororities and fraternities. Second, while *Keepin' It Hushed* does not assume a static, essential notion of Blackness and African American life and culture, and takes into account the quotidian and protean nature of the ever-changing same of Blackness, it is invested in exploring African American cultural continuities. As such, African American rhetorics and knowledges can be understood through a rhetorical method that is concerned with what circulates as Black, but is not limited to Black bodies, while avoiding becoming mired in the quicksand of authenticity.

While the testimony of slaves such as Charity Bowery and the scholarship of Lawrence Levine and Albert Raboteau provide evidence for the existence of hush harbors, Mark Anthony Neal illuminates their importance in the superb *What the Music Said: Black Popular Music and Black Public Culture,* where he convincingly argues that "the initial development and maintenance of covert social or 'safe' spaces of the antebellum South are at the core of the black critical tradition in America."[7] As Neal illuminates, these spaces are not merely metaphoric safety deposit boxes of history and culture, nor vernacular treasure chests of raw material awaiting cultural or rhetorical anthropologists to excavate meaning or to theorize them, these safe spaces are hush harbors and reside at the core of a critical, theoretical tradition in African American culture. In chapter 8, I discuss how President Barack Obama's distancing of himself from Rev. Jeremiah Wright inadvertently cleaved himself from this core, critical African American tradition, and how this separation, endemic to podium–auction block rhetoric, relegates African American knowledge to the periphery of public debate in the service of a more consumable neoliberal Blackness.

Gwen Pough in *Check It While I Wreck It* (2004) smartly deploys Neal as she connects this critical tradition of the hush harbor to both hip-hop culture and Black public sphere theory. Therefore, African American theory and critique that are unaware of, not informed by, or depart from, even in a gesture of disavowal, a critical genealogy of hush harbors and AAHHR are seriously compromised.

Toni Morrison's success as an internationally renowned writer is due in part to her familiarity with and understanding of the importance of hush harbors and hush harbor subjectivity in African American culture. All of her novels make at least one reference to the hush harbor. *Beloved* (1987) is paradigmatic in this regard. It provides an example of how African American literature fictively suggests the rhetorical, epistemological, and spatial intersection of the hush harbor and explores the fertile connection between unofficial and subjugated discourse, hush harbors, and African American subjectivity.

Beloved is a womanist-centered slave narrative where one of the main characters, Baby Suggs, "uncalled, unrobed, unanointed," and a woman, took all the Black folks who could gather in a "clearing—a wide-open place cut deep in the woods" to deliver a hush harbor sermon to a hush harbor audience. In this "wide open" outpost, "she told them that the only grace they could have was the grace they could imagine. That if they could not see it, they would not have it."[8] "Uncalled" and "unrobed" refer to her unofficial status as heretical and as a preacher. Yet, in the outpost in the woods, she speaks to an all-Black audience. Her unofficial status? Precisely what, in this clearing, enriches her status? In a clearing where masculine logic, the law of the father, and patriarchal expectations have been clipped, hacked, and burned away, Baby Suggs will be listened to. Heard. This is an all-Black audience that can gain knowledge and affirmation from her that they cannot gain elsewhere. And they follow her to the clearing because to attend her sermon in public is to risk discipline and punishment. Hush harbors served as spatialities where African Americans could see the grace, acquire the knowledge, and possess the subjectivity they could not have in the public sphere.

Literature is, of course, not the only modality in which hush harbors appear in African American expressive culture. Film has been a significant medium in addressing hush harbors and AAHHR. Julie Dash's film *Daughters of the Dust* (1991), Charles Burnett's *Killer of Sheep* (1977), Kasi Lemmons's *Talk to Me* (2007), and of course the *Barbershop* films (2002 and 2004) are just a few examples. The first *Barbershop* film makes explicit both its connection to such hush harbor urtexts as Paul L. Dunbar's poems in *We Wear the Mask* (1896) and *An Antebellum Sermon* (1895) and its understanding of the mainstream public sphere, not as an ideologically and racially neutral free-zone market of ideas, but, as scholars such as Nancy Frazer, Michael Dawson, and Michael Warner recognize, as an always-already racialized, gendered, and heteronormative space. So, when Eddie the barber makes the comment "Now I probably would not say this in front of white folks, but in front of ya'll I am going to speak my mind," that single sentence links the barbershop as hush harbor to African American rhetorical history, to a specific audience analysis, and to the continuing recognition that, over one hundred years after the end of the Enslavement, the public sphere and the free speech associated with it are still hegemonically White. It is not a surprise that scholar Michelle Wallace, the fictional Eddie, and Frederick Douglass all understand the continuing relevance of AAHHR and the difference that Black audience makes.

What Is a Black Audience and Why Speak to Them Differently?

Master orator Frederick Douglass made a habit of speaking differently in front of Black audiences than in front of White audiences. Certainly, Douglass was no racial essentialist who reduced race to mere phenotype. Nevertheless, when a large number of Whites came to hear him in a Black church, he altered his remarks. His explanation is worth quoting at length because it so accurately captures and resonates with the tactics and strategies of contemporary AAHHR: "There are some things that ought to be said to colored people in the peculiar circumstances in which they are placed, that can be said more effectively among ourselves, without the presence of white persons. We are the oppressed, the Whites are the oppressors, and the language I would address to the one is not always suited to the other."[9]

From David Walker's appeal to colored citizens and from "We Wear the Mask" to director Tyler Perry's films, African Americans through AAHHR distinguish between White and Black audiences. Tyler Perry's success in terms of his gospel plays and his movies is structured upon a scaffold of African American life, culture, and audiences. The distinction among White, non–African American, and Black audiences remains important both as a rhetorical tactic and as a recognition of the contingent nature of knowledge, its legitimization, and of the reception and circulation of Black perspectives.

What is a Black audience? Of course, a simple conceptualization would be a group of individuals who identify themselves as Black, are identified by others as Black, and are understood by the rhetor as being Black. While this is a necessary starting point, it is insufficient. AAHHR is sedimented in the ever-changing same of African American knowledges, experiences, histories, and subjectivities.

The Black audience is one that is persuaded by tropes, knowledges, and terministic screens anchored in African American life and culture. Therefore, although non–African Americans can be part of a Black audience, in general such is typically not the case in AAHH and other Black spaces constituting Black civil society. A rhetor identifies with an African American audience through performances linked to identifications such as speech, gesture, tonality, organization, image, attitude, and ideas anchored in the deployment of African American knowledges, hermeneutics, and understandings of the world. These knowledges, understandings, and worldviews are developed through distinctive terministic screens and nomenclature.

Philosopher and rhetorician Kenneth Burke understands that a terministic screen is both a reflection and a deflection of reality and that "any nomenclature necessarily directs the attention into some channels rather than others."[10] He further understands that, even if a given terminology is a *reflection* of reality, by its very nature as terminology it must also be a *selection* of reality; and to this extent it must also function as a *deflection* of reality."[11] Therefore, no stance or view, no claim to reasonableness, lies outside of the contamination of human perspective. This is neither to offer another version of radical postmodernism nor to argue against truth in both its uppercase or lowercase forms. Instead it is a simple recognition that worldviews and the knowledges and the rhetorics reflecting them are social nomenclatures. More significantly, Burke argues that terministic screens are not static perceptual lenses that lie dormant until activated by human will;

terministic screens *direct* attention. And while it should go without saying that African Americans are hardly monolithic, it should also go without saying that African Americans and Whites often deploy different hermeneutical frames emerging from different terministic screens constructed through distinctive experiences when it comes to crucial issues and interests related to African American life and culture.

AAHHR is tethered to viscous (not fluid) African American terministic screens. Whether it is voting, movie- and television-viewing habits, positions on affirmative action, Hurricane Katrina survivors as looters or refugees, the interpretation of events through a lens of African American newspapers and websites, sentencing fairness within the prison industrial complex, or a plethora of other examples, African Americans have particular experiences refracted through different terministic screens. AAHHR foregrounds and embodies theses screens and nomenclature through African American knowledges and worldviews that enhance African American subjective fortification through the *addressing* and *invoking* of Black audiences.[12] Black audiences are constructed around and can be persuaded through these terministic screens through an appeal to African American knowledges and opinions and through rhetorical forms and tactics such as signifyin', call and response, improvisation, and sermonic discourse.

This is not to argue that all phenotypically Black African Americans identify with or create and engage the world through the same screens or nomenclatures, nor is it to claim these screens and lenses are singular or dominant for every person who can be identified as African American; instead, it is to pose that AAHHR moves primarily Black audiences through deployment of rhetorics and worldviews usually identified with African American knowledges, experiences, and identities. Indeed, individual African American subjects can gain social capital in mixed audiences or when participating in hegemonic discourses by denying, ignoring, complicating, or remaining silent vis-à-vis African American knowledge, worldviews, and experience. Nevertheless, even when accounting for intraclass, caste, and sexual-orientation antagonisms, African Americans *generally* have distinctive terministic screens that enable them to engage in what, as I discuss later, Jon Cruz characterizes as *pathos-oriented hearing.*[13]

As most of the experts, knowledge producers, think tanks, foundations, entertainment, and financial institutions in the United States are shaped by, through, and or center Whiteness in the marketplace of ideas, references to the common good in political, economic, and social discourse do not necessarily include African American interests. In fact, one of the reasons that President Barack Obama was able to garner well over 90 percent of the African American vote while for the most part avoiding explicit discussions of race is that, when he refers to the common good, African Americans know that, unlike too often in the past, it includes them. So, within AAHHR, recentering African American standpoints is not about an atavistic Black nationalistic impulse; instead, it is to make visible and explicit African American knowledges and experiences that mainstream public sphere discourse often neglects under the guise of common good.

AAHHR functions on the supposition that Black audiences are more likely to be found and animated in Black civil societies and Black spatialities reflecting Black lifeworlds. African American publics, spatialities, and lifeworlds through the theoretical prism of *Keepin' It Hushed* deterritorialize space, public spheres, and discourses that situate the public sphere as mostly inclusive, rational, and static, and then reterritorialize them as political, ideological, and viscous categories. Still, important scholarship puts pressure on the self-evident existence of Black publics or counterpublics. Further, even if they exist, are Black public spheres and/or Black counterpublics *public* in the Habermasian sense of the terms?

2.

Hush Harbors
Spatiality, Race, and
Not-So-Public Spheres

Space is fundamental in any form of communal life; space is fundamental
in any exercise of power.

MICHEL FOUCAULT, *Power*

Race matters, but it is clear that space does too.

MURRAY FORMAN, *The 'Hood Comes First: Race Space,*
and Place in Rap and Hip-hop

POLITICAL SCIENTIST MICHAEL C. DAWSON ARGUES IN "A BLACK COUNTER-
public?" that a black counterpublic no longer exists if by counterpublic one
means "a set of institutions, communication networks and practices which
facilitate debate of causes and remedies to the current combinations of
political setbacks and economic devastation facing major segments of the
Black community, and which facilitate the creation of oppositional formations and sites."[1] Political scientist Melissa Victoria Harris-Lacewell disagrees
and offers the barbershop and beauty shop as sites that would "fall within
any definition" of Black public space.[2] Indeed, as Harris-Lacewell points

out, "Barbers and Hairstylists still constitute the overwhelming majority of entrepreneurs in the African American community."[3]

While Dawson's conception of a counterpublic is productive in its utility in directly intervening in the insertion of African American interests, it remains problematic in at least two ways. First, Dawson's theorizing around Black publics is too concerned with and dependent upon Black life and culture as resistance and opposition. *Keepin' It Hushed* privileges a theoretical investment in African American rhetoric and the manufacturing of African American knowledges in terms of their productive capacities. Black life and Black publics are vital to African American life and culture based on intracultural concerns, not solely in response to racial subordination. As Harris-Lacewell pointedly makes clear without any hint of essentialism, "Black public spaces are unique because African Americans come together in these areas because of their Blackness in a way that can, but does not necessarily, happen in other counterpublic areas."[4] Second, any definition of Black publics or counterpublics that does not take into account how informal sites such as barbershops and beauty shops function as substantial communication networks central to Black public space requires further elaboration. Therefore, I want to extend the Harris-Lacewell objection to Dawson, connect her formulation to my notion of hush harbors in general, and then put pressure on the Harris-Lacewell formulation to think about Black publics such as hush harbors as more than alternative publics or counterpublics. While necessary, such alternative formulations inadvertently hollow out the productive, epistemic, and affirmative qualities of hush harbors that exceed concerns with resistance or with countering mainstream conceptions of African American life. That is to say, hush harbors are rhetorical free zones of emancipatory possibility precisely because they are internally directed, working from the terministic screens of African American life and culture rather than being anchored in a concern with countering White or mainstream surveillance. Of course, any notion of public sphere theorizing must take in to account Jürgen Habermas.

Habermas's conception of the bourgeois public sphere can be understood as constructing *public* as an informal spatiality, not formally affiliated with the state, that serves a rhetorical/discursive purpose as both separate from and a conduit between civil society and the mechanism of the nation-state. This separation facilitates the ability of individuals to wrestle over questions of common good through the temporary leaving behind of *private* concerns through rational debate. Nancy Fraser makes a significant intervention into Habermas's conception of the public in her germinal essay "Rethinking the Public Sphere,"[5] to which both Dawson and Harris-Lacewell refer, as she complicates Habermas through her argument for multiple spheres and counterspheres.

The private concerns that Habermas brackets out of the domain of the public—race, gender, class, sexual orientation—mediate both its openness and its rationality. Therefore, Fraser's work is important because it does more than argue for inclusion; it recognizes that the very terrain upon which rationality, the public and, by extension, modernity is constructed *requires* the exclusion of certain social and political investments. In addition, while she is obviously concerned with gender and the inclusion of women, a larger or intersecting goal is to point out the limits of the public sphere within a particular version of liberal democracy. Fraser argues for a substantial democracy where the body politic of the United States goes beyond mere procedural democracy and the concern with everyone being eligible to vote, to struggling over and creating the political, ethical, and moral terrain over which voting is understood and practiced—a substantial democracy that is not sidetracked by the alibi of superficial participation. Fraser provides a different trajectory through which to discuss the danger posed by the public sphere for certain gendered and African American rhetorics and knowledges, as Whiteness and White interests in the public sphere circulate/masquerade as disinterested and rational. African American perspectives that make White interests legible can be disavowed under the guise that such perspectives are an appeal to special interests (for example, race discourse is identity politics and therefore not about the common good) or irrationality. So it is not surprising that President Barack Obama largely avoided an explicit discussion of race until compelled to by his relationship to a hush harbor space and a hush harbor rhetorician whose survival, by definition, does not depend upon *public* acceptance. It is also worth mentioning that Michelle Obama, who responded to her husband's legitimate chance for the presidency as for the first time truly feeling like an American, was infamously satirized with an Afro, weapons, exaggerated sassiness, and giving her husband a Black pound, on the cover of the sophisticated *New Yorker* magazine.[6] My point here is not to illuminate the circulation of racist visual rhetoric and representations (nothing new there). Rather, it is to make more tangible and relevant Fraser's and Harris-Lacewell's work around race and hush harbors, and how the public sphere continues to structure out, and remains dependent upon, the exclusion of African American hush harbor rhetoric (AAHHR) and not so easily consumable Blackness and African American subjectivities.

African American hush harbors (AAHHs), then, are not public spheres. They are, however, like fraternities and sororities, churches and clubs, Black publishers and record companies, and, as Harris-Lacewell theorizes, barbershops and beauty shops, Black networks in Black civil society. Hush harbors may, as an element of Black civil society, function as a conduit between civil society and the state in the way, say, a Black church might. So while hush harbors may not explicitly produce the institutions and social formations Dawson rightly values, hush harbors do wrestle over the common good—the American common good understood through African American terministic screens. Finally, hush harbors are Black publics where Black common sense, "ideology lived and articulated in everyday understanding of the world and one's place in it," is assumed to be hegemonic and normative.

Where *Keepin' It Hushed* slightly diverges from Fraser and Harris-Lacewell is in its investment in disrupting the normalcy and hegemony of the public sphere through public/counterpublic, mainstream/alternative concepts that inadvertently reestablish that which it attempts to challenge. The aforementioned binaries smuggle in through a theoretical back door the hegemony of public sphere discourses that privilege Whiteness, maleness, and heteronormativity. To wit: The hegemonic public sphere remains the center to which all other publics are alternative, and the sphere from which difference constructs its meaning and gains significance. Hush harbors are not just Habermasian public spheres with a Black difference. They are singularities—aspects of Black civil society. They are Black lifeworlds.

Othering Habermas: Black Lifeworlds, Meaning, and Cultural Rhetoric

Adopting the term from phenomenologist Edmund Husserl and sociologist Alfred Schultz, Michael Hanchard in his book about African American politics and communal expression, *Party/Politics,* deploys the term "lifeworlds." In Hanchard's usage, the *lifeworld* evokes the social networks and connections of community without the suppression of intracultural antagonisms and tensions that are often papered over in the interest of a nostalgic notion of community. Lifeworlds are the taken-for-granted bundles of beliefs, subjectivities, standpoints, and the language use that ordinary people engage in to create meaning.[7] And despite the pervasive misunderstanding of rhetoric as mere ornamentation, *meaning* is precisely a realm of rhetoric for, as James Berlin succinctly puts it, "Wherever there is persuasion, there is rhetoric. And wherever there is 'meaning,' there is persuasion."[8] Hush harbors, then, can be thought of as lifeworlds of Black meaning. AAHHR's link to Black meaning is partly what makes AAHHR a cultural rhetoric: it goes beyond rhetoric as techne to address what meanings can be and are produced within certain cultural configurations—in this case, a particular African American cultural configuration. This expands on Steven Mailloux's useful definition of *cultural rhetoric* as the "political effectivity of trope and argument in culture" by taking into account that political effectivity is linked to the maintenance and production of meaning, and to political rationalities. Of course, meaning and political rationalities and both are always contingent and tethered to culture.[9]

Importantly, hush harbors as lifeworlds "convey the vast array of identities and identifications associated with black subjectivity that are not reducible to nationality, gender, race, or region."[10] AAHHR can be viewed as a kind of literacy in that, while one of the primary functions of language is to scaffold the performance of social activities, as well as to scaffold human affiliation with other cultures, social groups, and institutions, the primary function of cultural rhetoric in general and of AAHHR as cultural rhetoric in particular is that they scaffold human affiliation *within* cultures, social groups, and institutions through rhetoric. As a term, lifeworld simultaneously evokes the inherently spatial elements of life and the protean openness and changeability of spatial meaning, use, and meaning production. The term resonates with the importance of spatiality to African American rhetoric, culture, and life. Hush harbors understood as lifeworlds are more than just the background upon which people act and upon which subjectivities and identities are performed; they are a significant geography within a network of ontological terrains upon which Black subjectivity, meaning, and existence are constructed.

For Hanchard, Black lifeworlds convey "the vast array of identities and identifications associated with Black subjectivity that are not reducible to nationality, gender, race, or region. Black lifeworlds are constituted by experiential knowledge and the lessons learned from such knowledge acted out in daily life."[11] AAHHR developed and nurtured in the Black lifeworlds of hush harbors animates and is animated by these vast arrays of identifications and knowledges. These vast arrays of identities are constructed, understood, valued, and normalized through African American life and culture.

In geographies such as the Chitlin' Circuit, barbershops, beauty shops, and some Black churches, AAHHR and identities circulate with distinctive intensities. Yet, Hanchard does not suggest some prelapsarian African American innocence or prepolitical take on African American experience sealed off or disconnected from other structures. Hanchard sutures lifeworlds to Black diasporic and African American cultures and identities while productively skirting either an uncritical essentialism or a facile fluidity. Indeed, Hanchard resonates for me precisely because he forecloses any notion of African American cultural purity while simultaneously articulating a possible architectonic of diasporic and African American cultural experience. It is important to keep Hanchard in mind as I shift to a discussion of spatiality, race, and AAHHR. Such a discussion is necessary because, in keeping with the theoretical trajectory of this project, I want to address how hush harbor spatialities can be thought of as raced in a theoretically and experientially informed manner disarticulated from the simple equation of epidermal signification and Black bodies equal Blackness and Black spatiality.

Spatiality and African American Hush Harbor Rhetoric

So what does Blackness have to do with Architecture?

DARRELL WAYNE FIELDS, *Architecture in Black*

Rhetoric and episteme are inextricably linked to space and place.

So is race.

The reception and evaluation of what is uttered by a rhetor is connected to where it is said and what has been said there before. Whether it is a courtroom, a bar, a church, or a classroom, spaces have material and discursive histories. Race and racism are a matrix of rhetorical, discursive, material, and spatial practices. Therefore, one cannot really be said to have substantially engaged African American life and culture, African and African American experience, without reference to space. Ideologically, racially and spatially charged terms such as the slave pen, slave holds (in ships), slave dungeons, whipping houses, *barracoons* (slave warehouses), slave quarters, and the various rhetorical standpoints that emerged from them illuminate the connective material and discursive tissue between spatiality, scenes of subjection, and race.

Terms such as the plantation, the suburb, the ghetto, and even that utopian spatiality of cosmopolitan porousness, the border, are fraught with racial connotations entangled in a nexus of class, caste, gender, foreignness, and race. Given the rhetorical terrains and spaces African Americans have occupied and continue to occupy in the face of continuing ex post facto segregation, it is clear that space still matters. And, if space and race still matter, and if AAHHR emerges from Black spaces and places, and if *Keepin' It Hushed* endeavors to resist the reduction of African American space to bodies, then it is productive to pause, theorize spatiality, and make explicit and theoretically tenable what it means to refer to space as racialized or as Black.

Critical and cultural geographers have replaced the term *space*, with all its Cartesian-Kantian implications of space as absolute, fixed, and static, a kind of backdrop or container in and upon which social relations occur, with the term *spatiality*. Significantly, as a term, spatiality addresses the notion that space is, in part, a relational *social product*. Spatiality also resists the Cartesian and Kantian positivistic notion of space as transparent, an empty Black box existing a priori to ideology, social meaning, and investment: space as objective and neutral. Influenced by scholars such as Henri Lefebvre, Doreen Massey, Daphne Spain, David Harvey, bell hooks, and Delores Hayden, the notion of space as manufactured and produced, as relational and in process, reflects a major theoretical shift in the spatial imagination from the previous paradigm grounded in mathematical abstraction, empty and positivistic in orientation. Lefebvre writes, "Could space be nothing more than the passive locus of social relations, the milieu in which their combination takes on the body, or the aggregate of the procedures employed in their removal?"[12]

Dolores Hayden writes in *The Power of Place,* "People make attachments to places that are critical to their well-being or distress. An individual's sense of place is both a biological response to the surrounding physical environment and a cultural creation, as geographer Yi-Fu Yuan argues."[13] All three critical geographers point beyond spatiality as more than a Cartesian-Kantian abstraction, as more than its material composition. While not denying the materiality of space, understanding spatiality as a social product foregrounds what commonsense notions of space tend to overlook—the social, epistemic, and ideological aspects of space. Space as social and ideological begins to carve out a site to place a notion of the hush harbor as a Black spatiality on more firm theoretical terrain. It frees Blackness from merely an epidermal and cultural question, and frees geography from the prison of the material, enabling both to be reframed under rubrics of social relations, the production of knowledges, and the circulation of power.

Again, although spatiality does not ignore that space exists prior to human encounter, it privileges the importance of how the conception, understanding, habitation, and use of the materiality of space and place mediate the encounter through power and ideology. Human encounter with space is never neutral. While space as social and ideological seems self-evident to some, it is often not so apparent to most because spatial constraints are repeated so often that they become encoded and familiar, rarely noticed, thereby ceasing to consciously matter—or, more precisely, making invisible how indeed a conception of spatiality always ideologically matters, masking how conceptions and descriptions of space are often used to serve hegemonic purposes. For example, when is a terrain a "frontier" and when is it civilized? Who must inhabit a frontier to make it a civilized territory? When is a neighborhood a ghetto? A suburb? Who then occupies a ghetto when it is reduced to a trope of violence and a commonplace for neglect, lack, and deprivation? And who occupies it when it is also understood as an a ethnic enclave with productive aspects? When is a neighborhood a "hood?" Although the reader must be wary of a kind of nostalgia, Cornel West in 2008's *Hope on a Tightrope* makes a spatial distinction in the following fashion: "I grew up in a neighborhood, not a 'hood. It was all Black. Our neighborhood was a place where there were wonderful ties of sympathy and bonds of empathy. The folks who lived there kept track of you. A 'hood is the survival of the slickest. They are obsessed with the 11th Commandment, 'Thou shalt not get caught.' That is what young people are up against."[14] Such questions, as well as West's description, unsettle uncritical, commonplace notions of space as ideologically and politically neutral, creating a bridge of understanding to how architectural history and form are not only social and ideological but also infused with racialist, classist, and masculinist assumptions.

Architectural theorist and critic Darrell Fields in *Architecture in Black* describes how G. W. F. Hegel, whose books *Lectures on the Philosophy of World History* (1837) and *Aesthetics: Lectures on the Fine Arts* (1835) continue to be pivotal in architectural schools, exiled Africa from history, and African/Black forms from architectural theory and history, when he shifted the Egyptian pyramid from the African style to the Asiatic. This gesture assisted in inscribing Whiteness and neutrality into the conceptual terrain of architectural theory and practice.[15]

Adolf Loos's germinal modernist manifesto "Ornament and Crime," argues for the suppression of ornament and decoration in the regulating of passion. Loos's tethers ornament and decoration to argue for the erasure of ornament from architectural form; he views ornament as a deflection from form's rationality, substance, and truth.[16] Just as the secret to the whitest white paint in Ralph Ellison's *Invisible Man* (1952) is a drop of Black paint, and just as Toni Morrison's *Playing in the Dark* (1992) unveils the African presence upon which American literature is constructed, Hegel's and Loos's projects making Blackness excessive and ornamental inscribe the absent-presence of Africa/Blackness in architectural theory. My reason for importing architectural history and theory into this discussion is an elaboration and extension of *Keepin' It Hushed*'s attempt to theorize AAHHR and Black spatiality beyond bodies. In terms of racialized space, Field's rereading of architectural theory and history chisels a space to move beyond Black space and built environments based on habitation and use by Black bodies to one that reads architectural *form* as being raced. Such a gesture moves hush harbors as Black space from the mere sociological to the theoretical.

The notion of Black space and architecture can be found in Robert Farris Thompson's germinal *Flash of the Spirit* (1884). Thompson describes the cultivation techniques and architecture of Black runaway slaves of the Mandé ethnic group of Mali in West Africa in Costa Chica, on the western coast of Mexico as "a momentous event in the history of African-influenced architecture in the New World."[17] Cone-on-cylinder techniques and multi-habitational "socially binding spaces" that continue to this day. As work by scholars such as Michael Vlach, Dell Upton, and Steven Nelson illustrate, African and African American forms such as the shotgun house, the porch, and the Mousgoum teleuk embody form and rationality, thereby challenging rationality as acultural. Black bodies and Black spaces in African American life and culture are more often than not viewed as epistemically empty or as outside of rationality. So when Muhammad Ali told Whites, in the introduction, that "you do not know me," it can be read as a synecdoche for the rationality and knowledge too often locked within a negative diacritical relation to Blackness, Black bodies, and Black spaces. *Keepin' It Hushed* wants to ensure that no such invisibilities and erasures are locked into a relation to AAHHR, hush harbors, and the theorizing of Black spatiality.

From the Enslavement and the Constitution to contemporary attempts at redlining and the rapid growth of gated communities, the partitioning of race and ethnicity has seeped into American settlement and spatial practices. In short, accompanying the much-touted linguistic turn of literature and critical and rhetorical theory is a spatial turn that increasingly recognizes space and knowledge as ideological and rhetorical. Pushing the argument further, Beatriz Columbia posits—the reader should take note of how her work intersects with that of Huxley's vis-à-vis spatiality and subjectivity—that spatiality not only contains social and ideological relations and the subjectivities to which they tend to be sutured but also *produces* them[18]—produces subjectivities. Therefore, even spatial design is ideological. For example, space and place are not equivalent: they function on different scales. A bedroom would be one scale, a block would be another, a neighborhood would be a larger scale. Spatiality, place, and scale produce subjectivities. So, as spatiality and place function on different scales, it is necessary to distinguish between them.

Although there are many ways to distinguish between space and place, for the purposes of this examination I understand place as *practiced spatiality.*[19] Hush harbors can be interpreted as practiced spatialities of Black culture or Black space.

Geographer David Delaney in *Race, Place, and the Law* cogently addresses race, spatiality, and the racialized practices of juridical institutions. Although Delaney is not specifically concerned with rhetorical theory, his concern with race and its connection to spatiality assists me in illuminating the significant interrelation of race, space, and rhetoric because his work illuminates "the central position that geography has occupied in the unfolding dynamics of African American history."[20] I would add to Delaney's formulation by making explicit that which his formulation assumes—the central position that geography has played in the unfolding dynamics of African American identity and, by extension, African American life and culture through the knowledges and identities of Black folks through spatial practices.

In chapter 4, I illustrate how what cultural geographer Christopher Airriess refers to as *ethnic landscapes* and *cultural autobiography*[21] construct and inscribe Blackness and identity on urban landscapes through signage such as marquees, advertising, magazines, and clothing. Hush harbors as Black lifeworlds are infused with signage, magazines, smells, tastes, feelings, memories, and histories. Further, hush harbors have particular discursive uses and functions imbricated in those histories. Expectations emerge around those histories. Those histories precede any individual performance and must be taken into account if the rhetorics are to be entertaining, persuasive, or pedagogical. Therefore, rhetorical performances and the African American life and culture in which they are entangled are mediated both at the point of production and at reception by the spatiality in which they occur.

Quite as Its Not Kept: Principles of African American Hush Harbor Rhetoric

Several rhetorical principles, terms and themes implicitly and explicitly inform and constitute my approach to AAHHR. However, here I want to focus on three primary principles of AAHHR: *nommo, parrhesia,* and *phronesis.*

Fundamental to any discussion of AAHHR and to any genre of African American rhetoric is the principle of *nommo.* Informed discussion of African American rhetoric in its public, literary, or hush harbor forms *must* take *nommo* (the power of the word) into account. Influenced by the work of Janheinz Jahn and Marcel Griaule, nommo was codified in speech communication through the scholarship of Afrocentric theorist Arthur Smith, who would later be known as Molefi Kete Asante.[22] Of course, to describe nommo as the power of the word does little for rhetorical scholars because the term *rhetoric* itself implies the power of the word and therefore remains conceptually vague. Fortunately, Adisa A. Alkebulan and Richard L. Wright in the excellent *Understanding African American Rhetoric* contribute articles providing analytic sharpness to nommo. Grounding nommo in this manner in *Keepin' It Hushed* is important because the entire discussion of hush harbors and AAHHR as they circulate in African American life and culture is informed by nommo. As hip-hip, spoken word, poetry, and the importance of preachers and public intellectuals—problematic masculinist logics notwithstanding—illustrate, orature remains vitally important to African American life.

According to Alkebulan and Wright, speech (rhetoric) is fundamental not only to the binding together of community but also to that community's understanding of reality.[23] Put differently, the material world is understood, constructed, impacted through language; language and rhetoric are not epiphenomenal to reality. Wright in "The Word at Work" uses the image of the plow to illustrate how nommo functions in and through the materiality of the world: "That is, like the plow, which parts the earth in preparation for the planting of the seed, the word does work in the world."[24]

Nommo is so significant to African American life and culture and to AAHHR that I explore the term in depth in chapter 3 and refer to it in several chapters. Nommo is practiced within a material and discursive terrain of asymmetrical power relations in the American context. As a result, understanding nommo intensifies the understanding of what is at stake in African language use and African American oppression when words are often the only or primary weapon left to a subjugated people advocating not only for their rights but also for recognition as being fully human. As such, while words and rhetoric have never been merely been epiphenomenal to material and political practices, this is particularly the case for African Americans and their life and culture in hush harbors and for Black folks occupying space temporarily in the hegemonic public sphere where they have been traditionally relegated backstage. For example, Muhammad Ali's words intensified what is at stake around African American language use and the construction of hegemonic masculinity when he asserted a Black masculinity that refused to acquiesce to mainstream or White expectations of decorum and civility.

Muhammad Ali's nommo emerged from distinctive African American spatialities, possessing distinctive assumptions about Black masculinities, their performances, and their meanings; it evolved from his privileging of African American standpoints anchored in African American life and experience.

Reverend Jeremiah Wright's hush harbor rhetoric was a centripetal force in the hush harbor spatiality of a Black church where the Black unsaid can be said, thereby challenging the hegemonic political rationality in front of a materially and discursively Black audience; the same force in which motion when entered into the public sphere is reversed, becomes centrifugal, creating such polarization that, after years of attending church, President Obama was required to distance himself from hush harbor rhetoric to facilitate his election. Nommo inserts a kind of undomesticated Blackness into the world. Conversely, nommo linked to African American knowledge and worldviews or standpoints is the lingua franca of AAHHR. As the hush harbor rhetorics and subjectivities of Muhammad Ali, Lani Guinier, Harry Belafonte, Rev.

Wright, and African American life and culture seep into the public sphere, those rhetorics must be domesticated or delegitimated as they disrupt the normative political rationality of the hegemonically White public sphere; therefore, hush harbor rhetorics are deemed *parrhesiatically* dangerous.

Parrhesia alludes to fearless, dangerous speech.[25] Influenced by the courage of Socrates and the boldness of Black folks such as Dr. Julia Hare attempting to dismantle the disciplinary gaze of a White audience, Cornel West and Michel Foucault address the centrality of *parrhesia* and of the *parrhesiastes* (the rhetor/speaker willing to engage in parrhesia). Parrhesia is important to any substantial notion of democracy that pushes beyond the procedural (e.g., electoral politics, reduced to voting) to fundamental questions of the good, justice, and power as they relate to the soul of the body politic that seriously pivots around knowledge, life, culture, and suffering. Parrhesia requires the rhetor to put herself at risk in speaking truth to power, to the dominant political rationality, or to a hegemony that could result in the loss of status, influence, resources, legitimacy, or life. African American parrhesia, then, embodies the aforementioned, but the African American parrhesiastes deploys African American truths and knowledges through African American terministic screens. Parrhesia is endemic to AAHHR, as not only are African American knowledges and ways of knowing privileged, but also as Black notions of civility, decorum, and permissible speech are dominant. African American parrhesia is often constructed as angry, militant, distorted, irrational, unreasonable, unpatriotic, divisive, and, of course, dangerous. However, the African American parrhesiastes who is willing to wedge African American knowledges and standpoints into the public sphere is highly valued.

The aforementioned begs the question of whether AAHHR knowledges and standpoints can or should be inserted into the public sphere. Such is a practical/ethical question that *Keepin' It Hushed* addresses in the last chapter, "Neoliberalism and the Domestication and Commodification of Hush Harbor Blackness in the Public Sphere." So *Keepin' It Hushed* attempts to heighten the understanding of the importance of the barbershop as a hush harbor where Black knowledges and American democracy are taken seriously, and where *both* a distinctive African American political rationality is manufactured and the dominant political rationality is affirmed and challenged and able to transmit rhetorical force as they are listened to with pathos-motivated hearing and engaged through practical knowledge and experience.[26] Several times *Keepin' It Hushed* has deployed the term *knowledge*. Prior to providing a short description of the remaining chapters in the book, I want to discuss the kind of knowledge to which *Keepin' It Hushed* refers.

Nommo invigorates the reception of Black rhetorical knowledge through phronesis. *Phronesis,* which refers to practical wisdom, intellect, or virtue,[27] embraces high theory but wrenches it down to earth around functionality and usefulness. Phronesis includes, but is more than, street smarts; it includes, but is more than, quaint wisdom because it coalesces theory within lived everyday experience and usefulness. Phronesis taps into the *sensus communitas*—the commonplaces—of African American culture and provides the *subjective fortification* so highly valued in African American communities.[28]

The *commonplace* is an important element of phronesis. Commonplaces, or Black commonplaces in the case of AAHHR, can be defined and understood in the following ways: a rhetorical place from which to invent or inform an argument (e.g., the Bible, the vernacular culture, the barbershop), a strategy of argument (e.g., call-and-response, signifyin'), or a Black cultural touchstone familiar to African American communities in a particular way within a constellation of African American social relations (e.g., the Chitlin' Circuit, Harlem, twenty-twos). A *Black commonplace* can be productively thought of as what literary theorist Stephen Henderson calls a mascon. The *mascon* is a commonplace that exudes massive concentrations of Black symbolic energy. This symbolic energy moves African American audiences because it taps deeply into African American terministic screens, experiences, memories, and meaning.[29] Phronesis, then, in hush harbor spatialities and as an element of AAHHR, taps into African American political rationalities informed by Black common sense thereby affirming African American ontology, knowledges, subjectivities, and the relation of all of the aforementioned to themselves as citizen subjects of the nation-state.

Keepin' It Hushed attempts to perform the danger it theorizes. It resists the current trend in academia to underestimate the epistemic status and political saliency AAHHR for Black folks and others who live and function at the lower frequencies of public culture. Such underestimation relegates the experiences of vast numbers of Black folks to the detritus of identity and difference.

While useful and well intentioned in the context of certain scholarship, politics, and uncritical investments in reactionary identity politics, pithy shibboleths such as "race is a fiction" and "race is a social construction" allow a retreat from the everyday politics of the racial state and White privilege. Race is not a social construct; it is not a fairy tale; it is a political rationality with material, psychological, and social implications and effects. *Keepin' It Hushed,* through its engagement with AAHHR, understands that the violence of identity politics for some is the mandatory refusal of invisibility and epistemic irrelevancy for others. It is these others, like Muhammad Ali, who refuse epistemic and existential erasure, that constitute the investment of *Keepin' It Hushed.*

Having set up the theoretical and rhetorical framework of the book, chapter 2 situates the barbershop trope within a genealogy/cartography of related, but distinct, iterations of AAHH sites. It shifts from rugged, unculti- vated terrains such as woods and swamps to physical structures (churches and jook joints) and organizations (burial societies) to connect the barbershop to a genealogy of hush harbors. Chapter 3 closely examines the barbershop chapter in novelist Leon Forrest's epic *Divine Days* (1995), and two novels by novelist and cultural activist John Oliver Killens: *The Cotillion; or, One Good Bull Is Half the Herd* (1971) and *Youngblood* (1954). One of the goals of this chapter is to understand more precisely how nommo, in conjunction with narrative sequencing and nomos (truth and reality as human and social con- vention rather than unassailable natural law), works to produce meaning and significance emanating from distinct African American political rationalities in African American life and culture. Chapter 4 shifts to the genre of poetry to examine the barbershop as a pedagogical site of rhetorical education through the transmission of knowledges, rituals, and identities in relation to the work of several poets, including Richard Wright, Sterling Brown, Keith Gilyard, Sonya Brooks, S. Brandi Barnes, Major Jackson, and Kevin Young. While hardly comprehensive, the chapter is useful in further establishing the depth and breadth of hush harbor rhetoric in African American life and culture.

While nommo certainly functions on a generative register within AAHH spatialities, rhetorics, and rationalities, it also produces damaging effects that point to the limitations of African American political rationalities and AAHHR in that both are hardly innocent of reactionary ideologies and practices. To that end, chapter 4 concludes with an exegesis of Sterling A. Brown's "Slim Hears 'The Call'" (1932) to illustrate the deployment of negative nommo. Of course, barbershops are immersed in the contradictions of Black culture. Barbershops can, of course, produce their own versions of oppressive discourse. The chapter addresses some of those contradictions. Chapter 5 uses Keith Gilyard's memoir *Voices of the Self* (1991) and Lonne Elder III's play *Ceremonies of Dark Old Men* (1969) to compare and contrast the African American rhetor speaking well and the African American rhetor who speaks badly because he lacks the practical wisdom of phronesis.

As popular culture increases in its importance as a public pedagogy in American entertainment (popular culture is the number one export of the United States), and in the reception and production of African American subjectivities, it is more than coincidence that the barbershop as hush harbor attracts attention. Chapter 6 tackles the *Barbershop* films to explore how the commodification of Blackness constructs an easily consumable, marketable, sellable Blackness increasingly disconnected from the histories and politics linked to the practical wisdom that provides meaning and substance to African American struggle. Chapter 7 in *Keepin' It Hushed* addresses what an AAHHR approach to pedagogy might look like. Chapter 8 concludes *Keepin' It Hushed* with an examination of the ethics and pragmatics of inserting AAHH rhetoric and knowledge into the public sphere in an epoch of neoliberalism. I believe this chapter takes on particular gravitas given the election of the first Black president of the United States.

3.

Wingin' It

Barbershops and the Work
of *Nommo* in the Novel

NARRATOR, PLAYWRIGHT, JOURNALIST, AND BARTENDER JOUBERT JONES IS
the protagonist of *Divine Days* (1993). Discharged from the military, Joubert has
returned to Forest County to "take over [his] own life," so that he can, "regi-
ment [his, i.e., Joubert's] emotional waywardness and [his] easily distracted
intelligence."[1] Joubert struggles to find meaning in his life through writing
a play about the soul within the voice of his recently deceased mentor, the
trickster, angel, and hustler Sugar Groove.

This chapter uses three texts: Leon Forrest's *Divine Days* and John Oliver
Killens's *Youngblood* (1982) and *The Cotillion* (1971). All three texts are written
by accomplished writers grounded in African American vernacular language,
knowledges, and experiences; all of these literary texts evoke the importance
and significance of the power of the word; all three are pivotal works in African
American vernacular-oriented literature; they provide a fecund context in
which to place chapter 1's more abstract discussion of nommo in relationship to the concepts of narrative sequencing and nomos, both important
sources of meaning making in African American life and culture; all three

novels are fertile sites for analysis because they are anchored in Black modes of discourse, African American rhetoric, and African American political rationalities; and finally, all three have significant barbershop milieus where African American hush harbor rhetoric (AAHHR) circulates. It is appropriate to begin with *Divine Days:* a barbershop scene is one of the first scenes Forrest wrote for the novel and evokes the importance of nommo.

Adisa A. Alkebulan establishes nommo's importance as a principle not only of classical West African and African American rhetoric, but also of African and African American cosmology and philosophy, by explaining nommo's significance to African philosophy: "Nothing exists without nommo."[2] Read alongside Richard L. Wright's notion of the term, here nommo is read as mutually constitutive of concrete, material reality, not external to such processes. Nommo is an elegant rendering in a single concept of how our terministic screens through which we create and interpret the material world shape its production, its circulation or reception, and therefore its meaning. In this view, nommo is both a resource of and lens through which Africans and African Americans encounter humanity and life. These resources differ from European traditional rhetoric in its connection to African American political rationalities and therefore use African American, European, and American rhetorical forms and tactics for African/African American ends. As such, nommo permeates both discursive and material African American reality.

Forrest's Joubert is an African American Odysseus traveling through the seas of Chicago's South Side, where he encounters a wide-ranging tableau of African American characters of Greek and Ellisonian dimensions. These include the trickster as Mephistopheles, W. A. D. Ford (an apparent satirical take on W. D. Fard, the mythical mentor of Elijah Muhammad, the founder of the Black Muslims), who will engage in a final, violent confrontation with Sugar Groove, Aunt Eloise (Joubert's guardian), and Imani, Joubert's girlfriend, whose search for authentic Blackness through her African roots leads to tragic consequences. Through his travels, Joubert attempts to come to grips with life's contradictions. In the end, he comes to the conclusion that reinvention, not double consciousness, lies at the heart of the African American experience.[3]

Ecstatic about his first haircut upon his return to Forest Grove, Joubert goes to see Oscar Williemain. Proprietor and head barber, Williemain has invited Joubert, who was ten years old when he shined shoes in Williemain's barbershop, to be an initiate for possible membership into the exclusive Royal Rites and Righteous Ramblings Club. Here, Forrest immediately situates the barbershop and its importance to African American culture as a conduit of class mobility. The barbershop is one of the geographies of African American civic culture that provides entrepreneurial opportunities. Oftentimes, in the ghettos and postindustrial wastelands of some segments of Black America, the barbershop thrives. When mainstream institutions will not hire and other Black businesses fail, Black men young and old can find employment in a barbershop. As a site of economic vitality, the barbershop provides a version of business success that is obtainable for many and that points toward economic possibility for those who play the game of life relativity straight as opposed to those playin' it crooked.

Askia Muhammad's "Conversations in a Black Barbershop" (2003) contains a narrative in which a barber talks about how controlling his own chair allowed him to schedule his own hours and kept him out of jail. The barbershop provides flexibility, status, and a place for some Black men to be themselves and construct their lives.

The initiation into the Rites and Righteous Ramblings Club was also significant for Joubert: "To be a man among men means, among other things, to be taken in the back of the barbershop after closing and for Williemain to offer you something from his private stock. Then you could converse until shortly after midnight about things usually unspoken of during the harsh light of the workday world, up front in the barbershop."[4]

Being a man among men is important for Joubert, who desires the rhetorical education and knowledge production in the hush harbor site of the barbershop in which Black male masculinity is taken up as a generative site of social and cultural agency. For example, Joubert is well educated, cosmopolitan, and well connected. He is mobile and not imprisoned in a deficit ethos of Black pathology. Yet, he and other Black men who have achieved success such as politicians, businessmen, and ministers in Forest Grove want to become members of the Royal Rites and Righteous Ramblings Club. With this gesture, Forrest expands narrow notions of Black masculinity typically affiliated with criminality, pathology, irresponsibility, and sexuality to include a variety of Black men from different social positions concerned with being a man among men. Black masculinity is struggled over, humanized, and made functional in the barbershop in *Divine Days*.

Joubert pines for membership in Williemain's Royal Rites and Righteous Ramblings Club because it is a barbershop hush harbor away from the light of day, off stage from the surveillance of dominant assumptions about Black men. Hush harbor sanctuaries enable Black men to bear secular-sacred witness, to explore, to disagree, and temporarily to transgress dominant assumptions. Membership in this club implies that Black men in his Black lifeworld, have legitimized Joubert on the terrain of Black male experience, subjectivities, rhetoric, and knowledge—not violence.

While a rigorous theoretical and scholarly engagement with Black masculinities is not within the purview of this project, the focus on Joubert's initiation through masculinity and rhetoric is not to trivialize or avoid the obvious symbolic and material violences inscribed in and through hegemonic masculinity, nor is it to trivialize how male hush harbors such as the barbershop can be incubators for male privilege. Instead, it is to make two points: One is to connect masculinity to the notion of ontology expressed earlier that tears both masculinity and blackness away from biology, situating both within a network of overall social and political structural relation and value informing a variety of social practices. Two, by doing so, the stage is set to argue for a progressive masculinity that recognizes that masculinity, as John O. Calmore argues quoting Michael S. Kimmel and Michael A. Messner, and that "men are not born, they are made. And men make themselves, actively constructing their masculinities within a social and historical context."[5] My focus, then, on Joubert's initiation without the denigration of women and the valorization of violence points to the possibility of a different rhetorical terrain for the formation of more generative forms of masculinities and femininities for males and females.

Once Joubert enters into the back room of the barbershop, Williemain sets the general course of the subject matter, but "Williemain welcomes variety" because "more than anything else, he wants to see your stuff and what you are made of."[6] He determines what a man is made of based upon his verbal, not his physical, skills. Like subjects everywhere, Black men fight in many places and spaces. But in the barbershop, as in the Black church, violence is heavily frowned upon and occurs infrequently. Barbershops as hush harbors are cherished bulwarks against the danger and chaos that threaten the street. Therefore, rhetorical conflict, not physical altercation, is the ground upon which African American male masculinities are performed and evaluated in these locales. In African American life and culture, as well as in American expressive culture, men are represented as feeling comfortable and safe in barbershops. Rhetorical exchanges there rarely lead to the kind of violence in other hush harbor sites such as jook joints, street corners, pool halls, and, unfortunately, domestic spatialities. For example, even the highly stylized, hyperviolent movie *Belly* (dir. Harold "Hype" Williams, 1998), which contains two barbershop scenes, relegates its violence to outside the shop. Also, no physical violence occurs in either of the *Barbershop* movies.

In African American male hush harbors like the barbershop, male masculinity is constructed partly through the nommo of conversation. Since nommo addresses African American realities, it is no surprise that it has been associated with American rap music, Negro spirituals, jazz, and their rhetorical forms and devices.[7] Joubert goes to the barbershop precisely to immerse and/or reacquaint himself with the experiences and knowledges that inform nommo.

The Royal Rites and Righteous Ramblings Club is exclusive. Nevertheless, as *Divine Days* illustrates, its exclusivity is not predicated upon social status; its exclusivity is connected to how deeply and how long one has been immersed in the commonplaces, tropes, forms, worldviews, and political rationalities of African American rhetoric and Black talk. When Williemain wanted to evaluate what the men in his exclusive barbershop hush harbor club were made of, he tested not their bodies, not their strength, but their rhetoric. When he judged Joubert's rhetoric, Joubert's words were interpreted as being connected to who he is and to what he practices.

Later in the week, Prof. Allerton Jamesway, Galloway Wheeler (the resident Shakespearean scholar), and other folks packed the barbershop as Williemain cut Joubert's hair and got knee deep into his story about the recently deceased Sugar Groove. There was one question on everyone's mind. What happened to Sugar Groove's body? It was missing, and Joubert wanted Williemain to get to the *truth* of the matter even as he knew that attempting to get to the truth of the matter through just the facts of the matter was sometimes like trying to hit a straight lick with a crooked stick. Sugar Groove is a mythopoetic figure and image, a commonplace and mascon that are deeply drenched in the rivers of African American literature, folklore, and rhetoric. Williemain's exordium about Sugar Groove's flight, his nomadic ways, and his hustling behavior signifies that Sugar Groove is a trickster figure, immediately establishing the narrative's ethos with his Black hush harbor audience.

Much has been written about African American trickster figures, their similarity to African and Greek myths, their importance as tropes of resistance, and their historical significance as figures of possibility. Trickster figures in stories like *Divine Days* often make marginalized folks and the rationalities motivating their exclusion legible. For example, at the stroke of midnight, while her husband was playing the numbers, Sugar Groove's Aunt Gracie made a deal with the angel Gabriel, allowing Sugar Groove into heaven: "There was even a divine proclamation to that effect," but Williemain heard that "the written contract over his soul" greatly confounded Sugar Groove's status in paradise, as "the covenant was quite restrictive."[8] Forrest signifies upon the amount of energy America has purposely invested in keeping Black folks and their rationalities in their discursive and material place, making the heaven of democracy possible for others. From the Constitution's limiting them to three fifths of a human being, to housing covenants, racial profiling, and prison, material and discursive restriction has assisted in the patrolling of the gates of African American male possibility. Sugar Groove's restriction, then, reflects a tangible communal experience, a blues communal "I" evoked by the tale. Even if the Sugar Groove narrative is a lie (and it may be), Williemain's narrative refers to a larger truth. As a literary narrative, *Divine Days* intersects with African American oral narrative reflecting what Geneva Smitherman describes as narrative sequencing.

One of the modes of Black discourse, *narrative sequencing* includes more than the African American storytelling tradition such as toasts, ghost stories, and tall tales; it also contains a characteristic register of Black communication generally alluding to how African American vernacular English speakers will "render the general, abstract observations about love, life, and people in the form of a concrete narrative."[9] Narrative sequencing is so important to African American rhetoric, life, and expressive culture that the notion that "a nigguh always got a story" circulates as a prevalent commonplace.[10] Smitherman rightly understands narrative sequencing as the African American rhetorical strategy of *invention* through which the rhetor persuades the audience to the rhetor's point of view. Narrative sequencing involves Black invention, delivery, and style. As cultural theorist Stuart Hall argues, "Within the Black repertoire, style—which mainstream cultural critics often believe to be the mere husk, the wrapping, the sugar coating on the pill—has become itself the subject of what is going on."[11]

Narrative sequencing, then, produces knowledge not only through the use of the trickster trope as an inventional strategy but also as a rhetorical topoi or commonplace immersed in African American culture. It functions as a technique of knowledge creation in that its deployment by a rhetor makes legible her or his connection to African American culture, values, and experiences—through its rhetoric.

Most importantly, narrative sequencing as an element of nommo does work in the world. It creates a discursive spatiality of agency, identity creation, and meaning. Narrative sequencing asserts I am, Black folks are, and African American life and culture are. Therefore, Williemain's narrative sequencing serves a pedagogical as well as a persuasive function. Its deployment alludes to the subtle and not-so-subtle modes of resistance and knowledge creation that infuse the ways of Black folks.

Sugar Groove is called to heavenly account in just his first week in paradise because, among many other instances of rule breaking, he was seen "jetting down the left-hand side of the Kingdom, up and down the wrong side of the track, sailing, and jetting and floating and flipping and zooming 100 miles a second, on Sunday Morning at Sabbath-tolling time."[12] Forrest deploys the flight trope that is so important in African American culture as a mascon with secular and sacred implications. From the Gullah Island myth of the flying Africans, Negro spirituals (plantation songs), and Bigger Thomas's obsession with planes, to Charlie "Bird" Parker's solos, Ellison's

"Flying Home," Milkman's leaps, and R. Kelly's believing he can fly, tropes of flight infuse African American culture and male existence with optimism and possibility. More specifically, Sugar Groove embodies the secular African folktale American of the rebellious *flying fool*.[13]

Divine Days' story references to St. Peter, wings, flight, and heaven, as well as the use of symbols of restraint and exclusion, resuscitate the afore-mentioned folktale of the flying fool. St. Peter forestalled Sugar Groove from entering the gates of heaven. When St. Peter went to relieve himself, Sugar Groove sneaked in, swiped some wings, and zoomed up and down, sideways and hisway until he crashed. The flying fool/trickster represents a tradition of African American resistance to oppression and the affirmation of African American culture. As with the sharecropper Jefferson in Ralph Ellison's "Fly-ing Home" (1944) or Sterling A. Brown's "Slim" poems (ca. 1930–33) the trope of the flying fool is a repository of African American knowledge, wisdom, and wit that provides psychic and cultural solace within the verb of Blackness.[14]

Sugar Groove's flying got fancier and faster until Gabriel had to send him a note: "You better straighten up and fly right, Sugar Groove."[15] When Zora Neale Hurston attempted to provide a taxonomy of Blackness in "Characteristics of Negro Expression" (1994), the Negro's penchant for angularity and the will to adorn were two primary characteristics. Sugar Groove's angular flight, his jetting down the left side while the other angels float down the right, exemplifies his will to adorn.[16] As I will explore more thoroughly in the next chapter, adornment or ornament circulates as more than mere decoration in culture in general and specifically in African American culture. Read through an African American rhetorical lens, adornment conveys aspects of Sugar Groove's Black subjectivity. By this I mean, African American rhetoric values and encourages energetic and animated bodily movement and gestures in a manner that exceeds that of public sphere and public spatial concepts of civility and decorum. While hardly monolithic, the Eurocentric mediated, rhetorical aesthetic of the mainstream public sphere dominated by corporate media interest tends to privilege the performance of rationality, logic, and neutrality through the lack of adornment, the containment of the body and bodily gestures (i.e., criticism of Michelle Obama wearing sleeveless dresses revealing her arms), and the suppression of emotion to convey objectivity and sober detachment. Angularity embodies an African American rhetorical criterion that encourages rhetorical performances that flow over the barriers and banks of categories of mainstream decorum, an excess that produces a difference(s) that Blackness makes. Jazz's improvisational hubris, the blues' flatted fifth, and hip-hop's verbal gymnastics all reflect rhetorics that deterritorialize public sphere conceptions of flying right. Sugar Groove's angular movement decenters Whiteness. For example, dance movements choreographed by Katherine Dunham and Alvin Ailey often embraced an Afro-modernist angularity. Groove's blackness is angular—a verb, not a noun. Sugar Groove couldn't straighten up and fly right because the political rationalities informing his subjectivities compelled his jetting down the left-hand side of the Kingdom, up and down the wrong side of the track. For him, the so-called wrong side of the track was the "right" side.

Containing Black improvisation in relation to the movement of the body was a tall order, even for Gabriel. St. Peter had to be brought in to restore some rationality, some order: "Negro, have you lost your cotton picking mind?"[17] Improvisation with a Black difference—flyin' and jettin' down the left-hand side of the Kingdom—disrupts normative assumptions. The improvising Black subject, an "uppity nigga" outside hush harbors of Blackness, is deemed as having gone insane. Sugar Groove improvises with a difference beyond the privileged channels of meaning and produces Black noise that St. Peter does not want to see or hear.

St. Peter continues to display his irritation at Sugar Groove's flying and jetting down the left side of the track because, as St. Peter put it, "You just got here on a wing and a prayer as it is. Your grand aunt prayed you into Heaven and apparently struck some shady deal between herself, her boss man, and Gabriel, behind my back. But limitations were placed upon your status in the beginning. And your travel was curtailed. . . . I'm thinking seriously about cutting down on your spare ribs."[18] Sugar Groove's response to St. Peter embraces improvisation with a glib and witty vernacular retort to existential and concrete constraint: "I just wing it."[19] Forrest's narrative just wings it on the currents of African American vernacular. Parrhesia in the barbershop makes a spatiality in which Black men can just wing it. Nommo and phronesis construct a function at a Black junction where Black men can just wing it. They can wing it with Black flava, Black insight, and Black hush harbor rhetoric. Just wingin' it is an African American maxim and rhetorical device transformed into a mascon that traverses literary, rhetorical, and musical boundaries. However, like improvisation in jazz or Jackson Pollock's drip-and-slash technique in modern art, to wing it in the barbershop does not minimize contemplation, skill, and thought. To wing it suggests that African American rhetorical situations and African American exigency often require one to have mastered one's art enough, prepared enough, to improvise, to verbally shake and bake, and to perform one's subjectivity quickly and confidently in response to the assertions and interrogations of interlocutors on all sides of the racial fence.

Williemain explains how St. Peter time and time again not only attempts to convince Sugar Groove to stay in his place, but also tries to compel him to describe how he manages to wing it. Sugar Groove's refusal to divulge how he wings it is a metaphor for the resistance to appropriation of Black culture by Whites. Of course, the very success of African American rhetorical forms in the public sphere means that some appropriation is inevitable, possibly even desirable. Yet, since Black culture is not static, it will continue to invent and improvise novel or distinctive forms that temporarily escape appropriation. *Divine Days* satirically inserts White appropriation of Black culture into the afterworld of the promised land that Black folks have traditionally viewed as emancipatory.

White angels appropriate or bite Sugar Groove's style. They start three Sugar Groove fan clubs, one in which the members try to nap up their blonde wigs. Of course, the increase in the appropriation of Black culture has some White angels disconcerted. Since even St. Peter is denied access to hush harbors in which such knowledge is maintained, he keeps harassing Sugar Groove for the information. Unlike St. Peter, no character in the barbershop asks Williemain how the mythical Sugar Groove wings it; they either already know how or understand that the telling of the story is a pedagogical method to teach them how Sugar Groove does what he does.

Heaven appears to be in great disorder because Sugar Groove, as angular as a cubist painting, seems to be coming "from opposite directions."[20] In frustration, St. Peter performs a heavenly lynching: he clips Sugar Groove's wing. But *Divine Days* does not stop with this tragedy. It cannot. The historical and pedagogical function of folklore reflects how, despite the circumstances, Black folks keep on wingin' it. So does Sugar Groove.

St. Peter loses his cool when he discovers that Sugar Groove has been doing all his wingin' and jettin' with just one wing! He cannot believe that Sugar Groove flies with such style, grace, angularity, and adornment with one wing: "In the name of the lord and how supple you can dip down, as you get low, in your quick-silver-satin-soul—I'll amaze your grace."[21] Williemain is on a roll as he tells the men in the barbershop how Sugar Groove's braggadocio so amazed and surprised St. Peter that St. Peter suffered a heart attack. Sugar Groove is the only man who can transport St. Peter to the emergency room in paradise, so the angel Gabriel regenerates Sugar Groove's wing. Like a Black Icarus who uses improvisation with a Black difference to keep from falling, Sugar Groove wrote his name "upon the Proscenium of paradise." At this point, another barber, Galloway Wheeler, continues the story in the African American call-and-response pedagogical tradition and then hands the story back to Williemain, who proclaims that St. Peter's heart attack, due to Sugar Groove' improvisation, was the first time that anybody ever suffered a coronary in paradise. He ended the tall tale with his usual "Gentlemens, I ain't never lied."[22] Joubert responds to the tall tale with his own rhyme:

Raccoon, you know, he was an engineer
Possum, he always tend the switch.
Streamlined man from Sugar-Ditch?
Nothing but—a high-flying-son-a-bitch.

All the barbershop laughed in deep remembrance.[23]

Mascons and rhetorical forms not only have persuasive effect upon audiences but also create the expectation of certain kinds of experience. Joubert and Williemain met, flipped, and exceeded the expectations of the men in the hush harbor barbershop. *Divine Days* and Sugar Groove as trickster trope and mascon generate the power and force of nommo through commonplaces, maxims, the flight trope, improvisation, the raccoon, and the possum. Joubert explicitly locates Sugar Groove in the tradition of tricksters such as

Brer Rabbit, Brer Fox, the Signifyin' Monkey, and Anansi. African American trickster figures swim, float, play, improve, and resist in a river with cultural retentions stretching back through time to West Africa. Enslaved Africans shared these stories in hush harbors to finger the jagged edge of possibility within the blunt trauma of captivity.

Sugar Groove's body is never found. Fortunately, the hush harbor audience in the barbershop did not require its recovery. Recovering Sugar Groove's body was not the point, the payoff, or the narrative's resolution, for Williemain's (and Forrest's), myth, story, tale, and oral scripture are not about Sugar Groove's mortal skin and bones; they are about his ethereal spirit and soul. They are about the spirits and souls of the invoked audience of the hush harbor barbershop and the addressed audience of *Divine Days*. Forrest ends the novel evoking the power of AAHHR through nommo and improvisation. Williemain tells the hush harbor audience in the barbershop about St. Peter and his ongoing attempt to discover how Sugar Groove flies the way he does, with the style, vivacity, and skill he does, and with the grace he displays. In exasperation, St. Peter says, "I can't find the proper words to express the meanings of all your carryings on, your cavorting . . . your." Joubert's response: "No, St. Peter you can't . . . that's my job."[24]

Divine Days' narrator, Joubert, decides to write about Sugar Groove as a way to reclaim his own life, to understand his own soul. As Forrest concludes his magnum opus, Joubert, through his search for the heart and mind of Sugar Groove, becomes a source of knowledge for Williemain and tells him: "See Sugar-Groove believed (like certain folks hold to Jesus as the answer) a man's life has to be reclaimed, somewhere along the line. You've got to recapture it, recover it. . . . Shake it, shape it; because most people are overwhelmed by their lot. Right?"[25] AAHHR and nommo help African Americans not only to keep from being overwhelmed by their lot, but also to keep from being overcome by despair.

As Joubert writes about Sugar Groove and Williemain's barbershop to reclaim his own life and understand his own soul in *Divine Days,* John Oliver Killens injects into the public sphere the AAHHR rhetorics and knowledges of the porch, the beauty shop, and barbershop, where Black folks reclaim their individual and communal lives and gain a more fertile understanding of how others do the same.

In *The Cotillion*, "Killens was preoccupied with the way people talked when they were not around White people," writes Alexs D. Pate in the foreword.[26] In Killen's novels, hush harbor political rationalities are the primary hermeneutical lens. In *The Cotillion*, an incisive satire of caste, class, politics, and bourgeoisie aspirations within 1960s' African American culture, as well as in the earlier *Youngblood*, Killens recognizes the heterogeneous voices reflecting African American perspectives. *Keepin' It Hushed* includes the novel to illustrate further the continuing significance of hush harbor rhetoric even when it is not explicitly defined as such, and to resist any suspicion that *Keepin' It Hushed* inadvertently smuggles in uncritical notions of monolithic Blackness and authenticity.

Youngblood is an in-depth examination through a fictive lens of the early-twentieth-century American South. Resisting the tendency during his era to construct Black characters as obsequious, as pathological, and as victims, Killens produced a heroic, committed, and sacrificing African American family struggling against racial and class constraints. Both novels contain a significant barbershop scene. These scenes will be examined in this section because they demonstrate various iterations of Black rhetoric that circulate in hush harbors, important political and existential issues that are addressed within the humor of the hush harbor barbershop, and the provocative mix of secular and sacred talk in hush harbor sites.

Culturally and politically conscious, *The Cotillion*'s primary protagonist, Yoruba Evelyn Lovejoy, crashes into the cultural confusion of Brooklyn's Black bourgeoisie. Daphne, her West Indian, mixed-race, caste-and-class–obsessed mother, enters her into a debutante ball called the Cotillion. Daphne pushes her daughter's participation as part of her continuous project to ensure that Yoruba would become a 1960s version of Black Victorian true womanhood. Killens tweaks up the satire and irony through Yoruba's Black-nationalist boyfriend Ben Ali Lumumba. Yoruba's obsidian-complexioned, Southern-born, working-class, "big, Black, and handsome!" father, Matthew (Matt) Lovejoy, is less than enamored with his wife's middle-class pretense. He considers Daphne's encouragement of their daughter to participate in the Cotillion as part of that pretense. For Matt, the Cotillion is little more than the empty mimicking of White culture. He satirically refers to the cotillion as the "Fat Ass Cotillion."[27]

Matt goes, not to church, but to the Jenkins Palace Barbershop and hush harbor to lay down his burdens and rejuvenate his soul after a hard day at work as a redcap at Pennsylvania Station in New York City. Killens's titling of the central barbershop chapter "No Hiding Place" inadvertently and ironically both embraces and resists Trudier Harris's construction of this male hush harbor as primarily a site of escape and disengagement. Killens's barbershop is more than a hiding place. Like most hush harbors, his barbershop is more often than not a refuge for rejuvenation and engagement rather than merely a place of retreat from reality. Killens makes it clear that the barbershop as a hush harbor contains a functionality beyond haircuts. This is not surprising because the trope of the barbershop as a refuge appears again and again in African American expressive culture. Killens names this chapter in tribute to what Ralph Ellison called plantation songs, but what are more commonly known as Negro spirituals. These sorrow songs that evoke the spiritual strivings of ordinary Black folk are usually linked to the church. Killens's framing of this chapter, as he does every chapter or major section in *The Cotillion* and *Youngblood,* with a Negro spiritual, links the sacred hush harbor of the church to the secular hush harbor of the barbershop.

Throughout this project, I have discussed the hush harbor as a secular-sacred site, a church, and a pulpit for men. Vernacular cultural forms permeate both secular and sacred spatialities but are deployed to different ends. If one reads these forms through a rhetorical lens, then the barbershop as secular church can be further affirmed. *The Cotillion* explicitly illuminates the sacred-secular nature of the barbershop as hush harbor and of Killens's narrative through explicating Matthew's name, the text through which he speaks, and the kind of rhetorical location from which Matthew performs: "Like his biblical namesake, who provided the first gospel of the New Testament, Matt preaches his own 'first gospel,' an amalgam of the Scriptures, still the most pervasive text in the Black community, and Black nationalist myth."[28] Matt is not said to speak, talk, or converse; Matt preaches. Earlier in this chapter, when I defined nommo as it relates to AAHHR, I discussed how it sustains Black folks. Matt preaches not only to others but also for himself, thus sustaining himself through nommo. When Matt gets ready to preach, he does so from the barbershop's version of the pulpit or the platform of wisdom—the barbershop chair. Killens spends several paragraphs exploring the function of the barbershop chair. The chair is viewed as a site of release, of emotional, physical, and spiritual reinvigoration. It is a leather-and-steel baptismal that can make Black men anew. It is a location where Black men can shed their hair and shed their old skin. Matt was so enamored with the barbershop chair that "sometimes he'd get so at home in his chair-of-chairs, he didn't want to give it up, even after it was over. In some ways it was like Aladdin's lamp rolled up in a magic carpet. It was Matt Lovejoy's special juju."[29] The barbershop chair in hush harbors conjures up a Black magic of memory and comfort, a comfort that enabled Matt Lovejoy to imagine new possibilities outside of White, public disciplinary spatialities.

In *Youngblood*, Killens offers a more telling, poignant example of the intersection of White spatiality, work, and oppression, and the barbershop as a site of release from these constraints. Joe Youngblood labors as a millworker in the South. As in other spatialities disciplined by White authority, the African American millworker had to survive the whims and vagaries of a White privilege that might be asserted at any time, any place, under any condition. For years, the White paymaster, Mr. Mack, cheated Joe out of part of his pay with arrogant impunity. But as Joe's son, Robby, approaches adolescence, Joe considers the example of manhood that he should set. He decides that he would no longer allow Mr. Mack to cheat him. Of course, Mr. Mack attempts to do just that. Unexpectedly, Joe calls him on it. Mr. Mack tells Joe, "Move along, boy. Move along now. Sign that paper and go 'long with you. Ain't no time for no discussion. Got to pay off everybody."[30]

As with many African Americans outside the safety of the hush harbor, in the face of White privilege Joe's internal dialogue tells him to do as requested—to provide a response that affirms the political rationalities of Whites, to ignore or jettison African American political rationalities to save himself a possible public slight or, worse, physical abuse. Instead, he engages in the parrhesia of AAHHR: "Yes sir, but how about my eighty-five cents? I work hard for my money."[31] Mr. Mack accuses Joe of calling him a liar. Joe stands steadfast. Whites and Blacks look on. Tension bends the backs of everyone watching. Nommo's power becomes palpable. To speak from one's sense of possibility that one's rhetoric might move an audience and produce certain effects, even if the desired persuasion does not occur, generates useful rhetorical, psychological, and spiritual energy. Nommo is almost as much about emancipation through the process of speaking the word as it is about the production of particular effects. Finally, Mr. Mack shoves all of Joe's pay toward him and tells him to move along. As he does, three other Black men walk with Joe, forming a gauntlet of sanctuary. Nommo has done its work. As Wright alluded to in his discussion of nommo, like a plow, nommo does its work in the world, planting a seed where one of men who walks off with Joe may be the next to bring African American rhetoric, agency, and knowledge into the public sphere. When Black men such as Joe and Matt go to a barbershop, it is the racial burden, the weight of survival, the load of the keep-on-keeping-on of which they temporarily relieve themselves or learn to engage in a new way. Killens's framing the chapter as "No Hiding Place," then, illuminates the barbershop as hush harbor—not all barbershops necessarily qualify—as a secular-sacred site of secular salvation, contemplation, engagement, and discussion where African American males often go to get saved at the chair or pulpit of African American male masculinities, subjectivities, and possibilities—where they feel valued and accepted in ways that even intimate female others often do not comprehend and sometimes do not care to.

Craig Marberry's *Cutting Up* (2005) points to the sacred-secular dimension of the barbershop. He is worth quoting at length: "African American men commune at the barbershop. It's where we go to be among ourselves, to be ourselves, to unmask, more than even the church, where reverence for God's house curbs one's enthusiasm, the barbershop is where we gather for true fellowship, for a respite from a society where black men are often scorned and excluded."[32] And where there is church, secular though it may be, there is preaching.

Preaching as a trope emerges again, but this time in *Youngblood*. It is linked specifically to resistance and African American phronesis. Joe Youngblood asks the barber Joe Jessup, "When you reckin white folks gon get offa our necks?"[33] When Jessup responds, "Brother Youngblood, these here crackers ain't gonna git offa our necks till we git together and knock their ass off," another customer responds, "Preach it."[34] Arguably, as Mayberry makes clear, the Black barbershop for a significant number of African American males rivals the Black church in importance for the production, negotiation, and transmittal of masculine knowledge. Even Cornel West argued during a presentation at Eso Won bookstore in Los Angeles that many Black men fail to embrace the Black church because of the perception that it suppresses Black masculinity.[35] The term *preach it,* then, points to rhetors who are deploying secular knowledge and truths reflecting African American standpoints in the Black spatiality of the barbershop as hush harbor.

The Cotillion informs the reader that these everyday, vernacular, secular-sacred spatialities are more than places to get a haircut, more than spheres of mundane, meaningless banter. As Matt ruminates, "The Palace always did a swinging business, as was to be expected. Your six bits not only got you a haircut, but you also got goo-gobs of philosophical conversation in the bargain. Soul talk baby brother."[36] Several of the texts in this project refer to barbershop discourse—and, by extension, African American rhetoric—as philosophy. Philosophy, in this formulation, is deconstructed and tied to bodies that philosophy, poetics, and rhetoric would normally deem to be outside of its theoretical domain. This is not to say that every conversation in a barbershop conveys such critical gravity, yet the deliberative, critical, logos-driven talk attributed to philosophy does occur in hush harbor places. Matt does not say that the barbershop has a little philosophical insight; instead, he argues that it has much philosophy, goo-gobs of it—philosophy anchored in nomos.

Like AAHHR and nommo, *nomos* is grounded in African American worldviews and perspectives that reflect what Killens refers to as the Black psyche. *Nomoi* are social conventions and beliefs. In a broader sense, *nomos* can be described as a "self-conscious arrangement of discourse to create politically and socially significant knowledge, thus it is always a social construct with ethical dimensions."[37] The intersection of nomos with nommo, political rationalities, Black lifeworlds, and AAHHR seems self-evident. Black political rationalities and AAHHR contain worldviews with explicit political dimensions. In both instances, ethics should be understood as a concern with public or communal good as opposed to morality and its focus on good and evil reflecting personal character. An important question related to the ethics of inserting the nomoi of AAHHR into the public sphere and its relationship to the commodification of Blackness is explored in the final chapter of *Keepin' It Hushed*. To invoke nomos is to foreground the rhetorical-philosophical and hermeneutical elements of *Keepin' It Hushed*.

Nomos is more effective than the term *worldview* within a context of rhetorical critique for two reasons. First, worldview can be reduced to mere opinion or *doxa* (belief). However, my use of the term *nomos* refers to the lens or terministic screen through which one apprehends the worldview; those inculcated assumptions or understandings that mediate a worldview. It is a screen so normalized that it ceases to be consciously apprehended by the subject possessing the lens. Nomos then can be understood as a constellation of political rationalities circulating as hegemonic and normative. Second, nomos facilitates two goals important to my project. Goal 1 is to increase scholarly understanding of how both African American and European rhetorical taxonomies and history might enhance the comprehension of African American rhetoric. Goal 2 relates to my disciplinary interest. Nomos inserts the African American rhetor into an ongoing discussion that reflects a tension between rhetoric and philosophy over two thousand years old.

Matt's reference in *The Cotillion* to *soul talk* in barbershops is useful. Soul talk pries out from discourse those elements of rhetoric inculcated with African American experience and worldviews. Soul talk—itself a term fraught with imprecision—could be argued to be a subcategory of nommo. Like "keeping it real" and "make it plain"—it is a significant commonplace in African American culture but contains an ineffable quality that makes a specific, singular definition difficult. Nevertheless, rhetoric provides a grasp of the term as one manifestation of nommo and nomos in that soul talk is talk that through form, tone, content, and inflections, evokes tropes, memories, and *intimate understandings* and *empathy* with and for the individual and communal experiences of Black folks in America. Like the "A-men" in a Black church, soul talk is a verbal tuning fork that, through its vibrations, touches the body, moves the spirit, and reanimates shared experiences. Soul talk obtains its energy from the nomoi informing nommo that reflect African American experiential, social, and spiritual rationalities. For example, both Melvin Murphy's *Barbershop Talk: The Other Side of Black Men* (1998) and

Derrick Gilbert's ethnography, "Shaping Identity at Cooke's Barbershop" (1994), discuss the barbershop as a site of ritual, education, Black male subjectivities, and identity construction.[38] So when someone utters to someone else that *they got soul,* that person has tapped into those African American social and spiritual rationalities conveying that the particular individual not only gets *it* but also embraces it.

Part and parcel of the "goo-gobs" of barbershop AAHHR, of the soul talk Matt refers to, centers on sports. Sports and the discussion of sports supply a physical and discursive spatiality into which African American men can infuse and perform their phronesis, subjectivity, and nomos. Entertainment and sports have been two of the few social fields under the gaze of White hegemony in the public sphere to which Black men bring their own subjectivities with aplomb, with directness, with parrhesia. In *The Cotillion,* Matt listens in on a frequent hush harbor discussion of whether an African American or a European American is the better athlete:

> "Willie Mays the greatest. He's the best that ever done it."
>
> "Dig it."
>
> "Who you Humping?"
>
> "Aw man!"
>
> "I'll take Mickey Mantle any day. You see, that's because I'm objective. I'm color-blind. To me, a man is a man."
>
> "And a tom is a tom is a goddamn educated fool."[39]

While often overapplied and misused as a topos of betrayal, the "tom" quote is a rhetorical strategy to interrogate whether a particular individual is aware of or invested in the rationalities informing African American life and culture.[40] More than a simplistic monitoring of Black authenticity, questioning whether someone is a tom/Uncle Tom is an attempt to evaluate the extent to which a particular individual is invested in or committed to African American rationalities informing Black ontology, phronesis, and memory, or the individual's willingness to trivialize or ignore them for personal gain. Therefore, the Uncle Tom charge in the hush harbor of the barbershop is not an appeal to some uncritical notion of essential Blackness; rather, it is a critique of an

African American rhetoric, of individual positioning, without obligation to African American nomoi and rationalities.

After the hotly contested conversation about sports, Willie Mays, Mickey Mantle, and color blindness, Matt fastens African American excellence in sports to anatomy, racism, and literacy: "Reason Black cats run so fast, most of 'em from down home, and they used to hauling ass when the law gets in behind 'em. Some towns have signs that read "Peckerwoods Read and Walk Fast, Niggers Read and Haul Ass."[41] While the aforementioned discourse can mistakenly dismissed easily as Ebonics or jive talk, it is grounded in history, resistance, and rationalities reflecting AAHHR in both form and content. In form, the dialogue represents what linguist John Baugh categorizes as "black street speech" (BSS).[42]

Baugh's definition of the term makes its connection to AAHHR more apparent. According to Baugh in the article "Black Street Speech," "Street speech is the nonstandard dialect that thrives within Black street (*urban*) culture which constantly fluctuates as new terminology flows in and out of colloquial vogue."[43] In Baugh's view, "street speech survives because there is a population of speakers who use it in their daily lives and know that it is the appropriate style of speaking for their personal needs."[44] BSS is not the only language of the barbershop as hush harbor. However, hush harbor audiences embrace the liberating and pedagogical elements of BSS—elements that meet their personal as well as communal survival needs. One of the pedagogical elements of BSS is instructing Black folks on how to read.

Matt's understanding and use of *read and haul ass* is self-aware and polysemic, as is the reception of the term by the hush harbor barbershop audience. Matt's rhetorical assertion is simultaneously pedagogical, culturally affirmative, humorous, and dangerous. Yet, it is dangerous in the right place—a place where informality has been formalized with an African American cultural inflection. As with many individuals and groups who are marginalized within a network of asymmetrical power relations, African Americans must both read—and *read* those who are privileged by power and/or superior social status. When Matt says, "They got signs in some of them towns that read: Peckerwoods Read and Walk Fast. Niggers Read and Haul Ass," Black folks and White folks are not reading different signs; they are reading the same signs differently.[45] These different readings go beyond play for play sake. Lives are held in the balance. *Read* here can be taken as a literal reading of texts. However, given that the term *peckerwood* is a derisive African American term for Whites, White folks would hardly put up such a sign about themselves. And Black folks of that era would not publicly display such a sign for anyone to see. Such a gesture would be akin to suicide. Yet, in this barbershop space, there are shared assumptions, shared hermeneutical frames. No explanation is necessary. Reading here is all about hermeneutics, subtext, and the connection of both to lived experience and uneven power relations. Matt conveys that Black folks bring their phronesis, nomoi, and knowledge to bear in their reading of signs. BSS conveys his message through both form and content. This is dangerous talk, Black parrhesia in a public sphere, but safe talk in the African American Black spatiality in the Black civil sphere of the African American hush harbor barbershop.

In *Youngblood,* Joe Jessup deploys the synecdoche of "neck" as a trope of the Black body under pressure of White domination. His strategy as a response to that oppression is drenched in BSS: "I mean it, Bruh Joe. Mr. Charlie gon always keep his foot on our neck till we git together and stick together, steada one group over here and the other over yonder and nobody not doing a damn thing for the race."[46] As in the Palace Barbershop in *The Cotillion,* what gets said and the way it gets said reflect a comfort through shared social assumptions that allow critiques that are silenced or trivialized as racist in the public sphere.

Not all Black male subjectivities filtered through BSS would be deemed socially enlightened. It is important to make this observation to resist sentimentalizing barbershops or AAHHR. As with all discourses and the spatialities from which they emerge, barbershop hush harbor rhetoric can reproduce, as well as resist, racist and sexist thinking. In *The Cotillion,* for example, soon after an argument about Malcolm X, Martin Luther King Jr., and the Civil Rights Movement, the dialogue shifts into full throttle: "Don't know what the young folks raising so much hell about. We ain't never made as much progress as we making now. I'm as much a race man as anybody else but after all——."[47] Before the old man can finish, a young man the narrator describes as "a hip young dude, process-sharp, do-rag pastel-green" interrupts with, "Pops, you ain't talking no sense at all. Revolution is like a man cunt-hunting."[48]

Certainly, in more public spatialities, such language in reference to Black women is vulgar and offensive. A form of symbolic violence that reinforces physical violence. As Askia Muhammad relates in his 2003 audio-ethnography "Conversations in a Black Barbershop," barbershop hush harbor rhetoric can be a profane spatiality. Based on normative (African American middle class) expectations for decorum, the rhetorical exchanges in hush harbors can seem uncivil. However, some observers who dismiss such Black male barbershop talk do not take into account that, like all practices, hush harbor exchanges are generative and productive, as well as unproductive. That is to say, uncivil and profane practices in barbershops reflect the epistemological and improvisational openness of these spatialities and the African American parrhesia that drive them. Such nomoi can be and are uttered in hush harbor spatialities and are taken seriously. They are not immediately dismissed because of some notion of political correctness. Even when the customer asserted he was color-blind, his argument was taken seriously. Though disdained, the argument was not foreign to barbershop clientele. Returning to the young man who made the sexist comment, he may or may not have been corrected about his objectification of women in a barbershop, but he and his primary argument about the nature of resistance would not have been dismissed because of it. Indeed, it is in the giddy rhetorical energy and force of Black men speaking their hearts and minds in a manner unsanctioned in public spheres that the uncivil, the profane, and the politically incorrect are often symptomatic of rhetorical freedom unhinged. I have heard Black women in a beauty shop make a comment about Black men when they did not know I was there, that if said in another rhetorical situation would have been intolerable. I could have gotten out of sorts and jumped on what I considered to be its debasement of Black men. But because it was uttered in a hush harbor, I deliberated about it in a much more sober, less defensive manner. The incivility that is sometimes found in BSS and AAHHR reflects a comfort and acceptance of African American nomos that may not always be accurate or enlightened, but it lightens Black burdens as African American men and women express themselves.

Matt Lovejoy laid his burden down by the riverside of AAHHR that, like the Sankofa bird, glides forward into the emergent traditions of the future and backward into the residual traditions of the past. Of course, just like a river, the rhetoric keeps on flowing as Matt rises to leave and brushes himself off. As he strolls through the door, he leaves the hush harbor audience with this bit of wisdom: "I know one thing. It stands to reason, if the rabbits took rock-throwing lessons, there wouldn't be all them many hunters pitching boogie in the forest."[49] Lovejoy left with his phronesis, "leaving the young upset philosopher and the laughter and the 'Amens' and the 'Tell it like it is!' and the 'That's right!' and the odor of hair tonic, the sound of buzzing clippers and the signifying, leaving all that behind him."[50] Killens's nonjudgmental rendering of the barbershop as hush harbor recognizes the importance of AAHHR and nomoi.

Matt's wisdom partakes in the ever-changing same of African American folklore. The rabbits are, of course, a metaphor for Black folks: if Black folks engaged in self-defense, hunters (White folks) would be less likely to engage in acts of official and random violence, less likely to pitch boogie in the racial forest. Once again, laughter permeates the barbershop, not necessarily because the men in the barbershop agree with his analysis, but because Lovejoy affirms their right to self-defense, a gesture associated with masculinity and self-assertion that, by contrast, the early public sphere rhetoric of Dr. King denies to Black men and women. In the barbershop as African American male hush harbor, the participants' response recognizes that all human responses that are available to others should be available to Black folks. Matt Lovejoy did not argue for the universal truthfulness of his position; he instead argued for the importance of African American rationalities and perspective, the material and discursive conditions that make certain positions necessary. Hush harbor rhetors are valued because they speak on terms that privilege African American communal experience, knowledge, and wisdom. Speaking on their own terms means that Black discourse typically domesticated, neutered, and made civil and tolerant in the public sphere is deployed in a manner reflecting African American decorum, nomoi, and knowledge. In "Cultural Heroes," Keith Gilyard notes that Malcolm X was John Oliver Killens's "standard" for African American leadership.[51] Even as he critiqued Black folks, Malcolm X took Black nomoi, Black parrhesia, and Black phronesis seriously; like Muhammad Ali, he performed them publicly.

African American tennis star Serena Williams was roundly booed at the 2003 French Open. Harvard psychologist Alvin Poussaint contended that the booing was in part due to the self-assurance of the Williams sisters because "sometimes that attitude in both Black men and women frequently is not accepted by Whites. They would like to see more docility."[52] In other words, in the racialized spatiality that circulates as the public sphere, a sphere that in practice is dominated by White fears and fantasies, they desire and reward domesticated, decorous, and compliant Black bodies, except in popular culture, where the excessiveness of Black cool and pathology are provided symbolic and material recognition. Like Muhammad Ali, Malcolm X, and Serena Williams, Joe Youngblood, Matt Lovejoy, and John Oliver Killens resist Black docility. They embrace African American rhetorics, rationalities, nomoi, and parrhesia, and then perform these elements publicly on African Americans.

4.

Poetic Hush Harbors

Barbershops as Black *Paideias*

SHARAN STRANGE'S POEM "BARBERSHOP RITUAL" BEGINS "BABY BROTHER can't wait / For him, the rite of passage begins early."[1] Strange's poem immediately disavows the reader of any notion of domesticating the barbershop to a place of male gossip, jive talk, and transitory banter through her linking of barbershop rhetoric and practices to ritual. Understandings of barbershops as spaces of gossip may account for overlooking barbershops as legitimate sites of rhetorical analysis. While the aforementioned gossip occurs, sometimes with great frequency, barbershops as hush harbors gain their significance in African American culture based on their importance as sites of rhetorical education—of Black rhetorical education. Like their antecedents in hidden literacy schools, praise houses, and beauty shops, barbershops are pedagogical; they are Black *paideias* of rhetorical education and ritual. Whereas *Greek paideias* were spaces and schools where disciplines were taught Greek notions of the good and what it means to be educated, barbershops as hush harbors are *Black paideias* of rhetorical education where African American notions of citizenship, culture, excellence, and meaning are inculcated through African American rationalities and knowledges. Barbershops as hush harbors are sites of rhetorical education and reeducation because they tacitly decenter and destabilize liberal humanist notions of objectivity and rationality through including disavowed African American subjectivities and knowledges. Within a broader national context, where African American perspectives and knowledges remain neither hegemonic nor understood as fundamental to conceptions of knowledge, history, or citizenship, hush harbors such as beauty shops and barbershops acquire increased pedagogical and educational gravitas in African American life and culture. And as the public sphere does not manufacture consent around African American knowledges the way it does around European American knowledges and fears, the educational and rhetorical force of barbershops intensifies. Barbershops become de facto schools of Black ritual, culture, and communal and individual subjectivities.

Beginning with Strange's "Barbershop Ritual" and concluding with Sterling A. Brown's "Slim in Hell," this chapter examines several poems grounded in the African American barbershop as a site of rhetorical education. Thematic in approach, the poems further illustrate the pervasiveness and importance of the barbershop trope in African American expressive culture. Written by men and women, young poets and poets over age fifty, and poets living and dead, the dates of authorship span more than seventy years and the breadth of the twentieth century, representing a variety of different approaches to poetic form.

The emphasis of this chapter is the barbershop as hush harbor and ground of rhetorical education and pedagogy. Therefore, conventional concerns with poetic exegesis such as rhythm and meter are not the primary focus. Instead I use these poetic expressions to explore the barbershop/hush harbor as a ritualistic spatiality where males proceed through a subtle rite of passage from the relative innocence of childhood through youth to manhood. As part of this process but not limited to it, social practices as mundane as a young man sitting in a barbershop chair and participating in a conversation take on special significance. Further, I will illuminate how phronesis, practical knowledge, and wisdom, circulate through and are shared in barbershops. As two of the poems substantiate, the cultural and class heterogeneity of African American barbershops provides enough variance and flexibility to make them useful as places of practical knowledge and rhetorical education to a number of Black men with various investments and politics. Barbershops produce education and pedagogy not only through the boys and men who work, commiserate, and are provided services, but also, as I discuss later, the building/spatiality itself manufactures pedagogy through location, place, and, most importantly, ornamentation and signage. Black male identities are shaped through such spatial ideologies, yet hush harbors are not utopian sites, sealed off from the pain and struggle of Black life and culture. Unethical individuals use the rhetorical education in barbershops and other hush harbor paideias for selfish ends or negative nommo.

Examining Sterling Brown's germinal "Slim Hears 'The Call'" assists in exploring the negative nommo of the African American rhetor speaking well to odious ends. Through addressing the aforementioned themes, I hope to make palpable the importance of barbershops as sites of rhetorical education to Black males, for the education they receive there will affirm and facilitate their social psychological survival in a manner that is the exception to more mainstream public educational institutions.

Why can't baby brother wait? He can't wait because the ritual of the Black barbershop, of hush harbor rhetoric and its attendant humor, wit, pathos, passion, pleasure, pain, and possibilities, are too alluring to long resist. Baby brother knows that the barbershop is a meaningful portal to manhood and masculinity. My use of the term *ritual* should be understood through the rhetorical lens of *parrhesia*—fearless, frank speech. Therefore, *Keepin' It Hushed*'s understanding of ritual traverses the notion of formalized, officially proscribed, centripetal practices given institutional sanction. Instead, *Keepin' It Hushed* attempts to excavate the more informal, unofficial, centrifugal practices of marginalized folks (in relation to the dominant culture). Such informal rituals and practices transform—albeit temporarily—scenes of subjection into sites of affirmation, inculcating meaning into African American life and culture through the banal of everyday. The marginalization of so

much of African American rhetoric and culture from traditional conceptions of theoretical and metaphysical significance, and the very particular
pervasiveness of hush harbors as refuges from such marginalization, make
hush harbors vital sites of ritual. As Mary Douglas writes, "The more drawn
from the common fund of human experience" is a particular behavior, "the
more wide and certain its reception from its margins and unstructuredness."[2]
Indeed, examining particular African American hush harbor (AAHH) practices
contributes to and expands the common fund of human experience. While
masculinist barbershop discourses may circulate and pivot on a structured
ignorance of, and a diacritical relation to, women-centered knowledges and
standpoints, which problematizes any claim of such discourses drawing from
a common fund of human experience, barbershop rituals and practices such
as chair sitting, haircutting, game playing (checkers, chess, dominoes, the
numbers), all of which exude alternative conceptions of decorum, make it
a Black spatiality containing rites of passages based on a common fund of
African American male experience.

"Barbershop Ritual" perceptively grasps the ritualistic aspect of barbershop behavior embodied in a young Black male beginning his experience
of climbing into the culture of the chair and further immersing himself into
African American culture. The following lines evoke how his ascent into the
barber chair metaphorically affirms his own sense of power, protection, and
agency in this Black and male sphere, an agency less available to him in the
public sphere: "Each week, he steps up to the chair / the closest semblance of
a throne he'll ever know."[3] The poem's reference to the chair as throne is not
surprising. References to the African American barbershop chair as a synecdoche for throne and the regal subjectivity associated with it are deployed in
several of the texts I examine. They make reference to the barbershop chair,
climbing into that chair, Black male subjectivity, and an increased sense of
comfort and agency away from the whim of White privilege and desire that
can transgress African American personal boundaries in an instant. While
anecdotal, the following example is illuminative.

Several African Americans (particularly African American women)
have discussed with me the desire of non–African Americans to touch their
hair; hair becomes a totem of otherness with which they are fascinated. I

have witnessed mesmerized Whites' hands unconsciously lift toward Black hair before they catch themselves. It has happened to me on more than one occasion. One is instantly made invisible. Temporarily, one no longer matters as subject. Of course, this is a metaphor of how easily Black folks and Blackness become objects of utility—terrain for the projection of desire and fear—whether it is a taxi driver, police officer, or another Black male. But in the barber chair, you are both sovereign and subject: your desires are what matters. Your boundaries are sacrosanct. Your fears are privileged. And no White person would dare touch your hair without your permission.

The second stanza of "Barbershop Ritual" reasserts the barbershop chair not only as ritualistic totem but also as a seat where one acquires phronesis as each week the brother of the poem's narrator

steps up to the chair
the closest semblance of a throne
he'll ever know, and lays in
for the cut, the counseling of older dudes.[4]

"Barbershop Ritual" constructs African American phronesis in two ways. First, the "c" sound of *cut* is compressed and collapsed into the "c" sound of *counseling*. Cut and counseling are collapsed into each other. A "cut" in the barbershop goes beyond the functional cutting of hair to the metaphoric cutting/counseling of heads to the shaping of thinking and consciousness with the shears of Black knowledge and experience. Second, the poem attaches counseling to experience as it refers to "older dudes" who are

cappin' players, men-of-words,
Greek chorus to the comic-tragic fanfare
of approaching manhood.[5]

The poem's invocation of Greek chorus resonates with the emergence of phronesis from Greek culture and rhetoric. "Barbershop Ritual" links its ritual to individual transformation and practical, communal knowledge through the trope of the Greek chorus. Counseling provided by the Greek chorus of older dudes conveys African American phronesis or what Harris-Lacewell refers to as *Black commonsensus.*[6]

One of the reasons for including "Barbershop Ritual" in my analysis is that it is further evidence supporting my claim about the pervasiveness and importance of the barbershop as a hush harbor trope. Despite its sometimes raucous banter and sexist discourse, Black women are also aware of the importance of the barbershop as hush harbor. The narrator of the poem is a woman who takes her brother to the barbershop; the author of the poem is a woman. African American women are in on the importance of the barbershop as both communal paideia and as Black male spatiality even as their presence changes the contours of the conversation. In *Barbershops, Bibles, and BET,* the ethnographer Harris-Lacewell sends in a male confederate because she knows that her very presence will alter the flow of the talk, the energy of the rhetoric, and the content of the knowledge. Just as heteronormative and queer Black men who possess any insight into the values and ways of Black women understand the importance of the beauty shop to Black women and enter the spatiality with a kind of deference or regard to knowledge, Harris-Lacewell and the female narrator of "Barbershop Ritual" understand the significance of the Black barbershop. "Barbershop Ritual" illustrates the importance of the barbershop, not only to Black men but also, more broadly, to Black culture.

African American women tend to be aware of the significance of the barbershop as a requisite site of a Black male rite of passage. For example, the barbershop as a spatiality of ritual is not only evident in the title but also evident in her belief that, "before obligatory heists / of candy & comic books from neighborhood / stores," it is the barbershop he must negotiate "before he might gain the title 'Man of the House'" and so that he will not gain it "before his time."[7] Having swiped a few comic books myself as a preadolescent, I understand how this act of masculine bravado is linked to a ritual of testing boundaries or of showing off for the fellas (or for simply getting sumpthin' for free). Snatching comic books is one of the more innocent markers of the passage into Black male community and culture. Barbershops both encourage and mediate such behavior. Yes, the ritual does begin early. Barbershop hush harbors can transform "early" into the appropriate and the timely.

Kairos (the opportune moment), is a significant concept in rhetoric and an important aspect of the rite of passage in the barbershop as hush harbor. In short, it is not just the deployment of African American hush harbor rhetoric (AAHHR) that matters, it is when it is offered where and by whom that makes all the difference. Young men learn when they should speak. Even adults have to earn speaking privileges in some circumstances. This mirrors the narrator's desire in "Barbershop Ritual" that her brother not gain the title of man of the house before his time. AAHHR, phronesis, and kairos, then, intersect in a nexus of practical wisdom, time (opportune moment), and geography. Age and/or experience, of course, make it more likely that one possesses the characteristics to be a "man," but possession does not necessarily make it so. Therefore, although young folks often remain silent in barbershop discussions, this does not mean that they are always silent or take a backseat in hush harbor discussions. In fact, S. Brandi Barnes, in "Gentleman in the Barber Shop," precisely invokes the barbershop as a ritualistic, discursive space that shifts its focus to take young Black men into account:

> When I take the little one to get
> his haircut: They call him champ,
> size me up quickly,
> and change the conversation from
> men talk to small talk.[8]

Small talk resonates beyond the trivial and inconsequential. In this poem, small talk could be read as a metaphor for the phronesis and rhetoric that make the talk relevant for Champ. The poem conveys an understanding that, in this instance, small talk isn't really just small talk, because the men in the barbershop "always, always, give / instruction to the young."[9] The barbershop as hush harbor is a site of both lofty small talk and talk that is sometimes mundane.

A Richard Wright haiku illuminates the barbershop as a Black spatiality of the mundane, of ritual, and of lofty meaning. In his later years, Wright became enamored with the haiku, with its insistence on time, space, nature, and the extraordinary within the everyday. Wright composed over 4,000 haiku, 871 of which have been published to date.[10] Of course, as is the purview of artists immersed in the African American literary-rhetorical-musical-oral traditions, Wright rearticulated the traditional subject matter and concerns of the haiku to include African American spaces, places, and cultural investments. It is not surprising, then, that Wright would compose a haiku (haiku 450) about a barbershop:

> *In a barbershop,*
> *The stench of soap and hair,—*
> *A hot summer day!* [11]

Wright's haiku evokes the problems—the stench, the heat—and the wonder of the barbershop, and the epiphany of wonder for which the boy in "Barbershop Ritual" cannot wait. The stench of soap and hair connects the barbershop to the everyday: to its smells, to its pain, to its struggles. What struggles? For the young man in "Barbershop Ritual," for example, it may simply be his inability to compete verbally with other boys in the barbershop. Young boys and men go for what they know through signifyin', tall tales, narrative, and other forms of AAHHR. Those who are not verbally quick can experience the deflation of the ego visited upon the hush harbor habitué who does not know how to talk that talk. Wright wrenches the barbershop out of sentimental nostalgia. Subjectivities are at stake. Egos are at stake. Knowledges are at stake. Yet the dash (—) in the haiku is a symbol of possibility—it is summer. Like a Negro spiritual that offers light within darkness, resistance within loss, Wright leaves us with an epiphany—the enlightenment of summer and the possibilities that emerge from it.

Keith Gilyard's "Barbershops and Afros" also alludes to the barbershop as ground for ritual, possibility, and epiphany—illumination within the realm of the everyday:

> *Brink-filled*
> *Saturday morning barbershops*
> *pose stern tests*
> *for naturals/minds hearing* [12]

Gilyard discerns the myriad tests entangled within the possibilities that are part of barbershop ritual. Where Sunday is the day of ritual in the sacred-secular church of AAHHs, Friday afternoons and Saturday tend to be the days of secular ritual in the barbershop: work ends, the weekend begins. New possibilities, with the release from the stress of life on the horizon. While African American barbershops tend to be open each weekday except Sunday and Monday, Saturday is the main day for the barbershop as a hush harbor. Kids are out of school. Fathers can bring their kids for a cut while they themselves get a trim. Teenagers roll into the barbershop with their posses. "Barbershops and Afros" disabuses the reader of any notion that frivolity is the mainstay of barbershop ritual. "Stern" signals that these tests, these rituals, are serious endeavors. Too often, as in movies such as *Barbershop* and *Coming to America*, barbershops are reduced to sites of lively banter: jive, tall tales, and humor. Although these characterizations are not without merit, for wry humor is highly valued in African American culture, they are reductive in that they trivialize the pedagogy and rhetorical education occurring in the barbershop as hush harbor. "Barbershops and Afros" disrupts such notions.

Young Black men need information to survive, function, and prosper when, even in the barbershop, the discourse of Whiteness sits down right next to you in the guise of a Black body, as in "Barbershops and Afros":

Sad dismay sinks in when
A throwback process
with kinky skin
silently thinks that your bush
reminds him of sheep
while you reply unheard
"sheep? But don't they come in Black too?"
and neither of you
understands the other.[13]

"Sad dismay sinks in" deeply in this struggle over Black subjectivity and identity that evokes the pathos and the trauma of the tension of Black-is–Black-ain't authenticity. Comedian Chris Rock's documentary *Good Hair*

(2009) was motivated by one of his daughter's posing a simple question: "Daddy, why don't I have good hair?" Within the question are a variety of issues around authenticity, what is and who is Black enough, self-worth, caste politics, and other issues that cause Black women and the two boys who misunderstand each other dismay. What is important here is that the dismay and alienation that young Black men must navigate as part of the human condition embodied in Black ontologies and rationalities are addressed and sometimes ameliorated through the information, instruction, and empathy imparted in the paideia of barbershops. As I alluded to earlier, Black men can feel under siege in the public sphere. Their individual longing, desires, dreams, and fears are often masked by a veil of hegemonic masculinity, gangsta attitude, and Black-don't-crack hubris. Labor and the lack of it can bend some men's spirit the way age can bend the spine; racism eats away at the resolve of some the way rust wears away metal. Nevertheless, in the barbershop as hush harbor, in-da-back and in-da-front, there are men all around you who share their pain, their struggles, and their hopes. One knows he can make it because others are making it. Their talk—loud, funny, profane, boisterous, nappy, cool, hip, silly, profound, dirty, clean, depressing, and uplifting—conveys to you that you can make it and make it in your own way. You are worthy because they are worthy. Gilyard's "Barbershops and Afros" conveys Black male worthiness.

"Barbershops and Afros" perceptively taps into the heterogeneity of the barbershop but with an epistemological difference. Heterogeneity is attached to the knowledge and *doxa* (beliefs) of Black folks:

Brinked-filled
Saturday morning barbershops
pose stern tests
for naturals/minds hearing
56 independent interpretations
of the Bible in
one ear while the other
soaks in the numbers runners without
losing 2-eyed-sight of the

grandfather face trying to
peep under the bikini
of the bathing queen
in Jet *magazine*
she looks like his downfall.[14]

"Barbershops and Afros" delves into the heterogeneity of bodies, as well as the protean vitality of thought, in the barbershop. As mentioned earlier, for many Black men, the barbershop is often valued over the church as hush harbor spatiality because the territory of discourse in the church as hush harbor tends to be overly decorous (admittedly, for some good practical reasons). The aforementioned claim is worth mentioning again because "Barbershops and Afros" concerns itself with hermeneutics and, where there is interpretation, there is rhetoric. In the Black church "56 independent interpretations of the Bible" is heretical, whereas in the Black male barbershop 100 independent takes on the Bible is exegetical. Barbershops are far more rhetorically emancipatory spatialities for Black male rhetorics and rhetorical education than are Black churches.

Ironically, though the discourse of the Black church is gendered male, its pulpit a masculinized spatiality, its power embodied in the figure of the preacher as Black male, the membership of most denominations of Black churches are primarily female. Fifty-six interpretations, then, do not reflect a lack of commitment. Instead, barbershop discourse reflects a more flexible rhetorical hermeneutic that can be more democratic, more critical, and more affirming, for better of for worse, of African American male ways of knowing.

In barbershops, Black males dream about, wrestle with, and struggle for their social, political, and spiritual lives, as "Gentleman in the Barber Shop" makes clear:

At the Barber Shop
men rehash dreams, settle wars, and politics
and talk about mothers or ugly women.
They discuss the fate of the Union
joint around the corner,

and advise on child support.
Gentleman in the Barber Shop
relive the great love affair
they didn't marry,
and always, always, give
instruction to the young.[15]

Clearly, the barbershop in this poem and the other texts we have examined provide rhetorical education anchored in the ground of practical rhetorical education of phronesis, not the rarefied air of escape.

While the barbershop is a safe refuge of rhetorical education, it is not a communal narcotic to escape pain. Earlier I discussed the tragedy of psychological and spiritual pain in relation to Richard Wright's haiku. Many barbershops as hush harbors unfortunately occupy deindustrialized, disinvested, deteriorating urban cores ravaged partly by the uneven effects of globalization, outsourced offshored jobs and hope, and by insourced crime, death, and self-hatred. Major Jackson's elegiac "Mr. Pate's Barbershop" captures the unsentimental memory, sharp-edged loss, and persistent pain of a blues tragedy:

I remember the old Coke machine, a water
fountain by the door, how I drank
the summer of '88 over & over from a paper
cone cup & still could not quench my thirst,
for this was the year funeral homes boomed,
the year Mr. Pate swept his own shop
for he had lost his best little helper Squeaky
to cross fire.[16]

Pain and suffering dart through Mr. Pate's barbershop door with a wasp-ish sting. Jackson's writing connects Mr. Pate, tragically, to the bone and sinew of communal loss and despair:

He suffered like most barbers,
suffered, quietly, his clippers humming so loud

he forgot Ali's lightning left jab, his love
for angles, for carpentry, for baseball. He forgot
everything & would never be the same.[17]

Mr. Pate's reaction is not that of someone who has simply lost a helper; he has lost a surrogate son.

Despite the raw suffering and searing despair, Jackson's blues and jazz sensibility concludes the poem on an affirmative register that recognizes the educational value of barbershops as sites of rhetoric, philosophy, and knowledge. The poem offers the possibility that, through personal sacrifice such as Mr. Pate's, redemption is possible:

I remember the way the blade gleamed
fierce in the fading light of dusk and reflection
of myself panned inside the razor's edge
wondering if I could lay down my pen, close up
my ledgers and my journals, if I could undo
my tie & take up barbering where
months on end a child's head would darken
at my feet & bring with the uncertainty
of tomorrow, or like Mr. Pate gathering
clumps of fallen hair, at the end of a day,
in short, delicate whisks as though
they were fine findings of gold dust,
he'd deposit in a jar & place on a shelf, only
to return Saturdays, collecting, as an antique dealer
collects, growing tired, but never forgetting
someone has to cherish these tiny little heads.[18]

The narrative persona considers giving up his profession. Educating countless African American male children has seduced him; the loss of so many children to the chaos of the streets has shaken him. Yet, Mr. Pate remains. So does the poem's narrator.

Earlier, I alluded to how cuttin' heads is a double-voiced reference to physical heads, to the actual cutting of hair, and to metaphoric heads, the cutting and shaping of minds. Mr. Pate would collect the hair—memories, experience, knowledge, and dreams—of his surrogate sons. The poem's narrator wonders whether he could take Mr. Pate's place, because "someone has to cherish these tiny little heads." Hair, and its cutting, falling, clumping, and collecting, serve as a visual trope of Black minds, Black spirits, Black cultures—of Black rationalities. Mr. Pate reaffirms both himself and the community when he muses about how barbering allowed him to intervene so that a child's mind, his "head," would be enriched with the knowledge from his barbershop. Mr. Pate's loss of the young Squeaky to violence may forever change him, but he will not be forever lost, because barbershops as hush harbors are occupied by so many different Black men with so many different experiences that someone will be able to help Mr. Pate make a way out of no way.

Kevin Young depicts the variety of Black men and women who occupy barbershops. In his poem "Eddie Priest's Barbershop & Notary: Closed Mondays," the generational heterogeneity of the African American chorus in Black barbershops where there is "a mother gathering hair for good luck," "peach faced boys,"[19] and

> grandfathers
> stopping their games of ivory
> dominoes just before they reach the bone
> yard[20]

Grown "men / off early from work" come to the ethnic enclave of the barbershop for sustenance.[21] Barbershop texts repeatedly refer to the variety of Black folks, and especially Black men, who cross the barbershop's threshold. Working men and unemployed men, pious men and drunks, pimps and preachers, fathers, teenagers, and grandfathers—all are hush harbor habitués.

"Eddie Priest's Barbershop and Notary" alludes to the Blackness of spatiality as the poet constructs the barbershop itself as a character. Young does not describe the barbershop or what occurs within with prepositions or adjectives such as *in, on, inside,* or *at;* instead, Young infuses the barbershop spatiality with ontology, with being, with life, with funky life, through the verb *is:*

> *is music is men*
> *off early from work is waiting*
> . . .
> *is having nothing*
> *better to do*
> . . .
> *is the dark dirty low*
> *down blues*
> . . .
> *is the quick brush of a*
> *done head*[22]

Building and life, habitation and culture, are collapsed into a vital life force. Therefore, a notion of *spatial nommo* could refer to how spatialities and places convey African American rhetorical and discursive force and power through built environments. Christopher Airriess, in "Creating Vietnamese Landscapes and Place in New Orleans," understands spatiality, place, and geography through a geographic lens with rhetorical implications as he refers to *landscapes* as "the ordinary or commonplace visual elements of a community that residents create to satisfy their needs, wants, and desires."[23] He extends his analysis to *ethnic landscapes,* which he describes as "cultural autobiography" reflecting visual symbols—"residential architecture, houses of worship, recreation and commercial establishments, schools, and street signage—that convey the cultural traces of the community that created them."[24] Cultural traces can be conveyed through commonplaces embedded in spatial form and ornamentation.

Gilyard's "Barbershops and Afros" produces the effects of African American spatiality with its use of ornamentation and signage as cultural autobiography. As with rhetoric, ornamentation, is commonly misunderstood. Whereas rhetoric is derided as deceptive or superficial language, ornament circulates as insubstantial, superficial, or the merely decorative. Such uncritical views of rhetoric and ornamental are curious in an age where spectacle, simulacra, and postmodern disruption of easy surface-depth distinctions are taken for granted. David Summers, professor of art theory, takes such facile notions to task in *Real Spaces*. According to Summers, ornamentation is more than decoration. Ornamentation makes "social hierarchy clear, in costumes and furnishings, and in the social spaces in which all these distinctions are evident as part of the enactment of relations of status and power."[25] Given how, in both architecture and rhetoric, ornamentation has been linked to race and ethnicity, Summers's formulation sculpts ground from which to read how AAHHR conceptualization of ethnicity and race are understood as ontologies where episteme and ornamentation intersect and intertwine rather than merely the intersection of the decorative and the social in the public sphere.[26] So mere decoration in a simplistic sense could be thought of as adornment that is self-referential or object referential in that it seems to function in, of, and for its own sake, disconnected from an ordering, framing, or epistemic function desutured from social hierarchy or social distinction. Ornament then can be considered more thoughtfully as scriptings, motifs, patterns, visual tropes, and other verbal commonplaces and visual images that order, frame, distinguish, and enhance the meaning of an entity. Ornament is shaped by semiotic, ideological, and discursive forces resulting in social distinction. Ornament functions to alter, reproduce, enhance, or camouflage the political or hermeneutical rationalities of aesthetics and meaning.

Ornamentation and signage, then, illuminate designs, objects (books, paintings, magazines, album covers, etc.), forms, and visual images that convey African American rationalities through distinctive knowledges, social distinctions, and meanings as a conduit for semiotic, ideological, and rhetorical forces reflecting and producing African American life and culture. These lines cited earlier from "Barbershops and Afros,"

the
grandfather face trying to
peep under the bikini
of the bathing queen
in Jet *magazine*

refer to more than just a magazine. *Jet* magazine became a trope of Blackness, a rite of passage for Black males.[27] *Jet* was at one time a required Black text in any Black barbershop. Most Black men, at one time or another, wondered what titillating image would be folded into the center of the magazine. *Jet* conveyed Black tropes, rationalities, and rhetorics of Black civil society just as magazines such as *Slam, Vibe* (though published by non–African Americans), and *Black Enterprise* circulate as contemporary commonplaces of Blackness. African American barbershops can be said to be ethnic landscapes of Blackness that enable such spatialities to be understood as Black through spatial form, ornamentation, and habitation that signify particular subjectivities and identities. The barbershop is a neutral zone for the gumbo of iterations of Blackness in the barbershop as hush harbor. Therefore, the Afros and *Jet* magazines in "Barbershops and Afros" are the visible traces of Blackness that are deeply sedimented in African American expressive culture, knowledge, ornament, and rhetoric. Because visible traces of Blackness are deeply sedimented in Black spatiality, Black barbershops are never neutral utopian spaces.

"Barbershop Ritual" does refer to the barbershop as a neutral zone of brotherhood. Yet, if understood within the context of the entire stanza, it is clear that the poem does not argue for, nor does it produce, some abstract, neutral conception of spatiality:

> Baby brother's named for two fathers,
> And each Saturday he seeks them
> In this neutral zone of brotherhood
> Where manhood sprouts like new growth
> Week by week and dark hands
> Deftly shape identity.[28]

Ideology, identity, and masculinity permeate the spatiality the poem constructs. Nevertheless, the poem claims that the barbershop as hush harbor is a "neutral zone of brotherhood." Given my previous claim about the ideological nature of spatiality, how can the shop be neutral? What makes the spatiality neutral is that the barbershop is one site in which African American male topoi, tropes, and phronesis are consistently contested, but privileged. In other words, the barbershop is one place where Black masculinity and manhood are valued, not devalued; praised, not simply feared; desired, not despised. In this way, despite age differences, the barbershop is a level field in relation to how Black masculinity is negotiated in the public sphere. Unlike in the public sphere, far more can go unexplained and accepted in relation to African American experiences and knowledge. White worldviews that masquerade beneath a cloak of reasonableness, rationality, neutrality, objectivity, and civility in the public sphere are challenged in the African American barbershop. Class distinctions are left at the door, creating a neutral zone for distinctions/antagonisms. When class and other distinctions are not assumed, they must be asserted and argued. Of all the subjectivities that are asserted in barbershops as hush harbors, one of the most important is identity. In African American barbershops, African American hair circulates as a trope for identity.

"Barbershop Ritual" conjures up the nexus of hair as a visual trope of ritual, masculinity, subjectivity, and identity:

Head-bowed, church-solemn,
he sheds hair like motherlove & virginity
weightier than Air Jordans & designer
sweats—euphemistic battle gear.
He receives the tribal standard:
a nappy helmet sporting arrows, lightning
bolts, rows of lines cut in—New World
scarification—or carved logos (Adidas,
Public Enemy) and tags, like hieroglyphic
Distress signs to the ancestors:
Remember us, remember our names![29]

First, "Head-bowed, church-solemn" alludes once again to this Black geography as a sanctified secular-sacred spatiality. "Church-solemn" connects the act of cuttin' hair/heads to a ritualistic seriousness. Then the customer is baptized in the waters of culture and identity as he "receives the tribal standard: a nappy helmet sporting arrows." Recalling Chris Rock, his documentary *Good Hair,* and the question from one of his daughters that served as its catalyst, "Daddy, why don't I have good hair?" (nonnappy hair), hair for Black folk, particularly for Black women, is ornamental and more, identity and more—it is a site of trauma and relief, communal disdain and regard, individual confusion and coherence.

As with Pecola's desire for good eyes, as written about by Toni Morrison in her book *The Bluest Eye* (1970), based on a pervasive White standard of beauty circulating in both high culture and popular culture, the quest for good hair as a trope of beauty involves a Faustian bargain that makes the quest for its illusory assurance, along with notions of romantic love, according to Morrison, two of the most dangerous ideas in the Western world.

Dense tropes of excessive Blackness (in the mainstream public sphere) are embodied in nappy hair because the nappy signifies Blackness and African-Americanness on their own terms; Blackness as singularity. Singularity is the very foundation for any informed discussion of hush harbor rhetoric.

Nappy hair and African American identity are worthy of book-length elaboration. From the "kitchen" to the Afro, from the conk to the "Nubian lock," the coarse, the wild, and the nappy are all tropes for undomesticated, wild, assertively articulated, parrhesiatic, and energetically expressed Black subjectivity. Tribal (ethnic) standards are embodied in nappy hair because nappy hair as form and as symbol signifies Blackness on its own terms—the very foundation for any discussion of hush harbor rhetoric. "Roots," a poem by mawiyah bomani, targets the heart of the matter with humor, pathos, and purposeful catachresis:

> there
> is a revolution
> brewing
> within
> my hair
> and that's
> no lye[30]

"Roots" plays with the notion of nappiness and Blackness. Henry Louis Gates Jr. and bell hooks have both written essays about the hair on the nape of the neck, referred to as "the kitchen." The *kitchen* is the site of the hair that most transgressively resists processing, straightening, and conditioning. The "no lye" is a painfully comedic, sly but important nod to the chemical that burns the neck and singes the skin. Lye dissolves a Coke can in less than twenty-four hours but is useful for squashing the revolution of nappy natural Black hair. Revolution brews there because the hidden transcript of African American discourse always threatens to emerge (and does with a little sweat or water). While it may not be televised, the revolution is always goin' on in the kitchen.

Nappy hair illustrates perfectly the significance of AAHHR, its hidden transcripts, and how, whether by Lani Guinier, Muhammad Ali, or Rev. Jeremiah Wright, when a hush harbor storm makes landfall, it unleashes suppressed African American rationalities and knowledges, disrupting the racial calm dependent upon such suppressions and exclusions. Sooner or later, somewhere, somehow, nappy rhetoric, like nappy hair, percolates into the public. Nappiness must be dealt with in the American consciousness because the nappy as a trope throws Blackness on the table as trump; all other definitional cards that would sublimate Blackness under some broader category are, temporarily, tossed out of the game. Black hair signifies upon normative meanings with an ironic, funky twist: Black hair becomes real because it's wooly. "Barbershops and Afros" ends with an affirmation of the wooly:

> *yeah, there is a lot of pain in here but*
> *pain is a living thing*
> *like hair*
> *so all in all*
> *everything is on the upswing* [31]

Yes, things are on the upswing because, although Black folks playfully wrestle with Blackness in the hush harbor, hair ornamentations—arrows, bolts of lightning—are Americanized African retentions of practices of identity stretching through the Enslavement. AAHHR exhumes Black subjectivities trivialized, erased, suppressed, or ignored in normative conceptions of the public sphere. As with any single practice or set of practices, AAHHR can incur negative effects. Nevertheless, its effects are far more positive and productive in affirming African American subjectivity and enabling African American agency based on social, spiritual, and cultural rationalities informing African American culture and life. Revolution brews in the hair of the narrator of "Roots" because there is no lye—so the hair does not lie about its subjectivity. Black style is inherently political. That is to say that style always represents some cultural evaluation or investment. However, because an individual is wearing a style does not indicate that she or he has any investment in the politics of the style adorning their body. So processed hair that is lyed, fried, and laid to the side does not necessarily indicate a processed mind. Further, although natural hair does not always indicate progressive politics, the connection of natural hair and nappy hair to less domesticated Black subjectivities and identity as singularity retains rhetorical power and force:

> For naturals/minds hearing
> 56 independent interpretations
> of the Bible in
> one ear and out the other [32]

While conked hair has become a symbol for the lack of cultural or political commitment, Gilyard constructs the natural as a synecdoche for undomesticated Black minds. His gesture is not utopian, nor does it reflect a vulgar form of nationalism. Instead, through an AAHHR lens, the hair and minds are natural because Black men are freer to express them through a nappy rhetoric, a rhetoric that is less disciplined, less processed, than that which is authorized in the public sphere. [33]

Like other poems in this chapter, Gilyard's "Barbershops and Afros" creates nappy rhetoric, Black noise, as it tweaks Enlightenment conceptions of Blackness and beauty that were often used to justify the less than human status of Africans and of African Americans. The poem reconnects Black bodies and Black hair to Black minds, Black thoughts, and Black hermeneutics. Yet, because AAHHs are contact zones of African American culture, hush harbor barbershops are not Disneylands in which one can freely ride Blackness, maleness, and masculinity on gossamer wings of Afrocentric certainty into the tomorrow land of Black bliss. Identities are wrestled over and challenged in hush harbors. Dismay and disillusion haunt African American subjects who struggle with socialized ambivalence. "Barbershops and Afros" succinctly compresses experience, history, analysis, emotion, and knowledge into an image—an image of sheep:

> Sad dismay sinks in
> A throwback process
> with kinky skin
> silently thinks that your bush
> reminds him of sheep

Black hair was often compared to wool or to the coat of a sheep as a synecdoche for the subhuman status of Black subjects.[34] Subhuman hair gets conflated with Blackness as subhuman body and as subhuman subject: African-Americanness as ontologically inferior. African Americans themselves are marked as subhuman. African Americans, of course, are not immune to an Enlightenment-driven rhetoric that associates degradation with biology, to phenotype, and to physical ornamentation conveying embody degradation and inferiority. Some Black men and women go to the hush harbor to shear or process away that no-good nappy hair that marked them as other—as subhuman.

Willie M. Coleman captures the ambivalence, the pull-push contradiction, of Black hair and Blackness in a Black spatiality in the poem "Among the Things That Use to Be" (1979):

> Use to be
> you could learn
> a whole lot about
> how to catch up
> with yourself

and some other folks
in your household
   Lots more got taken care of
      than hair
   Cause in our mutual obvious dislike
        for nappiness
  we came together
under the hot comb
    to share
      and share
       and share[35]

Caressing a complicated rhetoric of belonging (verbal discourse, as well as the physical styling of the hair), the poet evokes the possibilities, as well as the challenges, of Black hair and Black communal rituals and the sensibilities surrounding those hush harbor rituals.

Young's "Eddie Priest's Barbershop & Notary" evokes the density of the rhetorical education of the barbershop through combining several elements, including identity, meaning, and memory, with lines that speak to young and elderly African American men alike about life:

grandfathers
stopping their games of ivory
dominoes just before they reach the bone
  yard is winking widowers announcing
cut it clean off I'm through courting
and hair only gets in the way[36]

This extract illuminates the weighty issue of living, life, and meaning informing, burdening, and haunting the jovial talk and game playing of barbershops. Young poignantly alludes to the inexorable decline of youth to old age as the men drop bones, play dominoes—as they play out life's string to the boneyard. No need to struggle over identity; they know who they are, what they are, in their souls, in their performances. In their bones. No need to wear the mask. Lose the bit. In the winter of their lives, these Black men look at their reflections—reflections through the images of the young men who occupy the protean male spatiality of the barbershop as hush harbor.

Gilyard, Young, and Coleman avoid an uncritical, sentimental view of the barbershop as hush harbor. As I alluded to earlier, I want to avoid sentimentalizing the rhetorics that emerge for hush harbor sites such as barbershops, and I want to reassert that AAHHR forms, tropes, commonplaces, and knowledges can be used for ill or personal benefit, as well as for communal affirmation and uplift. Therefore, I shift my focus to an African American rhetor who uses the forms, style, and tactics of AAHHR to meet his own personal desires at the expense of African American communal ethics. In this way, the rhetorical education of the hush harbor can go awry.

Sterling Brown's "Slim Hears the Call" is part of the Slim cycle in the groundbreaking book of African American vernacular poetry, *Southern Road* (1932). As important as Paul Laurence Dunbar's "An Ante-Bellum Sermon" (1896) and his other African American vernacular poetry was to the transporting of African American dialect and rhetoric into the White, mainstream public sphere, the prevalence of the plantation tradition as a cultural and literary commonplace mediated its reception. More specifically, modernist or New Negroes often viewed Dunbar's dialect poetry as a rearticulation of an antiquated Blackness that modernist sensibilities should reject. However, Brown was able to transport African American dialect, rhetoric, and folk culture into the public sphere through an epistemological lens that viewed vernacular folks and their knowledge on their own terms—terms that Brown valued. According to Mark Sanders, "for Brown, liberating New Negro poetics must imagine that 'dialect,' or the speech of the people, is capable of expressing what the people are."[37] Here, Brown's *theorizing* of orality intersects with James Berlin's theorizing around rhetoric, knowledge, subjectivity, and ontology as imbricated in rhetoric and various rationalities, in his recognition of the tangled nexus of language, rhetoric, and ontology. Brown's poetry challenged Whites and others who would construct Blackness as vernacular fetish and fetishize African American vernacular language/rhetoric. In addition, he challenged African Americans who would engage in a kind of exceptionalism that would construct Black folks as naturally more emotional and expressive. Brown was able to construct the Black working class and poor folks with verisimilitude because he himself often visited hush harbors such as jook joints, mills, pool halls, blues joints, and, of course, barbershops. Brown's characters are rich, complex modernist Black folks who shed the clothing of a plantation tradition that would reduce them to the instinctual. According to Sanders, Brown wanted to liberate "New Negro poetics" so that they were capable of "expressing what the people are," not what White folks need them to be.[38]

"Slim Greer," "Slim Lands a Job," and "Slim in Atlanta" all precede "Slim Hears 'The Call.'" In the series, Slim mirrors Sugar Groove in *Divine Days* as a hero, trickster, and bad-man figure who circumvents and subverts White hegemony and authority through improvisation, irony, lies, or whatever tactics and strategies help him to survive and, sometimes, to flourish. Slim's character illustrates nommo deployed to unethical or individual ends. Slim deploys a deceptive nommo—the use of African American rhetorical forms, commonplaces, and knowledges for personal benefit—under the guise of Black communal interest. Slim is immersed in African American rhetoric—its *techne* (its art and episteme), its phronesis, its nommo—but uses it to unethical and selfish ends.

Brown introduces us to Slim in, where else, a barbershop, in the middle of a soliloquy:

> Down at the barbershop
> Slim had the floor,
> "Ain't never been down so
> Far down before."[39]

Here, the barbershop functions as a dense cultural trope and commonplace that signals to both an addressed and invoked audience that, at this moment, Slim is the center of the rhetorical occasion. The floor in the barbershop as hush harbor, like the pulpit in a Black church, is both a material and discursive Black rhetorical situation informed by African American exigency, decorum, and kairos. In other words, the poem signals that this is gon' be a hush harbor performance at the opportune moment, containing Black modes of discourse and African American rhetorical forms. But the stanza also suggests an ethical problem because the floor had never been so low. Brown's poem hints that Slim is driven by the low motivations of an unethical rhetor about to misuse AAHHR:

> Big holes is the onlies'
>> Things in my pocket,
> So bein' a bishop
>> Is next on the docket.
>
> Lawd, lawd, yas Lawd,
>> I hears de call,
> An' I'll answer, good Lawd,
>> Don't fret none atall.[40]

Slim's rhetoric offers clues that he is a bad rhetor speaking badly who speaks well but who uses the African American trope of the call to make his own selfish interests seem the better case.

Brown uses irony and humor to convey the poem's skepticism about the legitimacy of Slim's call:

> Lawd, lawd, yes Lawd,
>> I hears de call,
> An' I'll answer, good Lawd,
>> Don't fret none atall.
>
> I heard it once
>> An' I hears it again
> Broadcast from the station
>> W-I-N![41]

Enslaved Africans understood the importance of the call. In a culture that valued orality, it was important to distinguish between a minister who got the call from the Lord and one who spoke well but who was not believed to be inspired by the will of God. Later ministers were referred to as *exhorters.*[42]

Exhorters could lead one to God but had to be watched because they could persuade one in another direction.

Slim's call emerges from more earthly sources and motivations, which Brown makes clear in the next stanza:

Gonna be me a bishop,
    That ain't no lie,
Get my cake down here,
    An' my pie in the sky.[43]

Reverend Ike would be proud. Slim stumbles upon an old friend with a deep, rich, and resonant voice even "Called hogs in a way / Jes beautiful."[44] Brown's play on call/called and hogs reveals how the rhetorical force of AAHHR can be connected to both the sublime and the decadent. The lines also foreshadow Slim's own rhetoric of deceit and negative nommo. Brown picks up on the aforementioned concerns when the smooth-talking hog caller, Brotha Greer, is introduced to folks in the African American community as a "great divine."[45] Slim and Brother Greer become partners in a plan to separate Black folks from their money. Brown makes it clear that Brother Greer is a man of questionable ethics and even more questionable cognitive skills:

An' he de kind of guy
    Was sich a fool
Dey had to burn down de shack
    To get him out of school.

    When de other pupils
        Was doin' history
    He was spellin' cat
        With a double p.[46]

However, what Brother Greer lacks in formal education he makes up for through cleverness, street smarts, and the narcissism of a con man:

> *But he knew what side de bread*
> > *You put de butter on,*
> *An' he could figger all right*
> > *For number one.*[47]

Again, the poem drives home that Slim's rhetorical brilliance is based on verbal ploys like those of which Plato accused the Sophists.

A Brer Rabbit frolicking in the briar patch of self-aggrandizement and personal desire, the rhetorical force of Brother Greer's nommo was powerful:

> *A passel of Niggers*
> > *From near an' far*
> *Bringin' in de sacred bucks*
> > *Regular.*[48]

Brown avoids the romanticizing of nommo that occurs too often in rhetoric and speech communication scholarship. "Slim Hears 'The Call'" unveils how nommo can be deployed improperly to the disadvantage of African American communities. "A passel" of Black folks alludes to the large numbers who are persuaded by rhetoric that is mere cookery. Fortunately, phronesis embeds AAHHR and nommo into ethics.

Slim follows Brother Greer, watching him swindle folks with a rhetorical tactic that entails "a pint of good sense / An' a bushel of bluff."[49] Brother Greer becomes the president/bishop of his own school and raises thousands of dollars to keep it afloat. When the school runs into financial problems, he attends conferences all over the country, even in places where his school/ church has no members. Brother Greer, according to Slim, "Filled a Pullman wid de delegates / He liked the best."[50] Brown's poem now directly addresses how nommo in the sacred sphere is often misused for personal gain:

> *Las' words he said*
> > *As he rose in de air:*
> *"Do lak me; take you' troubles*
> > *To de Lord in prayer."* [51]

Brother Greer exemplifies the flying fool myth with a twist: he's fooling the fools with whose money he's flying off. "Slim Hears 'The Call'" is a poetic take on the tall tale. Brown both affirms African American culture and the folks like Slim who are anchored in its valuable phronesis.

Yet, it also is a scathing critique of the unethical use of nommo to selfish ends. Brown makes this critique explicit in the poem's final stanzas. Slim informs the folks assembled in the barbershop why he would be a good bishop:

> I kin be a good bishop,
>   I got de looks,
> An' I ain't spoiled myself
>   By readin' books.

>   Don't know so much
>   Bout de Holy Ghost,
>   But I likes de long green
>   Better'n most.

> I kin talk out dis worl'
>   As you folks all know,
> An' I'm good wid de women,
>   Dey'll tell you so . . ."[52]

Slim's deceptive use of African American rhetorical forms to meet his own ends is apparent. Slim's looks and his talk, his nommo, are all he needs. There is nothing his rhetorical skills cannot accomplish for him. There is no talk of phronesis, no talk of ethics, no concern with any commitment other than to himself. AAHHR may have limits, but it does not limit him. Brown taps into the tension that exists in a culture where the verbal is so highly valued because it has done so much and because, so often, it was all that some folks had. But Slim decouples AAHHR forms and tactics from ethics and community.

Brown takes a final shot at Slim and his use of African American rhetoric in his piece "Slim in Hell," which concludes the Slim cycle. While the poem can be read in isolation, it is also a comment on the Slim the reader has been

introduced to in the other poems, including "Slim Hears 'The Call.'" In "Slim
in Hell," Slim goes to heaven and meets St. Peter. In Leon Forrest's *Divine Days*,
St. Peter is taught a few things about African American phronesis, rhetoric,
and culture. St. Peter is clearly the outsider. In contrast, in "Slim in Hell,"
Brown gives the reader a St. Peter who is, even more than Slim, attuned to
the realties of Black life. St. Peter provides Slim with wings and tells him to
visit earth, and then report back. Slim flew and flew,

> Till at last he hit
> A hangar wid de sign readin'
> DIS IS IT.[53]

Slim enters a mansion where he encounters the Devil. The Devil takes
Slim to Memphis, New Orleans, and Vicksburg. He takes Slim to giant stills
where moonshine is manufactured and "a passel of devils / Stretched dead
drunk there."[54] There they find "White devils wid pitchforks"[55] throwing Black
devils in a furnace. After a while, Slim has seen enough. He returns to heaven
and reports to St. Peter, and St. Peter says,

> Well
> You got back quick.
>   How's de Devil? An' what's
> His latest trick?

Slim's response is telling:

> I really cain't tell
> De place was Dixie
>   Dat I took for Hell.[56]

When Slim informs St. Peter that he mistook Dixie for hell, St. Peter
just can't believe that a Black man such as Slim does not know where hell
is located.

Brown ends "Slim in Hell" with this response by St. Peter:

"You must be crazy
Be crazy, I vow,
Where'n hell dja think hell was,
Anyhow?

"Git on back to de yearth,
Cause I got de fear,
You'se a leetle too dumb,
Fo' to stay up here . . ."[57]

At the end of the day, St. Peter banishes Slim from heaven because Slim lacks the practical knowledge and wisdom, the ethical rhetorical education, one would expect from a hush harbor rhetorician holding down the floor at the barbershop. Slim lacks the critical consciousness that would enable him to see Dixie for what it really is through an African American rhetorical lens. Globalization, with its simultaneous enlarging and diminishing of physical spaces and communicative networks, exposes African American males, like everyone else, to a faster and smaller world. The rhetorical education of hush harbors is thereby influenced by the commonplaces and ethics of a more interconnected globe. As a result, hush harbors can produce Martin Luther Kings but can also produce Slims.

Unfortunately, Slim turns out to be a hush.

5.

Barbers and Customers

as Philosophers in Memoir and Drama

WHILE THE TRAJECTORY OF THE PREVIOUS CHAPTER ADDRESSED NEGATIVE nommo, this chapter takes a related, but different, angle. Drawing from Keith Gilyard's American Book Award–winning memoir, *Voices of the Self* (1991), and Lonne Elder III's award-winning play *Ceremonies in Dark Old Men* (1969), this section illustrates and explores not the word, but its purveyor: the *phronimos* (good rhetor of practical wisdom) and *denimos* (bad rhetor). The barbers in *Voices of the Self* produce a generative, phronesis-driven rhetoric because their rhetoric is grounded in African American knowledges and rationalities. Conversely, the barber in *Ceremonies in Dark Old Men* provides little practical wisdom, knowledge, or intelligence. In opposition to the phronimoses of *Voices of the Self,* Mr. Parker is a denimos whose rhetoric is hollow, disconnected from communal ethics, and informed by self-interest that ultimately hurts both his family and himself.

The barbers in *Voices of the Self*—Mr. Boone, Mr. Shortside, and Mr. Horton—are *phronimoses,* a term borrowed from Greek philosophy. A *phronimos* might be called a *griot,* or philosopher in classic African and African American rhetoric taxonomies. If *phronesis* is understood as practical wisdom, intellect, and virtue, then the *phronimos* can be said to be a philosopher of practical wisdom, intellect, and virtue. As I mentioned earlier, the term is important because it disrupts conventional philosophy: who can be a philosopher, who gets to speak as a philosopher, particularly in the spatialities of African American hush harbor rhetoric (AAHHR). The *African American phronimos* is a philosopher of the everyday, of the world of sense perception, and of the practical as understood by Aristotle.

Aristotle discusses the qualities of the phronimos extensively in his *Nicomachean Ethics.*[1] Phronimoses possess the kind of wisdom related to "practical thinking" that "is concerned with what we can do to change things, and why we might decide to do one thing rather than another."[2] Like conventional philosophers, phronimoses may contemplate or consider abstract universals or first principles. However, unlike Platonic philosophers, it is up to the phronimos to apply what passes as the universal or the general to particular circumstances based on experience, intellect, virtue, and judgment. This is not to imply that the phronimos, a figure ubiquitous to the African American barbershop as hush harbor who might understand himself or be understood by others to be a philosopher, will be found spouting philosophical jargon about abstract universals and particulars as they relate to ontological and metaphysical speculations. Instead, it is to say that, in barbershops that function as hush harbors, phronimoses, barbers—or indeed many people who do not officially function as philosophers—provide knowledges and truths of civil society that are just as valuable, if not more valuable, than those provided by people who serve the state and its related institutions. On one register, the foregoing can be read as an attempt to carve out a space for AAHHR as philosophy, a move to consider barbers as philosophers, or a quaint gesture for inclusiveness. Such a reading would be ahistorical, hegemonic, and both a misreading of *Keepin' It Hushed* and a misdiagnosis of the problem this book and chapter are pushing against.

Barbara Christian in her germinal and controversial essay "The Race for Theory" (1987) and the Content of Minority Discourse" critiques the emerging methods and approaches of critical or literary theory. Too often read as an antitheory diatribe, the essay can be more productively read as a cogent rhetorical critique of the language games and language rationalities of access to and legitimacy in the discourse and practices of critique and philosophy. Christian's piece intersects with *Keepin' It Hushed* in terms of both hush harbor rhetoric and the ongoing struggle over knowledge. What do I mean by *ongoing*? In "Theory," Christian discusses how those who would critique what she refers to as the hegemony of the new academic elites of her era (deconstructionists, postmodernists, post-structuralists) must usually do so "in hidden groups, lest we who are disturbed by it appear ignorant to the academic elite."[3] She goes on to describe how women of color, feminists, and others must speak in "muted tones." Take note of how her concerns mirror those of Michelle Wallace in *Dark Designs and Visual Culture* from 2004 from which I quoted in the "Overture/Head" and those of the grandfather in the first season of the hip-hop culture, comic book influenced, *The Boondocks* who informs his grandson Huey that "you bet not dream about telling White folks the truth": "Black intellectuals, cultural critics—whatever you want to call them—are still not free to speak their minds anywhere except in their living rooms. The secret of conquering the so-called public sphere, which is just another name for the White dominated marketplace of ideas, continues to be having something critical to say about Blacks."[4] The linkage between Christian, Wallace, bell hooks, Patricia Hill-Collins, and *The Boondocks* is self-evident and cannot be relegated to the important, but fossilized, thinking of another era. I will illuminate in a few moments how the current fetish with a postracial America where influential writers and publishers such a Tina Brown and the usually discerning Maureen Dowd argue that the election of a Black president has made race passé ignores how even academia continues to reduce Black women scholars, even at the graduate level, whose work is grounded in Black women standpoints, to mere difference and sociology vis-à-vis French, Italian, German, and European high theory.

Christian goes on to launch a powerfully elegant critique of what she considers the "new philosophers" and philosophy that, as they lose control of a hegemonic hermeneutic that is punctured, cracked, and in the process of being dismantled by women of color, queers, and others, immerse themselves in jargon that, while decentering other philosophers in the Western Platonic–influenced canon, recenter themselves upon a different road in the same Eurocentric, male-dominated terrain occupied by their philosophical fathers. Christian argues that she and thinkers who are fellow travelers with her are neglected, omitted, or disdained.[5] Admittedly, her brush cuts a broad swath that requires some narrowing. And the notion that the ends of theory should be pragmatic in its conception is problematic. Nevertheless, her critique cannot be dismissed as Black nationalist hysteria or narrow identity politics (Christian critiques both in no uncertain terms). Here she does not seem to be referring to intention; rather she is referring to *effect*. Rhetoric as methodology and practice, takes effect into account and does not carry with it the taint of disinterestedness (as does critical theory/philosophy). She goes on to posit how such jargon and theories discipline out of the order of things the following:

> For people of color have always theorized—but in forms quite different from the Western form of abstract logic. And I am inclined to say that our theorizing (and I intentionally use the verb rather than the noun) is often in narrative forms in the stories we create, in riddles and proverbs, in the play with language, since dynamic rather than fixed ideas seem more to our liking. How else have we managed to survive with such spiritedness the assault on our bodies, social institutions, countries, our very humanity?[6]

Keepin' It Hushed argues for a distinct genealogy of knowledge with and against the grain of philosophy through the fellow traveler with, and counterphilosophy of, rhetoric as "The Race for Theory" argues with and against the grain of the new philosophers through literature. Both argue that there are other ways to theorize and understand the world that are not a supplement or epiphenomenal to or an exotic sidetrack from the road of high theory. *Keepin' It Hushed* argues that the realm of philosophy does not belong most significantly to scholars with French, Italian, or European last names, nor does such knowledge issue only from the ivory towers of the academy or corporate-funded think tanks and foundations; but that, as *Voices of the*

Self argues, philosophy and philosophers practice in a variety of spaces in a variety of occupations, like the barbershop, and sometimes they are more important to most folks than a bushel full of deconstructing, postmodern, post-structuralists who sometimes, in the words of Thelonius "Monk" Ellison in Percival Everett's brilliant postmodern, post-stucturalist satire *Erasure* (2002), "you need to get laid."[7]

Gilyard's *Voices of the Self* is an African American sociolinguistic bildungsroman addressing the acquisition of philosophy, literacy, and voice by an African American man. Though published in 1991, *Voices of the Self* addresses the still relevant issue of so-called Black English and its values, utility, and relation to African American–language competence. *Voices* is a germinal text in the fields of rhetoric, composition, education, and sociolinguistics due to its protean mix of memoir, rhetoric, and sociolinguistic scholarship.

The arrangement and organization of the book as a rhetorical artifact embody and embrace a methodology anchored in phronesis. Both theory and practical wisdom are conveyed as the chapters alternate between theory and autobiography. *Voices'* concern with phronesis, pedagogy, AAHHR, and African American subjectivity is evident in the following: "A pedagogy is successful only if it makes knowledge or skill achievable while at the same time allowing students to maintain their own sense of identity."[8]

AAHHR tropes manifest themselves in various ways in Gilyard's text. For example, when his family moves to Corona, New York, from Harlem, he must enroll, for the first time, in a majority White class. When introduced to the class, his internal narrative entangles itself in the African American trope of "I got one mind for the master and another for self" that is endemic in AAHHR: "*They cannot meet Keith now. I will put someone else together for them and he will be their classmate until further notice. That will be the first step in this particular survival plan*" (Gilyard's italics).[9] Here is a hidden transcript in the late twentieth century that eerily resembles those of the Enslavement and points to contemporary takes on performance, subjectivity, and viscous identity. Gilyard guides the reader through a migration narrative of spatiality and Black male subjectivity. From his inability to come home on time, and the cutting of his sister's hair, to moving from Harlem to Corona, to his competence both in and out of the classroom as he wrestles with the angels and demons relative to friendship, sexuality, accomplishment, drugs, and college acceptance, readers are immersed in a literacy narrative that constructs itself from the epistemological bottom to the experiential top—with an African American male twist. Due to its alchemy of theoretical and practical wisdom, *Voices* goes beyond the self-help ethos of the legendary Booker T. Washington and the neo-slave narrative, and thug aesthetic of post–soul brother journalist Nathan McCall, to illustrate how a young Black man makes a way out of a lot of different possible ways.[10] Given Gilyard's concern with an African American male child's acquisition of literacy, his identity, his coming to voice, and both his informal and formal education, it is not surprising that we find the barbershop and other hush harbors in his memoir.

Before the reader even approaches the primary barbershop chapter "Big Fame and Other Games," the importance of the spatialities of the barbershop and the beauty shop are tropes that Gilyard deploys as he constructs and reconstructs the memories of his childhood. A story that initially begins with an almost Hallmark card sentimentality around Keith as a little boy—a cowboy outfit and his six-shooters—quickly enters into hush harbor humor and pathos when he receives a severe spanking for jetting out into a busy street when he and his mother were returning from the beauty shop. Later, he gets in trouble again after he describes being consistently late coming home from school as he and his friends stick their noses into "the barbershop, the shoe repair shop, the fish market, the bars."[11] Both incidents occur in the first chapter as he lays out the events he considers important to the construction of his language competency and to his subjectivity. Interestingly, of all the stories he might have told, of all the numerous spaces he could have integrated into his narrative, the importance of African American hush harbors (AAHHs) is revealed in his narrative.

Including "games" in the title of the barbershop chapter signals the importance of play and game to African American male ritual, affirmation, transformation, and rhetoric. *Game,* which is a tactic and strategy of survival, as well as an assertion of personality and agency, alludes to one's ability to situate himself or herself through verbal and physical rhetoric within a variety of rhetorical situations with various exigencies. The connection of play/game to jazz and improvisation—a primary techne of African American rhetoric—is difficult to ignore. Game can be play, and play may be fun, but both are connected to Black survival, and that ain't just a game.

As the reader navigates the AAHHR of the chapter, Gilyard illustrates how the barbershop, not Las Vegas, is the gaming capital for most African American males. Ironically, this chapter begins with Keith in Mrs. Holtzman's elementary school class. Gilyard thus contrasts the formal, centripetal education he obtains in public school to the unofficial, centrifugal education he obtains in the barbershop. In the conclusion of the barbershop segment, Gilyard recognizes, in retrospect, the barbershop as a site of knowledge and rhetorical education. He concludes the barbershop segment with a critique of Mrs. Holtzman's pedagogy in contrast to the praise he lavishes on the unofficial pedagogy and knowledge of the hush harbor barbershop philosophers: "Mr. Shortside and Boone became very special in my eyes. They gave current events much better than Mrs. Holtzman did. More *analysis* and *fervor* [italics mine]. My teacher stayed more on the side of soft regret and subdued hope. Whereas she was detached, they had definite points of view."[12] Mr. Boone and Mr. Shortside provide an embodied pedagogy that increases their ethos with Keith. Cradled in the barbershop as a site of African American rhetorical education, they communicate to him through a mode of argument and delivery that conveys experiential and personal investment in issues relevant to him and to his life. And significantly, the Black body, its rhetorics, its memories, its knowledges, are not erased into oblivion.

Keith's analysis of Mrs. Holtzman's pedagogy illuminates how rhetoric and the political and social rationalities of the public sphere and its institutions tend to privilege a performance, style, delivery, and diction that suggest an appeal to logos, an objective disinterested rhetoric imbued with civility. Yet, what cannot be overlooked is that a disinterested rhetoric is itself a performance, and that civility is not ideologically neutral but is steeped in nation-state rationalities of gender, race, sexual orientation, class, and power. In other words, civility serves the manufacturing of racial consent because, "among other things," according to David Theo Goldberg in *The Threat of Race: Reflections on Racial Neoliberalism* (2008), "civility serves as a pressure to confirm, playing a key part in the social reproduction of consent." Further, "civility is a genteel analogue, of the expanding hold of racial historicism on modernizing racial imaginaries across the globe."[13] So when Gilyard refers to and combines pedagogy, analysis, and fervor—the latter two characteristics often viewed as oppositional in American public sphere rhetoric, particularly in relation to folks of color and women—he makes visible in everyday language how AAHHR embodies different rationalities, social expectations, and ideologies in the service of African American knowledges, life, and culture.

Gilyard's position reveals that fervor in AAHHR as it relates to style and delivery not only is positively valued but also evokes serious engagement through experience. From Malcolm to Martin, from Ida to Eleanor Holmes Norton, emotion and personal investment are valued in African American rhetorical practices. This is not because emotion (pathos) or subjectivity is valued over the empirical and/or the objective, but because, in an African American rhetorical performance, the separation of the two is resisted. Fervor does not negate reason in AAHHR performances.

Mr. Boone and Mr. Shortside are thoughtful and engaged, and this engagement is displayed through their willingness to offer differing viewpoints. As he grapples with White folks beating, shooting, and killing Black folks in the South for simply registering to vote, Keith seeks what he refers to as "a striking adult view on this and other situations."[14] What is important here is that Keith does not go to school, he does not visit church, and he does not go to the street corner for insight; he goes to the barbershop. He expects to learn something at the barbershop that he cannot learn elsewhere. Mr. Shortside, Mr. Boone, and Mr. Horton are philosophers whose worldviews and ideas continue to be put to the test of the banal, the mundane, the everyday, to the making a way out of no way, or to the improvising of more ways out of the way one already has. In addition, the rhetoric of the three men is not limited to a concern with making a way for themselves. Their AAHHR is concerned with Black folks, Black perspectives, and Black American psyches.

Soon to make the transition from elementary to junior high school, Keith enters into the male hush harbor to be schooled at Horton University, otherwise known as the barbershop. Keith's father has informed Mr. Horton to expect his son. Horton warmly greets Keith and gently teases him about his hair: "I see you done let it git nappy enough, don't you think?" Keith responds, "Yeah I guess so. . . . How's business in general Mr. Horton?" "My father always asked him that question," Keith thinks to himself.[15] Again, nappy as a trope of Blackness appears as it does in the poetry examined earlier. Gilyard's motivation for the question—his father always asked Mr. Horton the same question—suggests the importance of the barbershop as a sanctified spatiality of African American male rhetorical education. Sanctified spatialities are sites of repeated secular-sacred conventions and rituals in which subjects acquire the distinctive, culturally specific values transferred from one generation to the next.

In chapter 3, I mentioned Derrick I. M. Gilbert's yearlong ethnographic study of a barbershop in Long Beach, California, "Shaping Identity at Cooke's Barbershop." It attempts to extend the numerous studies of the importance of local geographies and the construction of African American male subjectivity to the overlooked site of the barbershop.[16] Cooke's barbershop was the only barbershop Gilbert's father ever took him to get his hair and head cut from childhood through adolescence.[17] Many of the topics of conversation in *Voices of the Self* (race, sports, education, clandestine economy) are mirrored thirty years later in Gilbert's ethnographic study, as well as in all of the literary, popular, and visual texts used in this study. Keith travels down a channel of experience and ritual valued by generations of Black men. Keith's father guided him through a Black male spatiality in which he (Keith's father) himself had been, in which he is respected, and in which he knows his son can obtain some of that African American male phronesis.

After Keith settles in and begins to get his hair cut, customer and community elder Mr. Shortside discusses his personal tactics and strategies for dealing with a younger woman with whom he is in a sexual relationship. According to Mr. Shortside, the woman wants to have a discussion just before sex as a tool to leverage for something she wants. Mr. Shortside avoids anger as, in his words, "I just puts the intelligence in my head. I carries it around in my socks, only got a little bit and I needs to save it like that."[18]

Two points are worth noting. First, Gilyard provides a glimpse into AAHHR as a hidden transcript of tactics and strategies that circulate in African American male hush harbors. Discussions about African American male and female relationships occur with regularity in barbershops. And Mr. Shortside would be less likely to share such information in a non–African American male hush harbor spatiality or within a more gender-diverse site that might be less of a safe refuge for African American males to express their take on male-female relationships. My claim is not that the *truth* of African American male-female relationships can be found only in male hush harbors; rather, the claim is that views, anchored in African American male standpoints, shared by men in barbershop and hush harbor places are not shared elsewhere. Second, Mr. Shortside contemplates and *deliberates* topoi of Western philosophers, philosophy, and, more importantly, given the investments of *Keepin' It Hushed*, rhetoric. Attaching philosophy to barbershop spatialities, bodies, and rhetoric disrupts the signifying system of conventional categories and discourse around philosophy. Experimental jazz poet and novelist Nathaniel Mackey contends that noise is whatever the signifying system, in a particular situation, is not intended to transmit.[19] For me to refer to men like Mr. Shortside, Mr. Horton, and Mr. Boone as philosophers creates conceptual noise because it is a discrepant engagement with conventional categories of what constitutes philosophy and philosophers. Further, offering men like Mr. Horton as philosophers fractures petrified assumptions and cracks stiff categories determining what counts as knowledge and which bodies count as legitimate sites of knowledge production.

My project in AAHHR links James Berlin's attempt to couple rhetoric to episteme and rationality and recognizes that rhetoric both generates and transmits knowledge. I am not simply imposing the terms philosophy or philosophers on the texts under examination nor grafting them onto AAHHR. For example, *Voices of the Self* and *Divine Days* contain references to both individuals and to elements of barbershop discourse as philosophers and philosophy, respectively. For example, in *Voices,* Mr. Horton questions Keith: "You didn't know Boone was a philosopher, did you?" "Actually," Keith thinks to himself, "I did."[20]

How did Keith know? He probably heard Boone deconstruct issues such as the University of Mississippi before.

Mr. Horton asks Boone, the barber with transgressive knowledge and a transgressive (nappy) Afro, to give his take on the University of Mississippi and its refusal to enroll African Americans. Boone's interrogation of the name "University of Mississippi" includes his deconstructive riffing on the preposition "of," the excess beyond presentation, and the absence-presence that infuses Whiteness with meaning that would make Jacques Derrida proud: "So it's OF Mississippi and it's good, and it's OF Mississippi and it's bad. And then you can say that it ain't really the University OF Mississippi at all because a Negro might can use that school to get a job opportunity just like a White boy, and that definitely wouldn't represent what Mississippi is all about. So it is and it ain't. All depends on how you look at it."[21]

Mr. Boone as hush harbor philosopher uses AAHHR to crack categories of language and the language of representation. Boone's critique functions at the junction of White privilege and Black physical and discursive segregation. Like a signifyin' philosopher, Boone's rap creates paths to defamiliarize the familiar; it encourages hush harbor occupants to rethink not only what they think but how they think about what they think. AAHHs are part of a critical tradition in which Black folks get both critiques and metacritiques. Like Langston Hughes's Simple, Mr. Boone probably hasn't read any Isocrates; nevertheless, he deserves a fee for what he had just dropped in this African American lyceum. Boone's riff acknowledges how the University of Mississippi conveys a representation of all Mississippians, but he is also aware how its meaningfulness as a category is based on the fundamental exclusion, the absence-presence, of its Black population. Boone's performance of his signifyin' encomium to and about Mississippi is immersed in the Black-is–Black-ain't discourse of the Black preacher in Ellison's *Invisible Man* who trolls the sacred and secular waters of AAHHR and the African American sermonic tradition.

Marx believed that the problem with philosophy was philosophers and seemed to agree with Aristotle about the uselessness of philosophers because of the opaque language and politics, and their lack of relevance to the lives of everyday folks.[22] As a phronimos, Boone makes philosophy mean something to everyday folks. Boone proceeds to tell Keith what all that philosophizing means: "It means the stuff is so screwed up. Usually when you hear a whole buncha jumbled up philosophy, it means somethin real bad is goin on. You git halfway confused tryin to explain the shit."[23] Boone can be seen as a vernacular Ludwig Wittgenstein who "believed that modern philosophy was little more than the working out of word games that did not refer to reality as such but betrayed an imprisonment within a framework of concepts developed by classical philosophy."[24] According to Herbert Muschamp, the way out of the prison is to "recognize the rhetoric."[25] Boone recognizes the rhetoric. Further, Boone recognizes his audience. Keith knows men like Boone are philosophers because they observe, contemplate, engage the world, converse with others who have acted in the world, and then convey that knowledge to hush harbor inhabitants. Hush harbor occupants can discern a phronimos and his or her rhetoric because AAHHR requires the philosopher to break down his or her language so those folks in the harbor can discern the rhetoric contained in the philosophy—rhetoric that often provides Black folks with a strategy to break, dance, or talk their way out of their constrictions. And if one is aware of AAHHR barbershop discourse, one knows that all kinds of knowledge from all kinds of sources might enter the spatiality.

Mr. Shortside saves and deploys his reasoning when the rhetorical situation demands it. He does not just react. Intelligence and deliberation in this case are more than just descriptions; they reconfigure the Black male as both corporeal and mind. Mind and deliberation are typically applied to White and formally educated bodies. Intelligence and dispassionate decision making are rarely attributed to Black male bodies, particularly to those like Mr. Shortside. Nor are intelligence, mind, and wisdom typically associated with AAHH spatialities such as beauty shops, barbershops, and Chitlin' Circuit sites.

What is deliberated upon in hush harbor spatialities? Anything and everything that impacts the lives of Black folks. More specifically, a Black commonsense tradition is simultaneously developed and deliberated upon. For Harris-Lacewell a tradition(s) of *Black common sense* "is the idea among African Americans that blackness is a meaningful political category," and for Wahneema Lubiano it is "ideology lived and articulated in everyday understanding of the world and one's place in it."[26] For me, Black common sense situates the aforementioned within a *terrain of intelligibility*. Black common sense as a terrain of intelligibility is a protean site of Black memories, rationalities, politics, and possibilities in African American culture, a terrain where meaning, struggle, pain, love, and commitment coalesce into a distinctive experience that is broader and deeper than one individual, yet depends on individual subjects for its vitality. AAHHs are primary Black enclaves of intelligibility where Black commonsense understandings are posited, struggled over, and negotiated.

Mr. Shortside continues his narrative sequencing: "So anyway I puts it in my head and then I realize that all I gotta do is keep my cool and use a little indifference myself, you know, like I could take it or leave it myself."[27] Geneva Smitherman bridges the concept of narrative sequencing to African American rhetoric. According to Smitherman, "The relating of events (real or hypothetical) becomes a *black rhetorical strategy* [italics mine] to explain a point, to persuade holders of opposing views to one's own point of view, and in general to 'win friends and influence people.'"[28] Barbara Christian's perspective on the theorizing of everyday Black folks gains additional traction when reread through the lens of Smitherman and Harris-Lacewell.

Like Aesop's fables with a Black vernacular flip, narrative sequencing provides a pedagogical narrative with personal and communal implications. To the African American men in the barbershop, Mr. Shortside's line about keeping his cool and deploying a little indifference teaches a rhetorical tactic of detachment from a kind of masculinity that is more about policing one's ego than problem solving. In the streets, in engagements with the police, in conflicts with mainstream institutions, one's economic, psychological, and physiological life can be saved by keeping one's cool, the temporary shelving of the ego. On one hand, detachment as rhetorical tactic in this case is partly persuasive and manipulative to the extent it serves Mr. Shortside's own agenda of love and lust. On the other hand, Mr. Shortside connects detachment and, by extension, AAHHR, to logos and thought. If one recalls that, as a genre of narrative form, narrative sequencing conveys the abstract through the concrete, then narrative sequencing could be said to address both the more abstract, utopian concerns of Plato's *Phaedrus*, as well as the more concrete pragmatic concerns of phronesis.

As Mr. Shortside continues, he pauses for a minute and reminisces about the excellence of his sexual performance with the woman and then goes on to tell the men in the barbershop, as they laugh out loud, "Now I can't get rid of the chick. It done even got to where I'm actually duckin' her now. Girl trying to be on me tight as a orange peel be on a orange. She gittin peeled though, better believe that."[29] Mr. Shortside expresses a take it or leave it ambivalence toward the woman in question. She's all over him, but he is going to have to peel her off of him and out of their relationship. Mr. Shortside is not going to tear, rip, or yank himself out the relationship; he is going to peel himself out. Peeling signifies taking one's time to reach one's goal with panache and grace but with a single-mindedness of purpose.

As in African American women's hush harbors, African American men bring the noise (their standpoints) in a rhetorical occasion with a distinctive sense of decorum; the use of the word *chick* (a term I will return to shortly) does not get him banished, nor does the term shut down conversation. In addition, Mr. Shortside may or may not be selling *wolf tickets,* a form of braggadocio and exaggeration valued in male hush harbors. The truth or falsity of his assertion is secondary. Such a reading is possible because "Mr. Shortside grinned, having played his audience well."[30] Mr. Shortside *played* to his hush harbor audience's expectation, not around truth or falsity but around Black male agency, authority, and self-control. Mr. Shortside kept his cool. In a society where Black men may not be able to keep their job, their family, or their economic stability, maintaining one's sense of agency and keepin' one's cool are meaningful acts.

Coolness as an expression of Black masculinity functions as a form of social literacy. Coolness becomes more than the eroticized and othered Black body performing hipness for consumption by both African Americans and non–African Americans. Like all forms of literacy, coolness is entangled in power, ideology, knowledge, agency, subjectivity, and survival. Coolness and Black masculinity assert agency through verbal and physical masking, veiling (as Gilyard did when he was introduced to his class at his majority White school), and performing for effect, for dignity and respect. In a society in which one false move can land a Black man in jail, in which one step on another's shoe could cost an African American man his life, in which assertions of Black male masculinity (and, of course, the assertion of masculine behavior by African American women) is seen as angry or uncivil, coolness and detachment can save one's life.

Given the probable political sensibilities of many readers, I want to address the use of the term *chick* in Gilyard's *Voices of the Self* and my quoting of the term. I am aware that, even given the current popularity of chick flicks, the term *chick* objectifies and diminishes women. I am also aware that, in more "enlightened" spatialities, such a term would not only be critiqued but would cause Mr. Shortside to be both dismissed and silenced as unworthy to speak. AAHHR embraces *parrhesia* (fearless speech), precisely because, as in the barbershop in *The Cotillion,* comments such as Mr. Shortside's, though they may be violently disagreed with, are not cause for automatic dismissal as they might be in more public spaces. That these terms are available for debate is exactly one of the reasons hush harbor spatialities are valuable. I have seen Black men and women in hush harbors allow and vigorously participate in discussions for which they would not allow rhetorical space in other rhetorical situations. Parrhesia provides hush harbors with a rhetorical vitality that makes them important to understanding democracy on the ground floor of the everyday.

Scholarship by sociologist Patricia Hill Collins and sociolinguist Geneva Smitherman resonates so powerfully with many African Americans because it imports African American standpoints or African American parrhesia into academic discourse. For example, Smitherman's use of the word "nigguh" cuts against the grain of my own ideology in relation to academic writing. In my view, the term carries historical baggage that, despite parsing and recuperation of the term by scholars such as Michael Eric Dyson, I find the commodification and increased circulation of the term in the public sphere highly problematic.[31] However, I am down with AAHHR, and just like the word *chick* in the era of the barbershops in *Voices of the Self,* "nigguh" does get deployed, and sometimes challenged, in African American barbershop hush harbors. So I use both terms, *nigguh* and *chick,* in an attempt to convey to the reader a sense of how AAHHR challenges public sphere notions of decorum and civility. Except for the most vulgar linguistic displays and for claims that clearly genuflect to White and male acceptance, there is very little language that is excluded a priori from the male hush harbor.

Later, Mr. Shortside expresses skepticism of President John Kennedy's fair-housing bill, passed in response to the successful direct-action campaigns of the American Civil Rights Movement of the 1950s and the 1960s, when he says, "It don't mean nothin to the people right over here down the street in Honkieville. The bill shoulda been written on toilet tissue cause that's the amount of respect the average cracker gonna give it."[32] Mr. Shortside expresses his skepticism in a suppressed enthymeme with an unstated proposition or claim supported by African American history and experience: abstract law is one thing, actual practice, particularly when it involves Black bodies, another. From the Constitution, and literacy and vagrancy laws, to various Jim Crow and zero-tolerance laws, African Americans have always understood that what is written and what is enforced often ride in two different trains with one destination—White privilege. Mr. Shortside attempts to interject into Keith's consciousness the practical wisdom of not placing too much faith in rarefied abstract concepts of justice. Mr. Shortside's concern regarding the average cracker reveals a discursive orientation that is Aristotelian in that he is concerned with concrete ethics here on the funkified ground of earth, not only in the purified realm of the ideal and the abstract. This is why Mr. Shortside is a phronimos as philosopher. He prepares Keith to engage the world and its contradictions, its tensions, and its opportunities by encouraging him to think critically about the abstract principle of justice within the context of lived experience: phronesis. While the average cracker comment may be offensive to some outside a hush harbor context, for hush harbor habitués the comment functions as a critique of White privilege without the baggage of academic jargon. It takes into account the discourse of an organic intellectual and the communities to which he is committed that is too often relegated to the tail section of the elite plane of high theory.

After Mr. Horton testifies to both the correctness of Mr. Shortside's position on President Kennedy and to his wisdom, Mr. Shortside drops this bit of vernacular knowledge: "Yeah I knows I am. Man with smart socks can't be no all the time fool. Helluva situation we in, ain't it Boone?"[33] His statement is an assertion of unity and harmony of African American interest through the power of the word or nommo. His collapsing of the personal *I* into communal investment reveals how AAHHR in the thick spatiality of a hush harbor produces a rhetoric of commonalities grounded in African American standpoints and rationalities. It is what makes his socks smart. The communal *we* is not informed by an essentialist sense of unity or ethnicity; barbershops are too heterogeneous for that. Instead, understood through a rhetorical lens, the communal *we* is informed by a critical ethnicity that privileges shared beliefs, institutions, discourses, experiences, and spatialities. Mr. Horton and Mr. Shortside evoke a notion of common political and social exigency around African American bodies and the average cracker.

In contrast, Russell B. Parker's barbershop in Lonne Elder's play *Ceremonies in Dark Old Men* is not a place of tactics and strategies where African American males might learn to engage the world. Parker's barbershop is the kind literary critic Trudier Harris constructs as a spatiality of fantasy and escape, a site of ineffective rhetorical education. Unlike Mr. Horton's shop, Parker's barbershop is an utter failure.

Ceremonies in Dark Old Men was turned into a made-for-television movie and continues to be performed on stage throughout the United States. While reviews of the play understandably focus on the play's themes of respect, Black male masculinity, family disintegration, uplift, tragedy, and drugs, few refer to the importance of the barbershop in the play. None that I am aware of link it to a cartography of AAHHs and their significance in any consideration of Black male uplift.

Ceremonies provides another glimpse of the importance of a hush harbor barbershop in African American expressive culture but through a more negative, cynical valence. Certainly it is not the only play involving a barbershop. *Beauty Shop* (by Shelly Garrett, 1989), *Five on the Black Hand Side* (by Charlie L. Russell, 1969), and several August Wilson plays include references to a barbershop. However, most of *Ceremonies* occurs within the confines of a barbershop. This makes it a very productive artifact to examine. In addition, Elder's text arguably functions as a cautionary tale. The barbershop fails because of its lack of functionality as an AAHH in which Black men are affirmed and obtain a rhetorical education that enables them to engage society effectively.

Ceremonies in Dark Old Men is the story of ex-dancer, talker, and current barber, Mr. Russell B. Parker, his daughter Adele, his two sons Theo and Bobby, as the family struggles to survive in Harlem. He and his two unemployed sons are supported solely by Adele, who has returned home after the death of Parker's wife. Frustrated by the financial and emotional burden of taking care of the men who contribute little to the household, Adele warns them that they have six days to find jobs or she will put them out on the street. In response, the men hatch a plan to save themselves by turning the barbershop into a gin joint where folks can purchase illegal whiskey and play the numbers. The plan has tragic consequences for all concerned.

As the play begins, Elder immediately signals that something is not quite right. African American barbershops typically consist of two or more chairs; they bustle with the interactions and talk among folks coming and going. In contrast, Mr. Parker's shop contains one chair—in the basement of his home. The shop is as bereft of life as it is of commerce. Mr. Parker has one customer, Mr. Jenkins, with whom he plays checkers. Mr. Parker's character parallels that of Ralph Ellison's *Invisible Man*, another character who, in the end, occupies a basement. However, Mr. Parker is an invisible man with a difference. Ellison's protagonist engages and struggles in and against the world. He occupies the basement as a sanctuary in which to gain enlightenment. The novel suggests that he will reenter the world at some point, but on his own terms. Mr. Parker is different. He does not occupy the basement as a refuge of enlightenment from which he might emerge to carve out a space for himself in the world; instead, his basement barbershop is a static womb where he contemplates the world, not for his future rebirth, but to hide and cower from responsibility, from racism, and, most of all, from himself.

Mr. Parker's timidity becomes apparent when his friend, Mr. Jenkins, tries to convince him to go upstairs, face his children, and own up to be being made into a fool by a younger woman. Mr. Parker's reaction is telling:

MR. PARKER: Never! Upstairs is for the people upstairs!

MR. JENKINS: Russell, I—

MR. PARKER: I am downstairs people! You ever hear of downstairs people?

MR. JENKINS: *(Pause.)* No . . .

MR. PARKER: Well, they're the people to watch in this world . . .

MR. JENKINS: If you say so—[34]

The play ironically seems to suggest through the character of Mr. Jenkins that downstairs people, such as Mr. Parker, are exactly the kind of people one should not watch.

African American rhetoric and poetics contain many spatial references that are metaphors for the hierarchal, asymmetrical power relations Between White and Black folks intertwined within the fabric of African American life. *Ceremonies* deploys the spatial geography of *downness* when Mr. Parker responds to his daughter Adele's critique of his and his sons running numbers and selling corn whiskey out of his barbershop: "I did like you said, I went downtown, and it's been a long time since I did that, but you're down there everyday, and you ought to know by now that I am too old a man to ever dream that I . . . could overcome the dirt and filth they got waiting for me down there."[35] The repetition of *down* attempts to etch into the consciousness of the reader how crushed, how small and inconsequential, Mr. Parker feels in the public sphere. However, Mr. Parker's empathy about the alienation and the hardness to be found in the world does not seem to extend to his deceased wife.

Initially, Mr. Parker's attribution of his problems to outside forces (racism, White privilege, urban renewal) seems accurate. By the end of the play, the audience will view Mr. Parker's problem through another lens. For now, it is significant to note that, in the world outside of his barbershop, Mr. Parker feels himself to be less than a man. The one place where he has some sense of agency, a sense of power, is in his barbershop.

As in *The Cotillion* and in *Youngblood,* the trope of the barber as philosopher-king occurs in *Ceremonies in Dark Old Men.* Mr. Parker refers to his single barber chair as the throne. Unfortunately, Mr. Parker is a philosopher-king of the Platonic mode who contemplates life and ideas in the abstract but does not take into account asymmetrical power relations, so he offers little of use, phronesis, in the everyday world. In addition, Mr. Parker, too often, does not act. For the most part, he relegates his agency to the contemplative realm of Platonic perfection. As a result, his wisdom is of little use to himself or his family. It lacks the phronesis of the barbershop owned by Mr. Horton.

Russell Parker then, is a *denimos.* The denimos was the rhetor who was the impetus for Plato's wrath in *The Sophists,* in *The Phaedrus,* and for Plato's hegemonic and self-serving condemnation of rhetoric.[36] The denimos disconnects rhetoric from ethics, from civic and communal good, and from the quest for truth (which Aristotle's *Rhetoric* describes as the most useful rhetoric), thereby reducing rhetoric to *techne,* a denigration, that continues to haunt rhetoric to this day. Denimoses such as Mr. Parker, Slim, and Clarence Thomas, Larry Elder, and John McWhorter know the tropes, mascons, and forms of AAHHR. Yet, as denimoses, they manipulate these elements for personal good and benefit rather than African American communal good. Mr. Parker is the clever rhetor who speaks badly, the kind of barber with whom Keith's father would not leave his son.[37] Mr. Parker's rhetoric in *Ceremonies* lacks phronesis because his lack of immersion in the shared beliefs, institutions, and experiences that inform a tradition of Black common sense hollows out the resiliency and knowledge that would enable him to overcome the hegemony of White privilege that most Black folks encounter in their daily lives. His timidity disconnects him from the rationalities vital to African American life and culture.

When Adele arrives home from work, Mr. Parker makes a strange request of his friend, Mr. Jenkins, with whom he is playing checkers. Mr. Parker asks Mr. Jenkins to hide under the bed so that Adele will not think that Mr. Parker has been at home all day. Adele knows better:

ADELE: . . . You looked for work today?

MR. PARKER: All morning. *(Pause.)*

ADELE: No luck in the morning and so you played checkers all day.

MR. PARKER: No, I've been working on a few ideas of mine.[38]

Elder's text smartly connects Mr. Parker's malfunctioning barbershop to a domesticated, innocuous masculinity disconnected from practical wisdom, ethics, or action. Looking for work requires Mr. Parker to embrace a blues-jazz epistemology that would allow him to think, posture, position, and improvise and perform himself into the funky reality of a material world full of obstacles. Mr. Parker justifies his disengagement from life as a response to racism. A former dancer, Mr. Parker tells his children and Mr. Jenkins that he would shuffle around, act like a clown, and get patted on the head, and that "after all of that I was going to ask for more by throwing myself into the low drag of some dusty old factory in Brooklyn? All I could do was to stay here in this shop with you [Mr. Jenkins] my good friend. And we acted out the ceremony of a game."[39] *Game* in *Voices of the Self* is a trope of engagement; here, *game* is a dance of retreat.

Parker's explanation is a game because it neglects the realities of uncountable numbers of Black men (and women) who have thrown themselves into the low drag of countless jobs to play in, lose to, and win at the game of life. AAHHR generally provides Black men with an anchor in the wind of racial chaos. Elder drives home the point about the emptiness of Mr. Parker's hush harbor and eviscerated masculinity. Mr. Parker tells Theo that "lookin' for a job can really hurt a man . . . I was interviewed five times today, and I could have shot every last one of them interviewers—the white ones and the colored ones too. I don't know if I can take any more of this."[40] Mr. Parker's problem goes beyond the racial divide. He avoids pain and, therefore, possibilities. He possesses little practical wisdom. That Mr. Parker has handed his version of masculinity down to his sons is revealed when Theo responds, "Yeah, looking for a job can be very low-grading to a man, and it gets worse after you get the job."[41] Black men, young or old, do not patronize Mr. Parker's shop. After all, one can get his hair cut anywhere, but getting your head cut, obtaining some knowledge about Black common sense, is a more difficult proposition. In short, Mr. Parker does not have hair to cut because he does not cut heads. His shop is not really a hush harbor; it is Plato's cave occupied by a philosopher, a denimos, deceived by the shadows of an unfulfilled life.

Instead of testing his agency in the world with knowledge and rhetorical tactics and strategies gained in barbershop hush harbors, Mr. Parker stays in his basement, thereby compelling his wife to enter into the world and engage in a manner he was not willing or able to do. Mr. Parker's discourse consistently imposes his impotent brand of masculine privilege over his wife and family, revealing his own insubstantiality. For example, Theo tells his father that his mother was "the hardest-working person I ever knew, and it killed her!"[42] *Ceremonies in Dark Old Men* offers a critique of Mr. Parker's puffed-up, empty masculinity through Adele's dialogue—dialogue that connects her to African American women in general: "But then I found myself doing the same things she had done, taking care of three men, trying to shield them from the danger beyond door, *but who the hell ever told every black woman she was some kind of goddamn savior!*" (Elder's italics).[43] Mr. Parker hides from the world while behaving as an impotent king over the women in his home. In contrast to the barbershop and chairs full of folks in Mr. Horton's shop, Mr. Parker's empty barber chair symbolizes that he is the philosopher-king stripped of his power who reigns over nothing but a barren kingdom of disengagement.

Ceremonies in Dark Old Men invokes the barber, Mr. Parker, as a philosopher but does so indirectly. Mr. Parker reads Jean Genet's *The Thief's Journal* (1949) to better understand how to run his illegal whiskey and numbers business. A barber reading such a book might seem to be a fictional stretch bordering on the absurd or the comic. Also, an argument could be leveled that Elder's use of Genet's text is not reflective of a more general deployment of such highbrow reading material in hush harbor barbershops. Such perspectives would be incorrect. Forrest's *Divine Days* and Killens's *The Cotillion* both refer to high-culture texts and authors such as Shakespeare and Milton. I myself have had to explain why I was reading of particular highbrow text in a barbershop. Not because the folks there were surprised that such a text was brought into the hush harbor inner sanctum but to give an account of why it was important to read or was I just showing off. (I informed them as to why the text was important and, if I was showing off. I wasn't going to admit to it. My response was deemed adequate.) From Mr. Parker's perspective, had Genet become a thinker before he became a thief, Genet would not have been in jail to write the book. Mr. Parker considers himself both a thinker and a philosopher, as the following makes apparent: "But it is my logicalism; that you've got to become a thinker, and then you become a crook."[44] According to Mr. Parker, if one examines the background of crooked politicians, one would find that most first attended law school prior to doing their dirt. Of course, Elder seems to be puncturing Mr. Parker's philosophical pretension, given his use of the term *logicalism*. As a matter of fact, like the racial reasoning of many Enlightenment philosophers, Mr. Parker's logicalism is not that logical. Nevertheless, Mr. Parker's attempt to understand himself as a philosopher illustrates the pervasiveness of the hush harbor philosopher trope in African American expressive culture. As in Gilyard's text, Elder's *Ceremonies in Dark Old Men* illustrates how the barbershop can be viewed as a site of philosophical contemplation and deliberation in African American communities, but does so, in my view, by offering a negative example.

I want to conclude with a final comparison of Mr. Parker in *Ceremonies in Dark Old Men* to Mr. Shortside in *Voices of the Self*. Concluding in this fashion is useful because I believe it will hammer home more persuasively the difference between a barbershop grounded in the AAHHR of a phronimos and the one Elder critiques.

Mr. Parker meets a woman many years his junior. He says he loves her and even offers to marry her. However, once Mr. Parker runs out of money, she locks him out of their hotel room. She sleeps with someone else. His daughter Adele ends up with a drinking problem and a thug who beats her. Worse, during a burglary, Mr. Parker's son Bobby gets shot and killed by a night watchman. The final scene has Mr. Parker slouched in his barber chair like a king with no kingdom, a philosopher with no school or adherents, drunk and in despair. Adele has left the thug. Theo has closed down the illicit whiskey and numbers business. They both want to see their father, Mr. Parker. He refuses. "I know what they want—They want to tell me what an old fool I am," he tells Mr. Jenkins, who has come downstairs to speak on behalf of the children[45] and to ask their father to come upstairs. Mr. Parker shouts, "Never! Upstairs is for the people upstairs!" Finally, however, he does allow them to come downstairs. He tells them that he loved their mother, but all the hardship, the racism he had to deal with as a dancer, was more than enough. He did not want to deal with it anymore.

At the beginning of the play, Mr. Jenkins, who had never lost to him in checkers, tells Mr. Parker that the day he won a game of checkers would be the unluckiest day of his life. In his despair, he asks Jenkins to play him one more game. Mr. Parker wins. He staggers toward his room mumbling, "I'm tired, I'm going to bed and by the time tomorrow comes around, let's see if we can't all throw it into the river."[46] Mr. Parker wants to begin anew, throw all his burdens into a metaphorical, existential river and begin with the hope of a new day. This blues ethos is fundamental to the spiritual, psychological, and material survival and transformation of a once-enslaved, marginalized people. This would seem to indicate that in the end the denimos Mr. Parker has hitched his rhetoric to a communal ethos (through his familial relations). However, his closing song reveals a pessimism that belies his transformation:

I HAVE HAD MY FUN!
IF I DON'T GET WELL NO MORE

I HAVE HAD MY FUN

IF I DON'T GET WELL NO MORE[47]

Mr. Parker's final words, "Say, where's Bobby?" reflect a denial of his son's death, a continuing unwillingness to come to terms with the harshness of life.[48] Unlike the barber in Major Jackson's "Mr. Pate's Barbershop," whose hush harbor pedagogy chisels Black possibility out of the stone of African American male heartache, Mr. Parker leaves his hush harbor audience with a skeptical ambivalence purged of optimism.

Comparing Mr. Parker's exit in *Ceremonies in Dark Old Men* to Mr. Shortside's exit in *Voices of the Self* reveals the importance of the lessons and pedagogy of the philosopher-phronimos to AAHHs and African American culture. In the section titled "The Self, Advancing Literacy, and Sidewalk University" in *Voices of the Self*, Gilyard points both backward and forward to the importance of barbershops and other hush harbors in the construction of Black selves, Black literacies, and Black spatialities of knowledge and rhetoric. The section title alludes to the hush harbor barbershop, as well as the street, as sites of rhetorical education. He makes it clear that the barbershop is one of several spatialities fundamental in assisting him to develop a sense of himself as an African American man. Mr. Shortside's exit from the barbershop offers a look at his contribution to Keith's sense of himself.

After Mr. Shortside's critique of the Kennedy administration and what he feels is a terrible fair-housing bill passed in response to the Civil Rights Movement, he grabs his cane and prepares to leave the barbershop. After Mr. Boone concurs with Mr. Horton's opinion about the funniness of the country Black folks were claiming as their own, Mr. Shortside adds his five cents. Remember, Mr. Shortside is very much aware of the adolescent Keith's presence and is speaking at him, as well as talking to the other folks in the hush harbor, when he retorts, "Damn right. Helluva funny country. I wouldn't care if Uncle Sam and Baldy Red [Khrushchev] blowed this whole mother up as long as they let me and a few of those pretty young gals live."[49] Once again, Mr. Shortside may be selling wolf tickets, but that's just the bag—the men in the barbershop respond to the rhetorical groceries in the bag. On the down low, he's teaching folks that there is possibility and joy to be found in the most dire situation.[50] Negro spirituals, blues, jazz, gospel, rhythm and blues, and neo-soul all to one degree or another reproduce this sensibility.

Mr. Shortside's blues-vernacular humor masks (for outsiders) a deep existential optimism inculcated through the epistemology, forms, and mascons that make up AAHHR and African American expressive culture. Where Mr. Parker seems resigned to his fate, Mr. Shortside is going to take what a racist society gives him, leaves him, or what he swipes while it's not looking. He's going to get in where he fits in, a strategy African Americans have developed since the first enslaved woman and man worked a little less hard than she or he really could. When Mr. Horton asks, "Is that all you want from the whole deal?" Mr. Shortside replies, "Yeah Horton. Why not? Ain't nothin better to live for. Not how I'm lookin at it now."[51] As an African American griot or *phronimos*, Mr. Shortside recognizes the contingent nature of his own claims and how they relate to his own life experience. He does not camouflage his theorizing in a posture of disinterest. He knows the exigencies of his claim. Later he may need a little more but for the moment he's cool.

Ceremonies in Dark Old Men and *Voices of the Self* both deploy AAHHR as it is manifested through African American expressive culture and make constant reference to the environment that cradles it. As a result, both texts articulate the understanding that philosophy and philosophers inhabit the Black spatialities I refer to as hush harbors. Both texts address the barbershop as a site of rhetorical education and knowledge production. But whereas *Ceremonies in Dark Old Men* provides a useful example of the philosopher as *denimos*, whose AAHHR lacks practical wisdom, *Voices of the Self* offers us the African American *phronimos*, whose rhetoric is full of practical wisdom offering light in the racial darkness, agency within a Black masculinity too often reduced to a negative referent. Rhetorical theory and pedagogy will be greatly enhanced when it takes the barbershop more seriously as a site of theory and epistemology. But that's okay if it does not, as long as I can, in the spirit of Mr. Shortside, read plays like *Ceremonies in Dark Old Men* and memoirs such as *Voices of the Self* through a rhetorical lens.

6.
Commodifying
Neoliberal Blackness
Faux Hush Harbor Rhetoric in *Barbershop*

A WIDE ARRAY OF AFRICAN AMERICAN FILMS SUCH AS *FIVE ON THE BLACK Hand Side* (dir. Oscar Williams, 1973), *Coming to America* (dir. John Landis, 1988), *Joe's Bed-Stuy Barbershop: We Cut Heads* (dir. Spike Lee, 1983), *Hollywood Shuffle* (dir. Robert Townsend, 1987), *Belly* (dir. Hype Williams, 1998), *The Fighting Temptations* (dir. Jonathan Lynn, 2003), *Honey* (dir. Bille Woodruff, 2003), and *Malcolm X* (dir. Spike Lee, 1992) attest to the pervasiveness and the continuing importance of the barbershop trope to African American film culture and rhetoric. However, no popular culture artifact could be more timely for the study of the barbershop as an African American hush harbor (AAHH) than the movie *Barbershop* (dir. Tim Story, 2002).

Primarily written by, produced by, and starring African Americans, *Barbershop* seemed to promise a funky, irreverent, insider's view of African American rhetoric and culture located in a Black public sphere often hidden from public view. What is certain is that a critical maelstrom of almost *Color Purple*sque proportions swirled across the African American and American cultural landscape in response to the film on television, in newspapers, in books, and on the Internet. Jessie Jackson, Al Sharpton, Ron Daniels, Michael Eric Dyson, and others weighed in on the propriety of the humorous, signifyin', vernacular darts of African American rhetoric that targeted American Civil Rights Movement icons such as Rosa Parks and Martin Luther King Jr. Some filmgoers and critics thought the jokes were disrespectful at best; others felt that, disrespectful or not, no person was beyond criticism in a film about a barbershop. While the latter argument is the historically and functionally correct take on the film and the function of the barbershop, both sides ignored what I consider to be far more important concerns. *Barbershop* flips the hush harbor script by offering an easy-to-sell, easy-to-consume, commodified, domesticated Blackness. Here, *Keepin' It Hushed* compares and contrasts the movies *My Big Fat Greek Wedding* (dir. Joel Zwick, 2002) and *Barbershop* in relation to what I argue is the commodification of Blackness; then I argue how the movie *Malcolm X* represents the barbershop as hush harbor with a verisimilitude lacking in *Barbershop*.

While *Barbershop* perceptively and forcefully deconstructs African American icons, it obsequiously provides a hush harbor for White privilege and consequently for White audiences by its refusal to critique White icons and White privilege. White audiences are let off the rhetorical hook as little transgressive bait is thrown into the movie's representational and discursive waters of Whiteness because African American parrhesia might unsettle mainstream assumptions. Standpoints that might make White audiences uncomfortable are reduced to the personal or to mere opinion. *Barbershop* offers the audience hush harbor lite: Black spatiality and culture sanitized and neutralized. In short, *Barbershop* disconnects Blackness, Black culture, and African American *phronesis* from political rationalities, power, and obligation.

Thematically, *Barbershop* centers around Calvin (Ice Cube, the nigga who folks used to love to hate), a devout family man who owns a barbershop inherited from his father. Calvin is everyday people with big dreams: he wants to live large and do his own version of big pimpin' by producing beats for hip-hop artists in his home studio. Due to past failed schemes, Calvin sells the barbershop to Mr. Wallace, a smooth, stylish urban entrepreneur who some might call a loan shark. Calvin's desire to regain his shop drives the primary plot while an ancillary plot includes two cats attempting to heist and open a stolen ATM. Barbers in the cast include a sista (the rapper Eve) who is trying to find out who drank her apple juice and work through an unsatisfying relationship; a White barber with no Black customers; an African immigrant learning the trade and who is smitten with Eve; Ricky, an astute ex-con to whom Calvin has given a second chance and whom a police detective mistakenly believes stole the ATM machine; and a smug, formally educated African American male who sees the barbershop as little more than a way to get to someplace else.

Calvin sells the shop, but when Mr. Wallace reneges on his promise to maintain the barbershop business and instead wants to turn it into a gentlemen's club where the patrons can get trimmed and get some "trim," Calvin changes his mind. After a moving soliloquy by the barbershop phronimos Eddie, about the importance of the shop to the Black community, Calvin, with Ricky's help, manages to retain the shop.

Barbershop is the anti–hush harbor movie that refuses to privilege, however contingently, African American critical memory. Instead of the parrhesia-influenced rhetorical jazz of a Joe Youngblood or Aaron McGruder, we get the smooth jazz, and ultimately bad nommo, of Eddie. Eddie is the character played by Cedric the Entertainer. Folks in the barbershop trust him—he is one of them. An urban Quintilian, Eddie is the good Black man who speaks well—unless it comes to White privilege. He's ethical, concerned about the good of community, and provides those in the hush harbor with wisdom, experience, and tradition. *Barbershop* partly situates Eddie as a *phronimos,* a voice of cultural and generational authority. However, after Calvin says that the hush harbor folks have to "give it up" to the Black Panthers, Jessie Jackson, Martin Luther King Jr., and Rosa Parks for their contribution to the American Civil Rights Movement, Eddie asks in mock ignorance, "Who is Rosa Parks?"[1] He goes on to retort that Rosa Parks's sitting down on a Montgomery, Alabama, bus on that fateful December day was not an act motivated by courage or sacrifice but by simple physiological necessity: "She was tired, that's what you do when you tired, you sit your ass down."[2]

The filmmakers make it clear that Eddie's claim resists conventional African American nomoi and *doxa* (belief) as everyone else in the shop energetically attempts to shout Eddie down. *Barbershop*'s supporters claim that the cacophonous disagreement in the shop reflects resistance to Eddie's contentions. While this may be true, what is overlooked is how that resistance is articulated. No one in the barbershop offers a coherent defense based on history and information. Only a superficial, artistic appeal to propriety is offered. In contrast, later in the film, when an African American character accuses the sole primary White character of the appropriation of Black culture, the White character's succinct and clear rebuttal, with an insult added for good measure, is made without being immersed in a cacophony of agreement or disagreement. Indeed, the entire barbershop remains silent. Restless natives are rendered speechless when the exigency for the rhetorical occasion is White opinion.

As the audience in the hush harbor as barbershop disperses, the respect accorded Eddie is apparent. Even the young teens in the shop stop talking, return to their seats, and settle down to listen attentively to Eddie. When he begins to speak, he eventually utters a single sentence that links the barbershop as hush harbor to African American rhetorical history, to a specific audience analysis, and to the continuing recognition that, over one hundred years after the end of the Enslavement, the public sphere and the free speech attached to it are still hegemonically White: "Now I probably would not say this in front of white folks, but in front of ya'll I am going to speak my mind." Eddie goes on to argue that while he would give Rosa Parks her due as "her act led to the movement," Rosa Parks "damn sure wasn't special."[3] According to Eddie, prior to Rosa Parks, lots of other folks had sat where they were not allowed on segregated buses. Rosa Parks received special consideration because of her affiliation with the NAACP. Eddie overly trivializes Rosa Parks's motivation and her courage but makes a valid point. Signifyin' through some of the nostalgic romanticism surrounding the Civil Rights Movement, Eddie's position is supported by several scholars who have written about how Claudette Colvin and others refused to be seated in the colored section of the bus prior to Rosa Parks.[4] However, due to issues of caste, class, and pregnancy, the women were not deemed appropriate to be the public face around which Black folks could rally for civil rights.

Eddie does not stop with criticizing Rosa: "Black people need to stop lying. Three things that people need to tell the truth about. One, Rodney King should have got his ass beat for being drunk and being grown and driving in a Hyundai. Two, O.J. did it! Three, Rosa Parks did not do nothing but sit her Black ass down."[5] *Barbershop* begins to deteriorate into a discursive hush harbor for Whiteness that provides sanctuary and refuge for White nomoi while trivializing African American rationalities. Pointedly, Eddie argues that Black folks willfully and knowingly deceive themselves. While some in the audience understand that Eddie is engaging in African American rhetorical strategy, why frame the debate as a lie rather than a difference in experiences or as critically arrived at disagreement? Black discourse, Black community reasoning, and African American exigency get lifted out of the social, the political, and the networks of power to be resituated within the context of deceit and emotion. Eddie relegates Blackness to the emotional side of the emotion/rationality fence.

Eddie spends a good deal of time pontificating about what Black folks lie about, yet neither Eddie nor any other barbershop character discuss what White people lie about. Did George Wallace block the doors to the University of Alabama to support segregation, or was he, like Rosa Parks, just too tired to move? *Barbershop*'s obsequiousness around race and White privilege is startling. Since when are such issues avoided in African American male hush harbors? From Magnificent Brothers in Los Angeles to Visions in State College, I have never been in a Black barbershop frequented by Black men in which White folks were not stridently criticized for their treatment of African Americans. In fact, in the multicultural barbershop/salon Visions, such talk occurred in the presence of White customers underneath the buzzing of clippers. Almost every text I examined for this study made some reference to White racism/privilege, relief from oppression, or the struggle for social justice in ways that would make many White audiences uncomfortable. *Barbershop* domesticates these sometimes transgressive Black public spheres to such a degree that most White reviewers were more than comfortable with the movie's racial politics. *Barbershop* as a site of rhetorical education all but avoids the emancipatory possibilities of hush harbors through their transgressive standpoints and their embrace of African American nomoi that are often excluded from or marginalized in the public sphere.

Eddie knows the tropes, topoi, political rationalities, commonplaces, and tonal semantics—he can invoke nommo. Yet, in his avoidance of a discourse about White privilege, Eddie deploys nommo without connecting his rhetoric to communal ethics. By communal ethics, I refer to a rhetorical stance anchored in the interest of a community and taking its nomoi, phronesis, and experiences as legitimate and serious even when the rhetor disagrees with the communal perspective. I do not imply that African American icons are beyond critique. Eddie is correct when he provides this response to the assertion by a character that Eddie's critique of Rosa Parks is wrong and disrespectful: "Is this a barbershop? Is this a barbershop? If we can't talk straight in a barbershop, then where can we talk straight; we can't talk no place else. Ain't nobody exempt in a barbershop. You can talk about whoever, whatever, and whenever you want to. Ain't nobody exempt in a barbershop."[6] Eddie articulates one of the few rhetorical rules in the thick spatiality of the hush harbor: no individual, entity, ethnic group, or topic is immune to criticism in the barbershop as hush harbor—including God. Unfortunately, the makers of *Barbershop* exclude White somebodies from Eddie's hush harbor insights. In this regard, *Barbershop* is about a hush harbor but is not a hush harbor movie.

At least one actor and several critics compared Barbershop to the hugely successful *My Big Fat Greek Wedding* in that both were *ethnic* films with universal appeal. In both films, the authentication of race and ethnicity is addressed. *Authentification* refers to how subjectivities and identities are ascribed to certain bodies and subjects and authorized as legitimate through constant repetition, evaluation, and normalization. *My Big Fat Greek Wedding* offers a perspective on what it is to be Greek or Greek American in ways that are far more astute and less commodified than the version of African American culture offered in *Barbershop*. To illustrate this point, I focus on the films' two ethnic or racial outsiders, *My Big Fat Greek Wedding*'s Ian Miller and *Barbershop*'s Isaac Rosenberg.

Waspish Ian meets Greek American Fotoula "Toula" Portokalos, who attempts to free herself from what she perceives as Greek familial and cultural constraints by enrolling in college, changing her hairstyle, and switching to blue contact lenses. Ian and Toula's relationship is framed through a scene involving their tentative meeting at the travel agency of Toula's aunt.

They go to a restaurant, then become friends, and later fall in love. To marry Toula, Ian must go through official and unofficial Greek rituals in official and unofficial spatialities to gain an understanding of her culture. Ian attends her church, is baptized in the traditional manner of the Greek Orthodox Church, and participates in a family dinner during which he becomes acquainted not only with the family but also with Greek food. Ian even acquires a little of the Greek language so that he can better relate to the family. After Toula and Ian marry and become parents, they enroll their daughter, as Toula's parents enrolled her, in Greek school to ensure her connection to Greek culture.

Ian's character arc in *My Big Fat Greek Wedding* transitions him into becoming more Greek, more literate in Greek culture. Ian's acquisition of ethnicity is grounded in a politics of practice associated with culture and performance. Unlike Ian, Isaac Rosenberg's acquisition of African American ethnicity or Blackness in *Barbershop* is disconnected from critical literacy and a politics of practice, and is grafted onto a politics of spectacle and display. African American culture is reduced to a commodity. African American cultural literacy seems predicated on a shared viewing of hip-hop videos and shopping.

Isaac Rosenberg, who is White and Jewish, wants to develop a customer base of Black customers so that one day he might have his own barbershop. Although Calvin is very supportive of Isaac, like all new barbers in Calvin's barbershop, Isaac must start in the first chair. Customers avoid him both because he is new and because he is White. However, the filmmakers authorize and authenticate Isaac's Blackness through how they introduce and enframe his character. It is here that a commodification of Blackness, Black culture, and Black women begins.

Maurice O. Wallace's *Constructing the Black Masculine* traces the importance of enframement in the eroticization, fetishization, and commodification of Black bodies in photography, modernist art, literature, and film. Wallace illustrates how enframement, the process or function of framing or bracketing phenomena, is analytic, not merely adornment. According to Wallace, frames necessarily produce blind spots that make certain kinds of visibilities possible. *Barbershop* frames Isaac's Blackness through eroticization of a Black woman's body and through constructing hip-hop culture as a commodified image disconnected from history, politics, and struggle. Through constant repetition, African American and non–African American audiences have become increasingly comfortable with fetishized representations of Blackness that appeal to the White racial gaze.

Barbershop's camera focuses on the most formally educated of the barbers and the one most skeptical of Isaac: Jimmy James. Then the audience hears the bangin' beats from a radio. A sleek, silver-gray Esplanade with its front windows rolled down pulls into the frame. A White male and a Black woman female occupy the Esplanade. Isaac slides out of the car and walks with the angular, cool stroll associated with Black men. His gear is hip-hop fabulous: jersey, matching pants, tennis shoes, skullcap, chain, etc. Meeting the African American woman on the sidewalk, they engage in a long, passionate, slow, and deep French kiss. The camera focuses on the woman's ample derriere as Isaac grabs, squeezes, and then sensuously spanks her rear. *Barbershop* marks Isaac's Blackness in a diacritical relation to the blatant sexualization and objectification of a dark Black woman's body as Hottentot (Khoikhoi).[7] The film punctures the tenuous veil between pleasure and politics to reveal the not-so-hidden investments of class, race, and gender that are ignored by both White and Black audiences under the guise of viewing Black cultural representations as mere entertainment. Imagine an African American actor in a family film fondling the butt of his White lover as he pulls up into a White ethnic barbershop, grocery store, restaurant, or pool hall as a framing device to signal his acceptance into White ethnic culture. Such a representation would be deemed, at best, racially provocative.

Isaac tells the woman as she departs, "I love you, Boo" (making the public grabbing of her butt acceptable, I suppose). Isaac walks toward Jimmy to give him a pound (soul handshake), but Jimmy flatly refuses. Isaac has been enframed and marked as Black through verbal and body performance, and Jimmy has been framed as a border patroller of Blackness, yet the film seems to imply that Jimmy's class orientation disqualifies him from monitoring borders of Blackness. As a central canon of African American hush harbor rhetoric (AAHHR), performance or posturing does provide evaluative criteria to discern ethnicity. However, as alluded to earlier, Isaac's Blackness, his performance and posturing, is disconnected from ritual, politics, and communal ethics and instead linked to spectacle. *Barbershop* puts the issues of Blackness and representation right on the ethnic table when Isaac confronts Jimmy in the back of the barbershop and tells him that, despite what Jimmy thinks, he did not learn his behavior from television. For Isaac, his response to the accusation of cultural appropriation is put simply: this is who I am. *My Big Fat Greek Wedding* makes it clear that Ian's character could not have become more literate in Greek American culture by watching GET (Greek Entertainment Television), shopping for Greek American clothing, or performing a Greek American strut, yet *Barbershop*'s on-screen ontological struggle over Blackness suggests that Isaac can legitimately acquire Blackness through exposure to BET, *Jet* magazine, or a Jay-Z video.

Fortunately, in scene 23, the filmmakers provide a scene that undermines their contention that they are not offering a commodified, consumable, Blackness without the burden of obligation. *Barbershop* scene 23 is titled "No Blacker Than Isaac." Jimmy and Isaac come into direct conflict over who is the most Black. After Isaac laughs at Eddie's reference to Jimmy as Booker T., Jimmy signifies on Isaac: "Who are you laughing at, Kid Rock?" Anyone familiar with Kid Rock and his faux hip-hop hard-rock persona knows that this reference signals a conversation about the appropriation of Black culture stretching back from Eminem and Elvis to Paul Whiteman. Isaac responds by calling the college-educated Jimmy "bourgeois" and telling him not to "hate on me." He also lays the "sellout" tag on Jimmy: "You got the Black girlfriend and the pimped-out ride and I'm the sellout? Man, you are a minstrel show turned on its ear. Al Jolson in a Fubu cap. Blackface for the new millennium."[8] Blackness and subjectivity as merely performative are critiqued. Jimmy connects the performativity of Blackness to a history of asymmetrical power relations that reflects how performance is not commensurate with identity and how performativity can serve oppression, as well as transgress it. So, whereas AAHHR recognizes the importance of performativity, African American phronesis requires that material and discursive paths of thought and practice must always be considered.

Isaac shoots right back: "Man with all your high education, why are you always talking about me?" Jimmy informs Isaac that Isaac does not belong in a Black barbershop, that "The White barbershop is uptown." After Jimmy refers to Isaac as a "White boy" and tells him "you ain't Black," Isaac counters with "Jimmy, I am Blacker than you. And what's messed up is that on your best day you could never be me." "You gon' take that?" responds one of the Black patrons incredulously. Jimmy does, and so do the Black men in the film's hush harbor audience. When Jimmy steps to Isaac because of the serious insult, the tension is diffused when the sole African American woman barber steps in front of Jimmy. Music from a radio station, which apparently everyone in the Black section of town listens to, begins to soothe the savage beast. Whiteness has the last word—game, set, and match for White and male privilege and the reduction of African American culture to a commodity. Al Jolson rises from the ashes and is reincarnated with the complicity of the Black filmmakers and Black cast.

Director Spike Lee skewered such a notion of reducing Blackness to performativity without commitment to Black lives and struggle in *Bamboozled* (2000). For example, the sole White member of an otherwise all-Black activist rap group, the Mau Maus, yells, "I'm Black! I'm Black! Why didn't you kill me? Why didn't you kill me?" as all his African American friends are gunned downed in a hail of police bullets while the police ignore his attempt at identity fluidity.[9] He wants to die with his Black friends but is taken into custody. Apparently, he is not quite Black enough for the police.

Barbershop's filmmakers attempted to display the existence of White males who are culturally Black. This is a worthy project that shifts Blackness from phenotype and begins to link it to rhetoric and discourse. Nevertheless, Isaac's Blackness is deployed in a social-spatial vacuum. Whereas movies like *My Big Fat Greek Wedding* and *Bend It Like Beckham* (dir. Gurinder Chadha, 2002) understand ethnicity critically and display this understanding on screen, *Barbershop*'s filmmakers leave a sense of critical ethnicity off screen. Isaac's Blackness is not connected to Black geographies, familial formations, community institutions, or politics. His backstory does not indicate whether he attended a Black church, a Black school, or was a member of an African American fraternity. The audience is never told whether he lives in an African American ghetto and therefore must use the check-cashing services and liquor stores instead of the banks and shopping malls linked to suburban and mostly White places. Is a parent African American? Is he pulled over more than other Whites because of his Blackness? Is he less likely to get a loan because of his

Blackness? None of these issues are addressed. Such concerns might interfere with the filmmakers' communication of a domesticated hush harbor and a commodified Blackness that are easier for audiences to consume.

Later in *Barbershop*, after Isaac has feminized and insulted Jimmy in an African American male hush harbor through his "your bitch ass can't compete" reference, it is Isaac, not Jimmy, who locates himself as the injured party and who again takes up the who is better, who is Blacker, argument as the two men stand in front of lockers in the back of the barbershop: "Hey man, let me tell you something. Just because you go to some fancy college, that don't make you better than me. That don't make you better than no one. And despite what you may think, I ain't pretending to be someone on TV. This is who I am whether you like it or not. I probably won't even go to school, but I am going to do something with my life. I am going to open up a shop. This is who I am going to be tomorrow."[10]

In *Summer Snow* (2003), Trudier Harris argues against what she sees as an anti-intellectual strand in the African American community.[11] While her argument must be placed within a larger context of American anti-intellectualism, *Barbershop* provides fodder for her point of view. Jimmy has been framed as the least likable character in the barbershop. Unfortunately, the one character who directly challenges White privilege is both the least likable and most formally educated. He is the only character who attempts to complicate Blackness without the burden of responsibility, the one who most openly extols education as his way out. Conflating barbershop talk with a disdain for those who advocate formal education is confusing given that the first historically Black college was founded by barbers and that service-industry occupations such as beauty shops, barbershops, funeral homes, and insurance companies have been primary sources enabling the education of African Americans. That the only college-educated character in the movie is portrayed as the least Black seems odd. *Barbershop* seems to flip Toni Morrison's characterization of the educated teacher in *Beloved;* it is the educated Black, not the educated White, who is the most dangerous to a harmonious community. The movie seems to imply that Jimmy's education has disconnected him from working-class Black folks.

Jimmy puts Isaac's Blackness to the ultimate test:

JIMMY: Alright man, let's see it.

ISAAC: See what?

JIMMY: You say this is who you are, this is who you going to be. So prove it. Hook me up.[12]

Isaac accepts the challenge and provides Jimmy with a smooth, expert cut. Barbershops are hush harbors, in part, because Black hair is generally styled by Black folks in Black places. Historically, this phenomenon is associated with African American domestication in the public sphere, the refusal of Whites to bury Black bodies, and the development of efforts like burial societies, secret societies, and insurance companies to service African American needs. Even today, with all the discourse of porous boundaries and fluid identities, Black hair remains a distinctive trope of African American subjectivities, politics, and political economy: most Black men, women, and children still require their hair styled by Black hairstylists. Within the realm of the quotidian, the everyday, most non–African American hairstylists do not style Black hair. As with the church in African American communities, beauty shops and barbershops remain predominately Black public spheres.

African Americans with access to the public sphere can be incoherent about Blackness and African American males in ways unthinkable in relation to other identities. Consider a movie about the African American female hush harbor called *Beauty Shop*. In this movie, the most educated African American woman in the shop demands that the only White female working in the shop must style a Black woman's hair to be an authentic Black woman. Once the hairstyle is completed, the movie argues that the White woman, by performing this significant but single act, is authentically Black. This is reductive and absurd on its face, yet this is exactly what both movies, *Beauty Shop* and *Barbershop*, argue. No character argues that Ian in *My Big Fat Greek Wedding* is just as Greek American as is his Greek-school-educated wife. To do so would undermine a serious theme of transgressive identity formation in the movie, collapsing its cultural insight into the realm of buffoonery. *My Big Fat Greek Wedding* connects Ian's transformation to insight gained through experience, ritual, and understanding, not to some Wal-Mart notion of ontology. Unfortunately, in African American movies such as *Barbershop*,

Undercover Brother (dir. Malcolm D. Lee, 2002), and *Bringing Down the House* (dir. Adam Shankman, 2003), buffoonery, minstrelsy, and sentimentality pass for insight. *Barbershop* provides no backstory about how and where Isaac might have acquired his haircutting skills. It does not have to. As a commodity, Blackness is flat and self-evident and, therefore, does not require explanation.

Once Isaac whips away the smock, Jimmy checks out his cut: "Not bad. Actually it's pretty good." After giving his approval as a kind of reverse slave-narrative amanuensis, a remorseful Jimmy apologizes: "Hey man, I, uh, shouldn't have disrespected you in front of everybody like that." Earlier in the movie, after Eddie signifies on Dr. Martin Luther King Jr. and, according to Jimmy, disrespects Rosa Parks, Eddie answers that one can say whatever one wants in a barbershop. Eddie never apologizes to anyone for what he says. Ricky, the ex-con, refers to reparations as "stupid." The filmmakers do not require that he apologize. When the only woman in the barbershop is criticized for staying with her promiscuous boyfriend, the customer making the critique is not made to apologize. Why then is Jimmy made to apologize?

A White male in a hush harbor, a refuge for Black males, refers to a Black man in the hush harbor as a "bitch," and that does not call for an apology? Any Black male who has ever occupied a barbershop as hush harbor knows that such an insult calls for an apology, a retraction, or a fight. Isaac is not made to apologize because White privilege does not require it. The filmmakers' discourse ensures that White folks in the audience feel safe. And like the overseers of the Enslavement who were occasionally Black and who were often the agents of White privilege, the filmmakers of *Barbershop* unwittingly act as agents of White privilege by requiring the sublimation of African American phronesis, parrhesia, and rhetoric to White nomoi. Isaac's response to Jimmy's apology explicitly reimposes White nomoi as rationality and knowledge on African American hush harbor rhetoric and phronesis:

ISAAC: That's cool, man. Actually I am kind of glad you came to your senses.
JIMMY: Why is that?
ISAAC: Cause I was running out of insults.

A White man determines when Black men come to their senses. More significantly, I am sure a lot of Black folks were proud that Jimmy came to his senses. After all, identifying with Jimmy requires that Black folks come to grips with their own complicity in the dominant political rationality.

Barbershop provides useful takes on community, consciousness about language (the N-word and cursing are minimal), about the changing demographic and discursive terrain upon which barbershops and other hush harbors function, and about African rhetoric and the power of the word, yet its conception of the barbershop as hush harbor is antithetical to AAHHs and AAHHR. Jimmy is made a villain because he polices Blackness. Although border policing is sometimes frowned upon in the academy, AAHHR as a hermeneutic of the everyday that recognizes and supports a certain kind of policing concerned with the valuing of African American subjectivities. Jimmy, for all his faults, is, unlike the filmmakers, a hush harbor phronimos and griot in that he recognizes that the barbershop is not a safe refuge for Whiteness. That is not to say that AAHHs should be ethnically pure, but it is to say that Blackness is not merely a commodity that can mimicked, purchased, and performed with no regard for the burdens of Blackness. If *Barbershop*'s discourse were more concerned with AAHHR, African American phronesis, and African American history, maybe Eddie's character would have spent more time criticizing Isaac or White icons and politicians such as Strom Thurmond, Barry Goldwater, and Ronald Reagan, all of whom have, from the perspective of African American phronesis, blocked African American uplift. Of course, the movie might not have made as much money.

Unlike *Barbershop, Malcolm X* does not constitute an anti–hush harbor movie. From its opening sequence, with a slowly burning American flag and the beating of Rodney King, director Spike Lee frames the movie so that Black nomoi, tropes, commonplaces, and phronesis are central. As a result, it does not commodify Black clothes, music, style, or Black women in the manner of *Barbershop. Malcolm X* contains two significant barbershop scenes central to understanding Malcolm Little's reeducation and his transformation into Malcolm X.

In the movie's first sequence, the camera swoops through a vibrant, jazzy, noisy urban Roxbury section of Boston as it follows Malcolm's partner Shorty (played by Spike Lee) into the Toledo Club barbershop. Shorty arrives amid men talking about numbers running and women. Just as in *Voices of the Self*, *Ceremonies in Dark Old Men*, and several poems discussed earlier, alternative economic networks and resistant counterpublic rhetorics occupy the same spatiality. Wide-eyed and innocent, Malcolm is called out of a room to sit in a barbershop chair so that Shorty can apply the foul-smelling, hot, and painful mix of a "jelly-like, starchy-looking glob" of lye and potatoes, called *congolene*, that is used to straighten out the natural texture of Black hair.[13] Several men from different generations watch as Shorty begins the process. One of the older men makes fun of Malcolm's upcoming ordeal by pointing at his own head and telling Malcolm that he (Malcolm) is in the hands of an expert: "Look at what he did for me." He removes his hat to reveal a scalp with patches of hair missing as all the men in the barbershop laugh heartily. Malcolm plays it cool and informs the cats in the barbershop through word and body language that he's impervious to pain. Of course, the congolene begins to scorch Malcolm's scalp. The men in the barbershop attempt to hold him in the chair. Malcolm jumps up and, with Shorty's assistance, washes the skin-dissolving substance out of his hair with water, after having trouble finding it, and a towel.

Set up at the start of the movie, the barbershop scene frames the narrative as a signpost of African American culture, subjectivity, and transformation. Interestingly, this scene, like a later barbershop prison scene, is crucially important to Malcolm's character arc in the film but does not occur in his autobiography. A hair-conking scene does occur in the autobiography, but in the private sphere of a home where Shorty is renting a room. Malcolm X connects the frying of his hair to the "processing" and transformation of his identity, but Shorty and Malcolm are alone. The obvious question is why Lee included two prominent barbershop scenes in the movie. One answer could be that Lee's thesis project in graduate school was *Joe's Bed-Stuy Barbershop*, indicating that he had a long-standing directorial affinity for barbershop scenes. Whatever the motive, moving the hair-conking scene from the private sphere of the home and placing it in the quasi-public AAHH of the barbershop infuses the act with a ritualistic, communal resonance lacking in the book. As AAHHR and its practices produce nommo through communal exchange, the scene suggests the importance of such spatialities to the cocreation of the power of the word. The barbershop scene reveals through visual rhetoric the importance of rhetoric, ritual, and masculinities in these geographies. Filming the initial conking of Malcolm's hair in Shorty's room would separate the processing or disciplining of Black hair from communal and social politics, reconfiguring them in and domesticating them into the private sphere. Lee contextualizes the conking of Malcolm's hair to reveal the African American rituals, rhetorical education, rites of passage, outlaw economies, and other forces of African American expressive culture, including struggles over Whiteness and Blackness, swirling around the styling of Black hair.

The men in the barbershop function like a jazz ensemble or a Greek chorus of communal comment and epistemology as Malcolm's hair is processed. The mirror in the shot makes it clear that Malcolm's transformation is a rite of passage that the African American male community affirms. The men in the barbershop are all aware of the pain Malcolm must endure as his hair is transformed. Blackness as both a rhetoric embodied in hair, and as an embodied rhetoric is reconnected to the pain of the Black body and its historical material and discursive disciplining into place as both a scene of subjection and emancipation. Ironically, a question popularized by Louis Armstrong, "What did I do to be so Black and blue?"[14] receives a polysemic answer through Black hair that points to African American complicity. Whereas *Barbershop* commodifies the pain of Blackness and Black hair and, by extension, African American culture, *Malcolm X*'s visual rhetoric resists an easy commodification of Blackness as its cost, joy, and pain are made apparent.

When Malcolm bends over, all we see is his rear end. When he straightens up, the camera zooms in on the towel. As Malcolm removes the towel, the camera moves closer still but from Malcolm's perspective as he looks into a mirror. The audience can see all the men in the barbershop look on with Malcolm in anticipation of the final product. Everyone smiles as the congolene has disciplined the nappiness and Blackness out of his hair: it's straight. The quest for Whiteness is complete. Malcolm gives the soul slap to the group and triumphantly exclaims, "Looks White, don't it?" The men nod affirmatively. Lee understands the barbershop as a sanctified spatiality in which Black male ritual and rites of passage occur. However, Lee reveals that African American phronesis and the ethics that accompany it are fallible. When Malcolm says with pride that his hair looks White, the Black men look on in affirming awe. *Malcolm X* illustrates how oppression often resides in the habits of mind and being that constitute common sense. Hush harbor safe spaces such as barbershops are not utopian oases *totally outside* of oppressive discourses. Hush harbors can inadvertently reproduce the very hierarchical social relations they resist.

In contrast to *Malcolm X, Barbershop* participates in the domestication of Blackness by its hollowing out of the politics of Whiteness as it relates to hair as a trope of Blackness. In the film, the ecstasy and pain of Black hair are not discussed through a discourse of nappiness, nor is the style of hair explicitly associated with Black subjectivity as it is in *Malcolm X.* Instead, it, the pain of Black hair (read: Blackness), is reduced to an issue of personal taste as a mother becomes upset at Jimmy for mistakenly cutting a significant plug of hair out of her son's scalp. Hair as racial and class politics is ignored. Hair as the embodiment of African American subjectivities and identities is overlooked. Visually, a variety of Black hairstyles inhabit the film's tableaux, yet Black hair, its style and its texture, are not situated in the political sphere in the way they are in *Malcolm X.* Of course, the filmmakers are entitled to make any film they desire.

As mentioned earlier, Lee includes a second barbershop scene in *Malcolm X* not included in *The Autobiography of Malcolm X: As Told to Alex Haley* (1987). In the film, the prison barbershop functions as a liminal spatiality of identity and consciousness transformation. At this point in the film, thanks to the intervention of Baines (a fellow inmate), the always intellectually precocious Malcolm transforms from street hustler to a faithful devotee of the Black Muslims and Elijah Muhammad. Malcolm goes to the chair and asks the barber to cut off/out the congolene.

In the prison barbershop, the congolene—Whiteness—is cut out of Malcolm's core sense of himself. The transformation becomes mythical. The hero (Malcolm) enters or is forced into a dark place (sites such as a valley or a whale's belly are mythical places of transformation) and, with the assistance of a guide and or divine spirit, comes to enlightenment. Even though the prison itself is not a built environment constructed to produce

Black subjectivities, the ritual of haircutting, the Black barber, and the banter of the inmates invoke cultural memory and transcripts that evoke a Black discursive spatiality.

African American professor Fred A. Bonner II, in "Black Professors," wrote about how difficult it was for newly minted African American professors in primarily White institutions.[15] Many Black professors felt they were out of the academic loop; that they had to work harder than White professors and had to tolerate assumptions about competence and performativity in ways White professors could avoid. According to Bonner, the only places they could go to be themselves were barbershops and beauty shops. At first glance, my analysis of the prison scene and connecting the cutting of hair to myth and transformation might seem more affective than analytic. However, as Bonner illustrates, even some academics see the barbershop and other hush harbors as synecdoches of Blackness.

Barbershop and *Malcolm X* both address the importance of the barbershop as a Black male spatiality. Both deal with the visual rhetoric of Black hair. Yet *Barbershop*, a movie explicitly about a male hush harbor, lacks the edge of the barbershop scenes in *Malcolm X*. Lee's movie directly challenges White privilege and Black comfort through the politics of hair. *Barbershop* sublimates parrhesia and phronesis for the easy laugh. *Malcolm X* and *My Big Fat Greek Wedding* explore ethnic enclaves as places of rhetorical education and knowledge production in which ethnicity is not always easily achieved. Hush harbors are connected to history, cultural memory, and myth in ways that reveal how the struggle over ethnicity and knowledge is more than clothes, cars, and slang. *Barbershop*, for all its positive attributes, ultimately fails because its fetishized, commodified notion of Blackness makes everyone comfortable. Making *everyone* comfortable is the goal of Hallmark cards; the barbershop as an AAHH exists, in part, to make *Black men* comfortable.

7.

Hush Harbor Pedagogy

Pathos-Driven Hearing and Pedagogy

AS WITH MUHAMMAD ALI'S *PARRHESIATIC* DEMAND TO BE RECOGNIZED, *Keepin' It Hushed* demonstrates the pervasiveness and importance of African American hush harbor rhetoric (AAHHR) in the construction of African American subjectivities and in the production of knowledge. In what follows, I will reiterate my discussion on African American rhetoric as an epistemic project to resituate it in relation to the use of *pathos*-oriented listening/hearing to excavate the epistemic aspects of AAHHR more fully. Then, the discussion shifts to explore the utility of pathos-oriented listening/hearing in literature and WAC (writing across the curriculum) composition classrooms. In keeping with the theme of phronesis and practical use, the discussion moves to an examination of African American public spheres and the ideology of space as it relates to writing. Given the interdisciplinary nature of my project and importance of literature to the book, this chapter of *Keepin' It Hushed* moves to a consideration of the use of how rhetorical criticism in reading a canonized American literature text, Richard Wright's *Native Son* (1940), points toward the use of AAHHR as pedagogy. The chapter then concludes with three recommendations for scholars interested in African American rhetoric to expand its utility as an epistemic project.

A primary conclusion of *Keepin' It Hushed* is that AAHHR is central to a serious engagement with African American knowledge, subjectivity, and pedagogy. More specifically, as a contemporary manifestation of the hush harbor, the barbershop remains significant to the construction and understanding of African American male subjectivities. Consequently, rhetorical scholarship that does not take into account AAHHR and the spatialities, the quasi public in which such rhetorics and knowledges circulate, produces woefully partial understandings and trivializing receptions of AAHHR. Part of the trivialization of African American rhetoric stems from the undeniable fact that African American culture in general is still primarily valued more as a geography of difference, otherness, or alterity than as a Black singularity of spatiality, knowledge, pedagogy, and education. Put simply, the question of what it is that Black people know is never asked because, for too many scholars, Blackness—and by extension African Americans—functions as epiphenomenal—an epistemologically empty category.

In *Culture on the Margins,* Jon Cruz provides a taxonomy of hearing differently within the context of music. I believe this taxonomy to be useful in hearing African American rhetoric (Black talk) and culture as locations of knowledge production and critical thinking.[1] As with my work in AAHHR, Cruz is concerned with racialized audience, hermeneutics, and the hidden transcripts of African American culture. Cruz is in dialogue with James Scott's notion of the hidden transcript in that their content may be heard with even the most superficial, uninformed kind of listening, but for the transcripts content to be audible as knowledge, to be heard and listened to critically, another kind of listening is required. To better hear or understand the hidden transcripts within African American culture, Cruz defines three types of hearing: *incidental, instrumental,* and *pathos mediated.*

Cruz describes *incidental hearing* as the kind of "accounts logged by White slave holders and observers who did not intend to hear Black music, but who instead stumbled upon it."[2] This kind of hearing is embodied in comments that reduce African and African American linguistic, rhetorical, and musical practices to indecipherable babble, noise, or rhythm. In this context, African American knowledge circulates as Black noise—remaining the excess outside of hegemonic channels of normativity and order. Noise occupies the excess outside valued categories of meaning and knowledge because "it does not fit them; it is rejected sound that spills out of, or flows over, the preferred channels along which known, accepted, and regulated sounds occur. Sound that cannot be meaningfully placed is aberrant sound. Sound out of place."[3] Duke Ellington once surmised that African American's made dissonance a way of life.[4] African American hush harbors (AAHHs) and AAHHR are terrains where Black folks immerse themselves in normalized waves of Black dissonance. AAHHR, then, flows outside, over, and through the preferred channels of rhetorical meaning and epistemology privileged in rhetorical scholarship and in mainstream public spheres. As a result, some Black folks offer more timid, consumable Blackness in the public sphere for increased access and personal benefit.

The second category of hearing, *instrumental hearing,* involved attempts by overseers to use music for "non-musical objectives and revolved around the appropriation of Black music and culture to hegemonic ends."[5] For example, plantation owners might "hear," value, and approve of the use of Negro spirituals, fiddling, or drumming, not as a hermeneutic providing an angle of perception into African American subjectivities and knowledges, but solely as a means to disciplinary ends: to increase work speed, heighten the sale value of a slave, or as an entertainment safety valve, releasing pent-up frustration that the enslaved might transform into resistance.

Fortunately, Cruz notes the emergence of a third kind of hearing where the sound of African American subjectivity can be apprehended, and where a trumpeting of the "hermeneutic dimensions of black expressions is valued."[6] Cruz refers to this kind of hearing as *pathos-driven hearing,* which attempts to hear and interpret from the cultural, epistemic, and normative assumptions of the performer, rhetor, or group producing the performance. Apprehending AAHHR as knowledge requires scholars and others who overhear and underhear AAHHR to engage in pathos-driven hearing. Pathos-driven hearing provides a space from which rhetorical scholars may hear (read), examine, and interpret African American rhetorical performances through the taxonomies and assumptions of African American experience and memory. Pathos-driven hearing opens up AAHHR up to more serious investigations and considerations, and opens up writing and literacy to reconfiguring as kinds of thinking, pushing beyond reductive conceptions that would reduce writing and literacy to mere instrumentalities. Linking writing and literacy to thinking and knowledge are of course central, in my view, to writing across the disciplines (WAD) and/or WAC approaches to composition. As students "hear" themselves write in their heads, they often engage in a kind of instrumental production and deployment of writing. Such writing is frequently oriented toward providing the writing instructor with what he or she wants—writing as mere conveyance rather than as a production of knowledges and/or writing as thinking about thinking. Outside the genre of the personal narrative or biography, writing too often circulates as a practice of drill, skill, and skillful regurgitation rather than as an exercise in which students explore and examine their own thoughts.

An important element in WAC, according to Robert Samuels in "Reinventing the Modern University with WAC," student voice—their sense of themselves as speaking, thinking subjects—is domesticated and suppressed in the composition-as-instrumental skill classroom.[7]

Voice in the context of a pathos-oriented classroom is not anchored in a concern with the expression of a personal, authentic self (although this may be the motivation for some students), but instead addresses student and social episteme, *doxa* (belief), and assumptions mediating their thinking through their writing. In addition, the pathos-oriented classroom attempts to assist students in constructing what Barry Brummett and Detine L. Bower in "Subject Positions as a Site of Rhetorical Struggle" refer to as *authorial subject position*. Brummett and Bowers define authorial subject position as "a locus and source of thought, decision, and control over one's self."[8] Pathos hearing/reading compels composition instructors to go beyond literacy as grammar, sentence structure, organization, and arrangement. It prods literature instructors to push through regurgitation and the listing and identifying elements of literature, and it pushes students to take themselves seriously as sources of and resources for thought and for thinking. It pushes students to make certain writing decisions.

If we can assist students to consider those decisions in the context of understanding academic writing as a particular kind of thinking and literacy that conveys a particular kind of social capital, then composition might provide a platform of insight into how literacy is always contextual. Therefore, students must be aware of how the elements of a rhetorical situation such as ethos, invention, exigency, disciplinary requirements, and decorum should always be considered if they want a particular literacy to provide them with the social capital they desire. I do not claim that pathos hearing/reading is a new form of rhetorical listening, but I do believe it is a highly suggestive approach to listening/reading the writing of essays that can assist in producing not only more effective student writers but critical students better able to negotiate various literacies occupying the everyday of most of their lives.

Based upon its concern with African American culture and its relation to philosophical and hermeneutical concerns, several more inferences can be drawn from *Keepin' It Hushed*. However, three are most significant in my mind. First, and probably most obvious, is that taxonomies of classical or current-traditional rhetoric, while useful, are *insufficient* for comprehending or understanding African American rhetoric. Therefore, my method in *Keeping It Hushed* of using current-traditional terms or categories along with African American terms and categories is purposeful.[9]

On the other hand, when deploying current-traditional taxonomies, categories, and terms as though in their universality, they can be seamlessly fitted into a variety of rhetorical terrains and account for various rhetorical practices while the taxonomies and terms of ethnic, gendered, and queered rhetorics remain tethered to the particular, reducing their circulation to difference and identity inadvertently participates in the insidious ethnographic and epistemic exclusions I critiqued earlier.[10]

Second, Black public material and discursive spheres such as barbershops, beauty shops, newspapers, magazines, book clubs, Black radio, and Chitlin' Circuit cultural productions are more useful for the monitoring and evaluating Black subjectivities than are the rhetorics produced in more mainstream public spatialities. For most African Americans, it is these spatialities where Black meanings can be found, where Black folks go to rebaptize themselves in Black culture in ways often unavailable in the public sphere. This is becoming increasingly true across a number of ethnic and gender configurations. Time-space compression, glocalization, migration, immigration, and other flows of capital and people decrease the significance of rhetoric, space, and place for some, but increase their significance for most. My notion of Black public spheres as they relate to AAHHs and the AAHHR that emerge from them is more conceptually fertile than the potentially facile notion of bodies marked as African American occupying a particular place on a particular rhetorical occasion.

Informed by and developed from scholarship in critical geography and other disciplines from scholars such as Gillian Rose, Roxanne Mountford, David Harvey, Henri Lefebvre, Nedra Reynolds, Michael Dawson, and Nancy Fraser, I conceive African American or Black public spheres in Black civil society in relation to a post-Kantian, post-Cartesian insight of the social-political-rhetorical construction of space: space as ideological. Further, particular kinds of discourses and literacies are more likely to be produced and to circulate in some places rather than others because of a protean nexus of memory, experience, emotion, power, expectation, history, desire, and palimpsests of social practices. African American public spheres are sites where rhetorical and compositional practices, emerging from particular rhetorical histories, occasions, spaces, and paths of thought, provide sanctuary for African American angles of knowledge and thought within the American experience.

Nedra Reynolds, in *Geographies of Writing*, drawing from some of the aforementioned insights about space and place, makes explicit the importance of space to composition and writing:

> *Geographies of Writing* sees writing instruction as rooted in time and place and within material conditions that affect students who are often transient residents of learning communities; students pass through, and only pause briefly within classrooms; "they dwell within and visit various other locations, locations whose politics and discourse conventions both construct and identify them" (qtd. from Drew 60).[11]

We are all aware that literary analysis occurs in spatiality and place. Still, we often undertheorize how the *spatial is ideological.* The spatial produces subjectivities; it is not a neutral container or platform for them. Reynolds's work is significant for me because it smartly examines the ideological nature of any classroom, the significance of composition in the construction of subjectivities, and the connection of those subjectivities to literacies; it sculpts a space for the importance of WAC through its attempt to critically cross and inhabit a variety of disciplinary and discursive spaces and places; and, finally, *Geographies of Writing* provides a bridge for my conception of hush harbor rhetoric to reside in the nexus of theorizing about composition.

Postsecondary schools are diminishing as a primary inculcator of values. Arguably, college education is increasingly viewed by students and administrators in purely instrumental terms: it's about a job. Obtaining a job is not only seen as postsecondary education's primary purpose (which certainly isn't new) but is also, more problematically, viewed as its only purpose by many students. For example, in my classes, the vast majority of students raise their hands when I ask them how many of them would not attend college if they could enter their chosen profession without a college education. While this is not definitive proof supporting my claim, consider it along with the increasingly vitriolic nature of the culture wars in the public sphere, the emergence of cultural studies in academia, and the increasing significance of youth culture in the selling of products and the shaping of the media; all point to the transmittal of values from numerous sites that contest the importance of schools at all levels. This is why, in my view, composition studies and writing programs in their various configurations need to address the issue of public pedagogy.

Public pedagogy as both method and as object of analysis produces the following two useful insights influenced by the work of Henry Giroux. First, the pedagogical and cultural are political, and the political is pedagogical. By *political,* I mean that pedagogy is not merely the neutral, purely instrumental transmission of information; *pedagogy* embodies values, knowledge, power, and perspectives informing the political, social, and spiritual rationalities and logics informing our daily lives. Second, although schools and universities are certainly important—at least I'd like to think so given where I am employed—education and the transmission of values occur across a variety of terrains outside of the classroom. As universities become more corporate in orientation and students increasingly, and for some good reasons, value education through an instrumental modality, I would argue that the influence of universities in the inculcation of noninstrumental values and knowledges has decreased.

Henry Giroux in *Border Crossings* (1991) addresses how "the production, dissemination, and circulation of ideas emerge from the educational force of the entire culture."[12] Extending the education beyond the classroom allows us to consider how a variety of discourses and rhetorics we usually think of us peripheral to learning or lacking pedagogical effect indeed reflect and produce the educational force of the entire culture. Film, music, commercials, books, churches, newscasts, the Internet, and cable all contain pedagogical potential. Even neoliberalism is partially a pedagogical project on the very ground of human subjectivity. This not to say that any particular show or event always produces learning or conveys values that the listener or viewer understands as pedagogical. Instead, it is to posit that together these sites combine to create a network of pedagogy that normalizes a constellation of values.

Neoliberalism as a political rationality functions as pedagogy that normalizes a constellation of values around market logics. Movies such as *Crash* (dir. Paul Haggis, 2004) and music such as Kanye West's reflect and participate in neoliberalism as public pedagogy, as does, as I argue in the last chapter, President Obama's "A More Perfect Union" speech. Pathos-oriented hearing enables us to hear the knowledge-production capabilities of popular culture and other extraclassroom sites, enabling instructors to impact student learning more effectively.

This is not to imply that all composition or literature curricula should be refashioned as cultural studies. Nor do I mean to suggest that literature and composition classrooms should become primarily sociological or ethnographic in orientation; after all, my personal goal in the composition classroom is to develop more effective writers, critical thinkers, critical citizens, more competent users of literacies, and fewer citizen subjects as *Homo economicus*. Instead, it is to suggest that, as the pedagogical terrain expands through the Internet, social networking, and blogging, these sites need to be taken into account as affirming and competing spheres of pedagogy and those pedagogies need to be understood as, not mere techniques or neutral channels for the transmittal of knowledges, but as inherently pedagogical and political.

My earlier professed interest in phronesis (practical wisdom) requires that I link *Keepin' It Hushed* to some pedagogical utility in the classroom specifically and in the world in general. Given my interest in African American expressive culture (rhetoric, literature, popular culture, music, and art), and the historical relation of rhetoric to pedagogy and poetics, I first address rhetoric and AAHHR, and their relation to the teaching of literature. Then, I shift my focus and discuss AAHHR and its relevance to public pedagogy and the classroom.

Scholars in rhetoric and literature seem to be placed, or place themselves, in opposing camps. Of course, some of this agonistic logic revolves around disciplinary territory and tenure-track lines. In any case, it is an artificial division I resist. Rhetoric and poetics have been inextricably linked for centuries. Not only have both been used to entertain, but each has been used to enlighten, to teach, and to instruct. Therefore, it is not surprising that Aristotle wrote famously about both rhetoric and poetics and that Carter G. Woodson would write about both Negro orators and literature, as both authors were concerned with rhetoric, phronesis, pedagogy, and the use of curriculum to produce more critical citizen subjects. Along with other approaches to reading and interpreting literature (e.g., formalist, Marxist, blues, post-structuralist, and feminist) rhetorical criticism offers another useful lens through which to read literature.

Rhetoric as method, as distinctive form of analysis, is not a call to deprivilege formalist or close readings of texts. However, rhetoric as a hermeneutical activity serves as a distinctive complement to close reading. In Aristotle's view, rhetoric, like ethics and politics, is a practical art focused on practices and effects around the probable, with how and what texts function in an attempt to create certain effects, with what makes texts persuasive to specific audiences. In addition, rhetoric provides a critical lens and taxonomy that account for rhetorical elements, forms, and tactics in texts and how they function in terms of audience, spatiality, and occasion. Richard Wright's germinal novel *Native Son* is a useful text to illustrate how a rhetorical lens might contribute to an alternative evaluation of a literary text.

Generally recognized as a watershed novel in American and African American literature, the first novel by an African American to be a Book of the Month Club selection, and celebrated for its naturalistic aesthetic accomplishment and its sociological insight, *Native Son* phenomenologically traverses the interior of an alienated, urban, African American male struggling against White racism and his own existential angst. Bernard W. Bell alludes to the importance of the novel: "It was the interplay between Freudian psychology and Marxist social analysis in *Native Son* that established the naturalistic model for many Black novelists of the 1940s, including Ann Petry's undervalued *The Street*."[13] However, as well received as the text was then and now, one of the major criticisms leveled at the novel centers around book 3, "Fate," and the forensic rhetoric of Boris A. Max, Bigger Thomas's lawyer.

Some critics consider book 3 a flaw in the construction of the novel in that it offers dialogue and speech making in place of dramatizing its thematics. This is to say that Bigger's rhetoric in book 3 goes against the grain of literary expectation. And it is precisely Wright's reconfiguring of the literary through oral-based written expression that makes book 3 significant if read through a rhetorical lens. In this view, the character Max's closing statement seems extraneous; that is, a restatement of what has occurred in the novel, and a propagandistic, ineffective oral appendage external to the fabric of the novel. While this criticism has merit through a *literary lens,* when reading and interpreting the final chapter through a *rhetorical lens* the criticism has little, if any, merit and opens up a different angle of evaluation. More specifically, given the structural, material, and discursive domestication placed upon African Americans, bearing witness through the embodied rhetoric of oratory—for all its limits—enhances African American subjectivity.

As Irving Howe points out, the last word in the novel is left to Bigger—not the orator–lawyer Max. If Max's attempt to "save" Bigger can be read as an attempt by him to connect Bigger's forming consciousness to the more politically informed thinking of Marxist ideology, then Max's failure could be read as how even a resistance to the dominant political rationality submerged hush harbor pathos and knowledge in a manner that Bigger could only say or speak the unsayable through nommo, through the work only it can do in the world. This is to say that Bigger's rhetoric in book 3 without the constraints of literary expectations, the very transgression of the literary expressed through *orality* in literary form is exactly what makes book 3 (the final book) of the novel interesting rhetorically. Bell perceptively carves open a space for a rhetorical analysis of this element of the text when he writes, "Stylistically, the tension in book 3 is more dialectic than dramatic."[14] Aristotle theorized that rhetoric is the counterpart of dialectic, so if Bell's reading offers a productive entry point into the text, then a rhetorical lens would seem useful as Bell, through his reference to dialectic as argument, deploys a term that Aristotle would save for philosophy but that *Keepin' It Hushed*—as does Barbara Christian—relates to the philosophies or knowledges of African American rhetorics.

Native Son illuminates the rhetorical force, power, and materiality of African American rhetoric. After his plea for mercy for Bigger Thomas is denied, despondent defense lawyer Max tells Bigger, "I did the best I could."[15] However, Bigger is satisfied with Max's performance. For Bigger, "It was not the meaning of the speech that gave him pride, but the mere act of it. That in itself was something."[16] Here material effect of Richard L. Wright's plow metaphor of the word doing work in the world. Its material effect is embodied in Bigger's comment. Further, Bigger's analysis and theorizing—and that is exactly what Bigger is doing—point toward the recognition that the work that nommo produces is beyond the content of the word, but the very materiality of the words, the physicality of the utterance, its being spoken in a particular way in a particular syntax through a body marked in a particular manner.

Bigger understands that the very act of the Black male body speaking, the act of having one's Black experience projected into the world through parrhesia, is a physical, material act—the materiality of rhetoric and language. Here Bigger experientially and intuitively understands that parrhesia is a rationality, an ideology, and that the rationality functions, of course, as more than just a mimetic representation through language that does little more than reflect some abstract material base; that, indeed, the word spoken through parrhesia organizes matter itself. This is precisely an aspect of what Giles Deleuze and Felix Guattari argue in *A Thousand Plateaus* about "order words," language, and desire: they do things, they are productive in the world.[17] John Rickford and Toni Morrison offer similar theoretical insights in terms of African American rhetorical practices. In literature and composition classrooms, I believe teachers must endeavor to encourage our students to understand that writing, language, and literacy are not mere mirror reflections of reality, husks that transmit ideas. That writing is a site where they can think about their thinking, that language both shapes and is shaped by terministic screens, and that literacy is central to, rather than epiphenomenal to, the very ground of the human. Through his words, his rhetoric, Bigger achieves some ontological solace as his experience, as his subjectivity, his very life, is temporarily made to matter.

Max's pathos-driven hearing, listening, and rhetoric connect to Bigger's sense of self. As a character, Max goes beyond the incidental and instrumental hearing prevalent within both the interrelations of Blacks and Whites and in public sphere interactions. Max imperfectly enters the interior of African American and Bigger's subjectivity (imperfect because Max's empathy for Bigger ignores how bounded up in race is class in the context of the United States). Literary theorist and cultural worker Elizabeth Alexander describes the Black interior as "Black life and creativity behind the public face of stereotype and limited imagination."[18] Max's closing argument, then, if analyzed through an African American rhetorical lens, can be interpreted as a recognition of the limitations of literature as a productive art/method in the examination of a Black interior such as Bigger's.[19] From a rhetorical perspective, Max's speech does not diverge from the novel's thematic fabric. Indeed, it extends the thematic fabric as rhetoric places different questions on the critical table. AAHHR is less interested in the textual ontology—what a text is, and more interested in what a text and its rhetorical forms do, how they work, what effects they may produce—and broadens the kinds of critiques that can be applied to literary texts. In short, rhetoric is a practical art concerned with audience, whereas literature is a productive art that is not inherently concerned with audience and effects upon it in the manner of rhetoric.

AAHHR as a practical art expands the objects of study under the purview of rhetoric. It assumes that education occurs across a broad variety of spatialities. AAHHR, the Black interior, and public pedagogy intersect in this regard.

Public pedagogy extends beyond the classroom because, like AAHHR, it assumes that education "takes place across a spectrum of social practices and settings across society."[20] My use of film, newspapers, journals, animation, gossip, radio, the Internet, and music in my own classroom isn't primarily about entertainment; it is a recognition that valuable pedagogy, education, and knowledge are manufactured in multiple places. To gain access to these alternative sites of pedagogy in hush harbors such as cantinas (Mexican Americans), pool halls and billiard rooms (Filipino men), and baby-shower rituals (South Asian women) requires extra effort on the part of professors. However, I have found that pathos-driven hearing sometimes opens up students to sharing their lifeworlds through discourse and rhetoric.

Theories of public pedagogy assert that pedagogy always reflects and embodies knowledge, power, ethics, and culture. In both my literature and pedagogy classes, I often make visible the often hidden transcripts of pedagogy: I carefully engage in a hush harbor pedagogy. I might discuss how the spatiality of the classroom, the curriculum, the sequence in which I teach materials, what I teach and do not teach, my clothing, hair, rhetoric, and race all mediate and inform pedagogy. Within theories of public pedagogy, culture is understood as more than values, practices, or artifacts; culture is viewed as a site of contestation and struggle through which identities, subjectivities, and knowledges are constructed. Idealizing the importation of hush harbor rhetorics and knowledges into the context of the classroom is not my intent. Experience has taught me that importing the hidden transcripts of hush harbor rhetoric into a classroom sometimes transforms the classroom into an agonistic spatiality. It can become a downright agonistic discursive war zone when AAHHR parrhesia occurs.

This brings an ethical question to the forefront. Should African American rhetors share or insert AAHHR, and the knowledges and standpoints associated with it, into the public sphere? Should AAHHR be wedged into the public sphere to ensure the kind of deep democracy valued by Cornel West, Gilyard, and Foucault? Are there some Black knowledges or dirty laundry that, as Dionne Warwick argued to Charles S. Dutton as she walked out of a performance of playwright August Wilson's *Two Trains Running* (1991), Black folks need to keep to themselves? There is much at stake in this question in terms of how dominant rationalities and neoliberalism filter and domesticate Black knowledges and how Blackness is legitimized and authorized in the public sphere(s). What enables an African American rhetor to be acceptable and electable? What kinds of rhetorics are allowed for that Black rhetor to be listened to as a racially nonpartisan ideal or abstract citizen (concepts I will return to later)? What racial knowledge must that rhetor ablate, leave behind, or ignore, to be acceptable in the current political rationality mediating the political public sphere within the American racial imaginary?

On one hand, deploying AAHHR and African American parrhesia into the public sphere could alter, reform, or challenge the dominant political rationality in the public sphere, moving the body politic and the country a little bit closer what Cornel West and Keith Gilyard would refer to as *deep democracy:* the kind of African American *rhetorical membership* in the nation-state of the American imaginary that would broaden the terrain of the sayable and the intelligible—the dominant political rationality—through the inclusion of African American and other knowledges. By *rhetorical membership,* I allude to the implicit and explicit assumptions and rationalities mediating the terrain of visual, rhetorical, and political in the American imaginary that one must occupy to be a legitimate member of the mainstream public.

On the other hand, the parrhesia, nommo, knowledge, and counterknowledge of AAHHR and the dirty laundry that comes with it may used against Black folks and preclude them from a position or job—say the presidency of the United States—that the African American individual or African American civil society may covet in a *substantial democracy.* I go beyond procedural democracy that begins with and stops at participation through voting. Substantial democracy goes beyond voting to create new or usable knowledge by members of the body politic that offers some possibility of altering the dominant political and social rationalities. Substantial democracy holds out the hope that, through various kinds of participation, citizens can have a measurable effect on their daily lives. Substantial democracy, like Cornel West's deep democracy, is "not just a system of governance, as we tend to think of it, but a cultural way of being."[21]

So, the ethical question remains. Should AAHHR be inserted in the political public sphere? More specifically, should AAHHR and knowledge about the nature of race in the United States be inserted into the rationalities guiding discourse in the public sphere; would that move us a bit closer to deep or substantial democracy?

Ethical or not, hush harbor knowledge and tropes have already entered the public discourse. Thanks to the president of the United States and the Rev. Jeremiah Wright.

8.

A Question of Ethics?

Hush Harbor Rhetoric and Rationalities in a Neoliberal Age

MUHAMMAD ALI WAS ARGUABLY THE MOST POPULAR ATHLETE OF HIS ERA. Michael Jordan was and is one the most popular athletes of any era. Muhammad Ali embodied the zeitgeist of his era; Michael Jordan his. Because he is now an internationally beloved figure, because his marvelously dissonant, brave, voice has been stilled by Alzheimer's, it is easy to forget and to unremember the audacious, frank, fierce, dangerous, "I am America" Muhammad Ali to which *Keepin' It Hushed* refers. "I am America" is Black noise, dissonance that drops the mask: it is spoken through an African American terministic screen—a hush harbor rhetoric.

Unfortunately, we live in epoch dominated by rhetorics and rationalities of neoliberalism, what Cornel West refers to as free-market fundamentalism, or what I call African American or Black neoliberalism. In such an era, the ethics and ethos of the market where the social, political, and the human are increasingly evaluated based on their exchange value—privilege the sale of tennis shoes over the struggle for social justice. Michael Jordan embodies the ethos of Black neoliberalism; the dominant rationality, as I have argued, of our era—a rationality Senator Barack Obama had to navigate to become president. This is also the context into which Rev. Jeremiah Wright deployed his African American hush harbor rhetoric (AAHHR).

The substance of this chapter focuses on Senator Barack Obama's–Rev. Jeremiah Wright's rhetorical debate that was pivotal to President Obama's election. While their antagonisms would be an obvious and productive focus, I will focus on what the two men had in common: their knowledge and use of AAHHR. More specifically, in President Obama's "A More Perfect Union" speech and Rev. Wright's two sermons—"The Day of Jerusalem's Fall" and "Confusing God and Government"—that the public latched on to.

The two men attended the same hush harbor: Trinity United Baptist Church. I want to focus on this hush harbor commonality for two reasons: First, the brouhaha, of course, brings attention to the continuing importance of African American hush harbors (AAHHs) and of AAHHR, as *Keepin' It Hushed* incessantly argues. Second, in a Black neoliberal age where personal, private, and economic success trumps communal good, hearing two African Americans frankly and bravely discuss race as it relates to communal and societal benefit through hush harbor motifs invigorated the public sphere. In addition, the hush harbor subtext of the debate added some Black dissonance that placed African American life and culture at the center of the public debate that made the public sphere, with considerable resistance, more Black than it has been in a long, long time.

Before getting to the Senator Obama–Rev. Wright speeches, I think it is important to situate their discourse in the context of neoliberalism as a rationality to which I have been referring throughout *Keepin' It Hushed*. Specifically, I want to situate their AAHHR debate within the context of Black neoliberalism—to set up the terrain to read the speeches of both men on a productive register.

Neoliberalism and Black neoliberalism in particular make race, its associated hush harbor perspectives, and other social issues more difficult to discuss. Unlike capitalism, which functions on the assumption that self-interest is a phenomenon natural to human relations so government should not interfere, neoliberalism is interventionist: its supporters and policies encourage the government to privatize and reconfigure all human relations through a market logic or ethos. Neoliberalism constructs the market as the primary organizing principle for all social, economic, and spiritual phenomena. It depoliticizes politics itself and reduces public activity to the realm of utterly privatized practices and utopias, limiting citizenship to the buying and selling of goods. It collapses the public into the private, rendering all social problems as personal. As Toby Miller, an expert in media and cultural studies, said to me in a discussion about neoliberalism, "The key thing is that neoliberalism is more—or perhaps less—than an account and an ordering of an economic mode of production. It is about a form of subjectivity, of rational calculation and desire, that argues for all forms of life being subsumed to it, with everything from divorce to religious affiliation understood through its lens."[1]

Black neoliberalism, then, relegates race and other discussions to the private realm; racism is viewed as personal failing rather than a reflection of the nation-state and its institutions. Further, as Miller suggests, neoliberalism and Black neoliberalism do more than function as economic exchange and social relations: they seep into the very ground of subjectivity itself, where choice, individualism, success, and keeping it real—really pragmatic—seep into African American life and culture.

Kanye West's oeuvre consistently addresses the symptoms of Black neoliberalism in songs such as "All Falls Down" and in "Can't Tell Me Nothing," where the chorus repeats the refrain "La, la, la, la / Wait 'til I get my money right" and the first stanza reveals "I had a dream I could buy way to heaven / When I awoke I spent that on a necklace / I told God I'd be back in a second / Man, it's so hard not to act reckless."[2] Here West makes legible how the economic imperative is increasingly privileged over communal, ethnical, and even spiritual concerns. Here I return to Michael Jordan. When civil rights leader Harvey Gnatt ran against segregationist Senator Jesse Helms, Gnatt's campaign asked Michael Jordan for public support. Jordan said no. His reason: "Republicans buy tennis shoes, too."[3] No hush harbor rhetoric here; this is podium–auction block rhetoric: Blackness for sale. Domesticated

Blackness. Blackness without Obligation. It is so prevalent that it sublimates the Black subject as political citizen to the Black individual as entrepreneur subject or consumer citizen. It explains the commodification of AAHHR in the "barbershop" movies I examined in chapter 6. As a rationality, Black neoliberalism shapes the value of African American life and culture. It is within this context that Senator Obama addressed race.

Ultimately, White (and male) privilege remains too entrenched in the American imagination for even neoliberalism in any of its iterations to suppress. So it did not come as a surprise to any hush harbor occupant that, with a Black man running for president, race would be an issue despite then Senator Obama's best efforts. What was extraordinary is that the discussion took place about AAHHs, AAHHR, and the value of both in African American life and culture. As *Keepin' It Hushed* has argued throughout, hush harbors and AAHHR are critical to any discussion of Black knowledges, Blackness, and rhetoric. And what is fascinating was that both Rev. Jeremiah Wright and Senator Obama deployed hush harbor tropes, knowledge, and rhetorics but through distinctive terministic screens to make their case for a more inclusive America.

On March 13, 2008, Charles Gibson and ABC's *World News Tonight* showed snippets from four videos of Rev. Jeremiah Wright's speeches. According to Obery M. Hendricks Jr., in "A More Perfect (High-Tech) Lynching," after reviewing hours of footage from over 196 sermons, Rev. Wright was labeled a racist by the use of just 156 words, the most controversial elements from two sermons from the pulpit of the Trinity United Church of Christ: "The Day of Jerusalem's Fall" and "Confusing God and Government."[4] In these clips, the Reverend Wright excoriates the United States government and the nation for their complicity in African American suffering through its negligence vis-à-vis drug trafficking, the prison industrial complex, and three-strike laws. He then says, "They (Whites) want us to sing God Bless America. No! No! Goddamn America." He goes on to damn America for its treatment of African Americans as less than human and for killing innocent people through its domestic and foreign policy. He samples from another hush harbor and African American jeremiad rhetor, Malcolm X, when he refers to the tragedy of 9/11 World Trade Center as a case of "the chickens coming home to roost."[5] As then presidential candidate Obama had attended Rev. Wright's church for years, he was required to give an account of himself, of why he attended the church of a hate monger. In short, Rev. Wright's words were deemed angry, uncivil, unforgivable, inconsumable Blackness—what Joy James refers to as an "unembraceable Blackness,"[6] a parrhesiatic hush harbor Blackness.

He responded well.

A watershed moment that will undoubtedly go down in history as pivotal in the discussion of race in the political public sphere, Senator Obama's "A More Perfect Union," otherwise known as his race speech, tapped into the sermonic form of both the American and the African American jeremiads—a form whose tropes are etched into the American imaginary as a shinning city on the hill of American exceptionalism. "A More Perfect Union" was presented in a context in which there was a robust discussion, particularly in Black hush harbors, of whether then Senator Obama's campaign discussed race enough as it relates to African Americans. While he strategically presented race in speeches in front of primarily African American audiences in hush harbor spaces, and then with a heavy dose of self-help discourse, as he did with his speech in South Carolina, Senator Obama generally avoided the topic. Of course, the rhetorical tension President-elect Obama had to traverse is obvious: a presidential candidate cannot win the office solely on the strength of African American votes. As a result, Senator Obama had to direct his rhetoric to at least two audiences—one Black and the other White—in addition to others. To do so, he chose a genre of rhetoric utilized since the Enslavement by rhetors as varied as Maria W. Stewart, Booker T. Washington, and Martin Luther King Jr. This genre I refer to earlier as African American public podium–auction block rhetoric.

Unlike with AAHHR, where the rhetorical goal of the rhetor is to identify with a primarily Black audience, their desires, and their political rationalities, podium–auction block rhetoric attempts to identify with at least two audiences. "A More Perfect Union" effectively appeals to the concerns, fears, and desires of those invested in the hegemony of dominant American rationalities (White folks) and those of African Americans. Preceding, during, and after the Enslavement, Black bodies on public display have to a least implicitly consider the spectacle of Blackness—the expectations, fetish, fear of, desire, and need for the Black body in the American imagination. Because of the aforementioned—the Black body that does not effectively speak to these issues, whether implicitly or explicitly—the mainstream political public sphere remains dangerous. So when I used the term *podium–auction block rhetoric,* it is not to imply the rhetor speaks like a slave or has sold out. Instead, I use the term to illuminate how the Black body and its rhetoric must offer a kind of more consumable Blackness—a Blackness that does not maintain its hush harbor dissonance. Therefore, when Frederick Douglass and Zora Neal Hurston caution African American rhetors to speak differently to White audiences than to Black ones, when bell hooks warns that the presence of Whites changes the shape of our words, the American imaginary is at issue, and President Obama had to take it into account. How did President Obama accomplish this?

First, he seamlessly connected the American democratic project to his quest for the presidency, and then both to a social-teleological movement toward a more inclusive American imaginary—an imaginary that for the first time could be read as implicitly including African Americans:

> This was one of the tasks we set forth at the beginning of this campaign to continue the long march of those who came before us, a march for a more just, more equal, more free, more caring and more prosperous America. I chose to run for the presidency at this moment in history because I believe deeply that we cannot solve the challenges of our time unless we solve them together—unless we perfect our union by understanding that we may have different stories, but we hold common hopes; that we may not look the same and we may not have come from the same place, but we all want to move in the same direction—towards a better future for of children and our grandchildren.[7]

Next, President Obama's speech moves from the public podium-auction rhetoric to the recognition of hush harbor spatiality, its rhetorics, and its utility. Such a move surely forges a connection with African Americans. And while he did not refer to Rev. Wright's church as a hush harbor, President

Obama's description of Trinity affirms it as a Black hush harbor spatiality, making visible and spoken what often remains masked and blocked. President Obama understood the significance of AAHH and AAHHR and their function as tropes of Blackness:

> Like other predominantly black churches across the country, Trinity embod-
> ies the black community in its entirety—the doctor and the welfare mom,
> the model student and the former gangbanger. Like other black churches,
> Trinity's services are full of raucous laughter and sometimes bawdy humor.
> They are full of dancing, clapping, screaming and shouting that may seem
> jarring to the untrained ear. The church contains in full the kindness and
> cruelty, the fierce intelligence and the shocking ignorance, the struggles and
> successes, the love and yes, the bitterness and bias that make up the black
> experience in America.[8]

Later, Senator Obama links the rhetoric and performances that occur here to the barbershop, kitchen, to Black anger, and to keepin' it hushed as a rhetorical tactic: "That anger may not get expressed in public, in front of white co-workers or white friends. But it does find voice in the barbershop or around the kitchen table." Here, Like Eddie in the barbershop, President Obama links Rev. Wright and his church to the genealogy of spatialities, rhetorics, and knowledges that *Keepin' It Hushed* argues remains important in African American life and culture. Reverend Wright, then, was hardly a fringe figure and neither is his rhetoric around race.

Reverend Wright's rhetoric emerges out of the AAHHR tradition I have theorized and illuminated in *Keepin' It Hushed*. His rhetoric embodies all of the elements and principles to which I have alluded: It is parrhesiatic; it conveys nommo (the mainstream response to Rev. Wright hammers another nail in the coffin of those who embrace trite notions of "it's just words" or that the material trumps the linguistic), embraces phronesis, the site where theory, practice, and worldviews merge to construct African American common sense; emerges out of a Black hush harbor space (a progressive Black church), delivered primarily for and in front of an African American audience; and is anchored in African American knowledges, worldviews, and history.

Reverend Wright's social gospel is very popular with his Trinity United Church of Christ on Chicago's South Side and nationally. As I mentioned earlier, he is a highly sought-after speaker, and his church programs have assisted people all over the country. His former importance to Senator Obama is self-evident: the Obamas attended his church for over twenty years. They were married at his church. He baptized both their children. President-elect Obama even credits Rev. Wright for the title of his memoir, *The Audacity of Hope: Thoughts on Reclaiming the American Dream* (2006). Reverend Wright's sermonic technique and delivery are anchored firmly in the tradition of American and African American jeremiad that David Howard-Pitney maps the genealogy of in his germinal *The Afro-American Jeremiad* (1990). According to Howard-Pitney, the American jeremiad is made up of three basic elements: citing the promise of criticism of the present *declension,* or retrogression from the promise; and a resolving prophecy that society will shortly complete its mission and redeem the promise."[9] Like the Puritans, Frederick Douglass, Ida. B. Wells, Malcolm X, Martin Luther King Jr., former president Ronald Reagan, and Alan Keyes before him, Rev. Wright borrows in part or whole cloth from foundational American quilt of narrative and myths that make up the American and African American jeremiad. He participates in a rhetorical tradition of American lament, indignation, reform, faith, and warning that America must live up to the promise of its special founding as a shining city on the hill of American exceptionalism or face grave consequences. The difference between the reception of Senator Obama and that of Rev. Wright was that Senator Obama believes in the possibility of American redemption, whereas Rev. Wright demands change, does so with a parrhesia-mediated tone, and seems more suspicious of America's will to change so as to enable redemption.

When further elaborating upon and describing the hush harbor experience in "A More Perfect Union," as mentioned earlier, President Obama says the following about Trinity and other Black churches: "They are full of dancing, clapping, screaming and shouting that may seem jarring to the untrained ear." The untrained ear is the ear of instrumental and incidental hearing that Jon Cruz referred to earlier. Whites and other non–African Americans are influenced by a rationality that produces a structural ignorance, a problematic that rarely hears African American sound/dissonance as a site of knowledge production. As a site of difference? Yes. A site of pathology? Yes. A site of resistance, spectacle, sexuality, criminality, entertainment, humor, religiosity, tragedy, special pleading, and danger? Yes, yes, and yes again. But as a site of knowledge? No.

American rationalities tend to preclude the pathos-oriented hearing referred to earlier that would allow the body public to take Blackness and Black people as sites of knowledge transmittal. When Senator Obama observes that Rev. Wright's church is not particularly controversial, he means that it is not particularly controversial for the trained ears of many African Americans. For the untrained ears of many Whites, Rev. Wright's hush harbor rhetoric and knowledge is simply too Black—too grounded in African American worldviews to be heard as emerging from ideal citizens able to invest in what's good for the American common good.

Two African American women, whose names were not provided, who are members of Rev. Wright's hush harbor church, made this clear in interviews with an ABC News crew. They summarized with pithy, African American vernacular–influenced hush harbor knowledge exactly what President Obama, Joy James, and what *Keepin' It Hushed* have been trying to make clear. When asked whether she thought Rev. Wright was "radical," she responded, "He speaks the truth and continues to speak the truth and people can label that as radical, but I see it as insightful."[10] Another woman, intersecting with *Keepin' It Hushed*'s linking of hush harbors and AAHHR, had this to say in answer to the same question, "Nah, I wouldn't call it being radical. I call it being Black in America. It's not radical, how radical is that?"[11]

To President Obama's credit, he repudiated any characterization of Rev. Wright as a hate monger, refusing to trash Rev. Wright and referring to him as an uncle with whom he disagreed. He refused to disown Rev. Wright: "I can no more disown him than I can disown the black community."[12] Interestingly, however, then–presidential candidate Obama disagreed with Rev. Wright's suggestion that racism is endemic to the United States: "But the remarks that have caused this recent firestorm weren't simply controversial. They weren't simply a religious leader's effort to speak out against perceived injustice. Instead, they expressed a profoundly distorted view of this country—a view that sees white racism as endemic."[13] Distorted for whom? Where?

For good or ill, Rev. Wright's claim is a commonplace in AAHHs and in AAHHR. While not a monolith, most African Americans understand White racism/privilege to be endemic to the American nation-state. And even if most African Americans did not agree with Wright's position, they certainly understand that position as legitimate rather than distorted or irrational. Reverend Wright and ordinary African Americans are not alone in this view. Scholars as disparate as David Theo Goldberg, Ruthie Gilmore, Cedric Robinson, and Elaine Richardson have written about the centrality of Whiteness and racism to the development of the American the nation-state, so Rev. Wright's claim is not a distortion. However, Rev. Wright's claim is a distortion for the dominant rationality in America that views issues such as racism and White privilege as unfortunate but not sewn into the fabric of American life. And to the extent that both issues are understood to have been structurally linked or endemic to the nation-state, the American imaginary constructs them as the residual effects of a bygone era.

"A More Perfect Union" courageously discusses an issue rarely taken seriously in the political public sphere but often expressed and discussed in Black hush harbors: Black anger. "A More Perfect Union" wrestles with Black anger in a manner rarely seen on a national stage:

> The fact that so many people are surprised to hear that anger in some of Reverend Wright's sermons simply reminds us of the old truism that the most segregated hour in American life occurs on Sunday morning. That anger is not always productive; indeed, all too often it distracts attention from solving real problems; it keeps us from squarely facing our own complicity in our condition, and prevents the African-American community from forging the alliances it needs to bring about real change. But the anger is real; it is powerful; and to simply wish it away, to condemn it without understanding its roots, only serves to widen the chasm of misunderstanding that exists between the races.[14]

This affirmation of African American anger and its roots that is often expressed in AAHHs is significant and should not be downplayed, especially within an American imaginary where Black anger is deflected, disallowed, or constructed as pathological.

Both President Barack Obama and Rev. Jeremiah Wright introduced AAHHR and rationalities into the public sphere, for a moment legitimating African American worldviews, knowledges, fears, hopes, and hush harbor spatialities. Importantly, they both put a dint, however small, into a neoliberalism and a Black neoliberalism that reduce human social value and worth to the logic of the market. Reverend Wright and President Obama were discussing how to make the country live up to its promise based on social good, not market logics. They carved out a public space where African Americans are not compelled to wear the bit and wear the mask because Republicans buy tennis shoes—a space where market logics of Black neoliberalism are not natural. Like Muhammad Ali, in the end, both men used hush harbor knowledge and rhetoric for something larger than themselves. They both removed their masks, ceased to grin and lie, and moved the country just a bit closer to a substantial democracy. And they did it around hush harbor rhetoric and tropes.

While AAHHR continues to, and—until some kind of postracial promised land is a reality—will and should continue to circulate primarily within hush harbor Black civil society, its knowledges, memories, and experiences are needed if democracy is going to be substantially meaningful, particularly for African Americans. So, in the dangerous public sphere, the bit and the mask are worn less often. African American life and culture will be the richer for it.

And *that* is something that should not be kept on the hush.

Notes

OVERTURE/HEAD

Epigraph to this chapter quoted in Harper and Walton's *Vintage Book of African American Poetry*, 76.

1. Hartman, *Scenes of Subjection*, 11.
2. Ellison, *Invisible Man*, 471–72.
3. See BrainyQuote.com.
4. Michael Leff, quoted in Berlin, *Rhetoric and Reality*, 165.
5. Giroux, "Critical Theory and Rationality," 331–32.
6. Brown, "American Nightmare," 393.
7. Ibid., 693.
8. Huxley, "Geographies of Governmentality," 195.
9. Hardt and Negri, *Commonwealth*, 57.
10. Ibid.
11. West, *College Dropout*, 2004.
12. Scott, *Domination and the Arts*, 11.

13. Kanye West, quoted in de Moraes, "Kanye West's Torrent of Criticism."

14. Harry Belafonte, "Harry Belafonte on Bush, Iraq."

15. hooks, "Straightening Our Hair," 28.

16. Iton, *In Search*, 3–4.

17. Rank and Hirschl, "Estimating the Risk of Food Stamp Use," 994.

18. Butler, *Frames of War*, 2–3.

19. Hartman, *Scenes of Subjection*, 116.

20. Fields, *Architecture in Black*, 7.

21. Gilmore, *Golden Gulag*, 28.

22. Wallace, *Dark Designs*, 325.

CHAPTER 1

1. Telephone conversation with Melba Boyd on 10 June 2008.

2. Charity Bowery, quoted in Williams, *Self-Taught*, 7.

3. Lefebvre, *Production of Space*, 350; and Massey, *Space and Gender*, 136.

4. Levine, *Black Culture*, 41.

5. W. B. Allen, quoted in Berlin et al., *Remembering Slavery*, 55–56.

6. Scott, *Domination and the Arts*, 14.

7. Neal, *What the Music Said*, 14.

8. Morrison, *Beloved*, 88–89.

9. Frederick Douglass, quoted in Howard-Pitney, *Afro-American Jeremiad*, 21.

10. Burke, *Language as Symbolic Action*, 45.

11. Ibid.

12. Ede and Lunsford, "Audience Addressed," 155–71.

13. Cruz, *Culture on the Margins*, 45.

CHAPTER 2

1. Dawson, "A Black Counterpublic?" 201.

2. Harris-Lacewell, *Barbershops, Bibles, and BET*, 9.

3. Dawson, "A Black Counterpublic?" 9.

4. Ibid., 8.

5. Nancy Fraser, "Rethinking the Public Sphere," 65–69.

6. *New Yorker*, cover, July 21, 2008, 84.

7. Hanchard, *Party/Politics*, 6–8, 223–24.

8. Berlin, *Rhetoric and Reality*, 65.
9. Mailloux, *Rhetorical Power*, 28.
10. Hanchard, *Party/Politics*, 6–7
11. Ibid., 7.
12. Lefebvre, *Production of Space* (1992), 11.
13. Hayden, *Power of Place*, 29.
14. West, *Hope on a Tightrope*, 76.
15. Fields, *Architecture in Black*, 45–51.
16. Adolf Loos, "Ornament and Crime," 29–36.
17. Thompson, *Flash of the Spirit*, 221–26.
18. Colomina, "Excerpts," 314.
19. Spatiality as practiced place is useful as it unhinges racialized place from bodies and connects it to practices in which bodies engage. Conceptualizing places as Black or public spheres as Black then becomes more theoretically and practically useful.
20. Delaney, *Race, Place*, vi.
21. Airriess, *Creating Vietnamese*, 228–29.
22. See Asante, *Afrocentric Idea*.
23. Jackson and Richardson, *Understanding African American Rhetoric*, 28–29.
24. Wright, "Word at Work," 85.
25. For useful explanations of the Greek term *parrhesia* (fearless speech), see West's *Democracy Matters*, 28; and Foucault, *Fearless Speech*, chap. 1.
26. Cruz, in *Culture on the Margins* (57–64), describes three types of hearing or listening: instrumental, incidental, and pathos. These terms are important for scholars in rhetoric and communication because they reinsert hearing and audience into culture and power. Pathos-motivated hearing is an attempt by a hearer to listen or hear on the epistemic or cultural terms of the rhetor.
27. For a more elaborate explanation of nommo, see Flyvberg's *Making Social Science Matter*, chap. 5.
28. Subjective fortification carries significant force in African American culture because that culture becomes "conceived as national identity, religion, and language" (Kelley, *Head Negro*, 94).
29. Childers, *Columbia Dictionary*, "mascon words."

CHAPTER 3

1. Forrest, *Divine Days*, 9.
2. Alkebulan, "Spiritual Essence," 23–40.
3. Forrest makes several references to what is in his view the confining nature of the trope of double consciousness. Forrest assumes that reinvention constructs Black identity in relation to a broader field of possibilities than does the fragmentation he associates with double consciousness.
4. Forrest, *Divine Days*, 42.
5. Calmore, quoted in Mutua, *Progressive Black Masculinities*, 137.
6. Ibid.
7. Cummings and Abhik Roy, "Manifestations of Afrocentricity," 59–76.
8. Forrest, *Divine Days*, 98.
9. Smitherman, *Talking and Testifyin*, 147–48.
10. Gilyard, *Voices*, 82.
11. Hall, "What Is This 'Black'?" 27.
12. Forrest, *Divine Days*, 98–99.
13. Hurston, "Characteristics of Negro Expression," 80–83.
14. "Verb of Blackness" alludes to how Sterling Brown moves away from a static notion of Blackness as he represents Black characters with complexity and depth.
15. Forrest, *Divine Days*, 99.
16. Ibid., 99.
17. Ibid.
18. Ibid., 100.
19. Ibid., 103.
20. Ibid.
21. Ibid., 105.
22. Ibid., 106.
23. Ibid., 108–9
24. Ibid., 110, original ellipses.
25. Ibid., 117.
26. Pate, foreword, xii.
27. Ibid., 48.
28. Gilyard, *Liberation Memories*, 89.

29. Killens, *The Cotillion*, 20.
30. Ibid.
31. Killens, *Youngblood*, 210.
32. Marberry, *Cutting Up*, 3.
33. Killens, *Youngblood*, 215.
34. Ibid.
35. Presentation by Cornel West at Eso Won Books attended by the author, February 11, 2004.
36. Killens, *The Cotillion*, 21.
37. Jarratt, *Rereading the Sophists*, 61.
38. See Gilbert, "Shaping Identity."
39. Killens, *The Cotillion*, 22
40. Ibid., 2.
41. Ibid., 23.
42. Baugh, "Black Street Speech," 92.
43. Ibid.
44. Ibid.
45. Killens, *The Cotillion*, 22.
46. Killens, *Youngblood*, 215.
47. Killens, *The Cotillion*, 25.
48. Ibid.
49. Ibid., 33.
50. Ibid.
51. Gilyard, "Cultural Heroes," 89
52. Quoted in Le Batard, "Open Look," 22.

CHAPTER 4

1. Strange, "Barbershop Ritual," lines 1–2.
2. Douglas, *Purity and Danger*, 141.
3. Strange, "Barbershop Ritual," lines 1–3.
4. Ibid., lines 1–4.
5. Ibid.
6. Harris-Lacewell, *Barbershops, Bibles, and BET*, 23.
7. Strange, "Barbershop Ritual," lines 3–8.

8. Barnes, "Gentleman at the Barbershop," lines 22–26.

9. Ibid., lines 10–11.

10. Wright, "The Word at Work," 127.

11. Wright, "Barbershop."

12. Gilyard, "Barbershops and Afros," lines 1–4.

13. Ibid., lines 15–23.

14. Ibid., lines 1–14.

15. Barnes, "Gentleman in the Barber Shop," lines 1–11.

16. Jackson, "Mr. Pate's Barbershop," lines 10–17.

17. Ibid., lines 17–21.

18. Ibid., lines 22–37.

19. Young, "Eddie Priest's Barbershop," lines 17, 20–21.

20. Ibid., lines 28–31.

21. Ibid., lines 1–2.

22. Ibid., lines 1–2, 8–9, 13–14, 24–25.

23. Airriess, "Creating Vietnamese Landscapes," 228.

24. Ibid.

25. Summers, *Real Spaces*, 99.

26. For two of many scholars in a variety of disciplines who theorize the ideological and racial nature of spatiality, see Fields, *Architecture in Black*, and Berry and Henderson, *Geographical Identities*.

27. Gilyard, "Barbershops and Afros," line 24.

28. Strange, "Barbershop Ritual," stanza 3.

29. Ibid., stanza 4.

30. bomani, "Roots."

31. Gilyard, "Barbershops and Afros," lines 30–34,   32. Ibid., 15–19.

33. The term *nappy rhetoric* intersects with AAHHR in that, like nappy hair, the reception and production of such rhetoric are, rightly or wrongly, assigned a more organic connection to Blackness in that they disrupt or transgress White standards of decorum or propriety. However, nappy rhetoric circulates in the public sphere with far greater frequency.

34. Byrd and Tharps, *Hair Story*, chap. 2.

35. Coleman, "Among the Things," lines 1–16.

36. Young, "Eddie Priest's Barbershop," lines 28–34.

37. Sanders, *Afro-Modernist Aesthetics*, 9.
38. Ibid.
39. Brown, "Slim Hears 'The Call,'" stanza 1.
40. Ibid., stanzas 5 and 6.
41. Ibid., stanzas 6 and 7.
42. Raboteau, *Fire in the Bones*, 98.
43. Brown, "Slim Hears 'The Call,'" stanza 8.
44. Ibid., stanza 10.
45. Ibid, stanza 11.
46. Ibid., stanzas 22 and 23.
47. Ibid., stanza 25.
48. Ibid., stanza 27.
49. Ibid., stanza 32.
50. Ibid., stanza 39.
51. Ibid., stanza 40.
52. Ibid., stanzas 44–46.
53. Brown, "Slim in Hell," stanza 7.
54. Ibid., stanza 19.
55. Ibid., stanza 21.
56. Ibid., stanzas 25 and 26.
57. Ibid., stanzas 26 and 27.

CHAPTER 5

1. Aristotle, *Nicomachean Ethics*, 110–18.
2. Hughes, *Aristotle on Ethics*, 87.
3. Christian, "Race for Theory," 53.
4. Wallace, *Dark Designs*, 325.
5. Christian, "Race for Theory," 53.
6. Ibid., 51–52.
7. Everett, *Erasure*, 37.
8. Gilyard, *Voices*, 11.
9. Ibid., 43.
10. See Nathan McCall's *Makes Me Wanna Holler.* By neo-slave narrative, I do not mean in the technical sense as perceptively described by Bernard Bell

(*Contemporary African American Novel*). Here I refer to the popular prison trope as a crucible of self-reflection and redemption where incarcerated Black men often remake themselves and reenter society.

11. Gilyard, *Voices*, 20.
12. Ibid., 84.
13. Goldberg, *Threat of Race*, 43.
14. Gilyard, *Voices*, 81.
15. Ibid.
16. Gilbert, "Shaping Identity," 20–25.
17. *Head cut* is a vernacular reference to the function of many barbershops as places where African American males go to obtain knowledge.
18. Gilyard, *Voices*, 82.
19. Mackey, *Discrepant Engagement*, 20–21.
20. Gilyard, *Voices*, 83.
21. Ibid.
22. Aristotle, *Nicomachean Ethics*, 109–10.
23. Gilyard, *Voices*, 84.
24. Muschamp, *Visions of Utopia*, 34.
25. Ibid.
26. Harris-Lacewell, "Barbershops, Bibles," 23–24.
27. Gilyard, *Voices*, 82.
28. Smitherman, *Talkin and Testifyin*, 148.
29. Gilyard, *Voices*, 82.
30. Ibid.
31. Listen to Cornel West's *Street Knowledge*, track 9, for Michael Eric Dyson's rationale.
32. Gilyard, *Voices*, 84.
33. Ibid.
34. Elder, *Ceremonies*, 172, 173–74.
35. Ibid., 179.
36. Here of course I refer to Plato's denigration of the Sophists and his position that they made the worse seem the better case by disconnecting rhetoric from truth and ethics.
37. I refer to Keith Gilyard as "Keith" at points in the narrative that focus on him as

participant. "Gilyard" will be deployed to emphasize him as a scholar.

38. Elder, *Ceremonies*, 19.
39. Ibid., 179.
40. Ibid., 63.
41. Ibid., 63.
42. Ibid., 38.
43. Ibid., 164.
44. Ibid., 110.
45. Ibid., 172.
46. Ibid.
47. Ibid., 180.
48. Ibid.
49. Gilyard, *Voices*, 84.
50. While, the term *on the down low* has taken on connotations in relation to the hidden sexual behavior of heterosexual Black men, my use of the term makes reference to hidden talk.
51. Gilyard, *Voices*, 84.

CHAPTER 6

1. Story, *Barbershop*, scene 19.
2. Ibid.
3. Ibid.
4. Garrow, *Bearing the Cross*, 15–16.
5. Story, *Barbershop*, scene 19.
6. Ibid.
7. Indigenous South African women were given the denigrating designation "Hottentot" by Dutch colonizers. Of course, the term is linked to the public spectacle and display of Sarah Baartman at World's Fairs in London and Paris.
8. Story, *Barbershop*, scene 23.
9. Lee, *Bamboozled*, scene 24.
10. Story, *Barbershop*, scene 23.
11. Harris, *Summer Snow*, 47.
12. Story, *Barbershop*, scene 28. Dialogue is hereafter cited in the text from this scene until otherwise indicated.

13. In this context, *congolene* is a hair product associated with the Black male hairstyle called the *conk,* in which the hair is straightened, flattened, or slightly waved. The product could literally burn the scalp as an individual attempts to process out its natural texture.

14. Louis Armstrong, "(What Did I Do to Be So) Black and Blue" (1955), composed in 1929 by Thomas "Fats" Waller, with lyrics by Harry Brooks/Andy Razaf.

15. Bonner, "Black Professors," 3–11.

CHAPTER 7

1. Given the common origins of African American music and rhetoric already established by numerous scholars, Cruz's utility in exploring AAHHR should not be surprising.

2. Cruz, *Culture on the Margins,* 143.

3. Ibid., 48.

4. In the CD that accompanies Cornel West's *Hope on a Tightrope.*

5. Cruz, *Culture on the Margins,* 144.

6. Ibid., 61.

7. Samuels, "Re-inventing the Modern University."

8. Brummett and Bowers, "Subject Positions," 125.

9. Clearly, Whiteness is a recent historical creation. Greeks and Romans did not consider themselves White. However, it is also abundantly clear that Western notions of European and White superiority have been scaffolding for constructions of White supremacy. Therefore, how Greek or Roman rhetoricians constructed themselves (around nation, country, or city-state) is irrelevant to this discussion and ignores how White superiority and privilege function.

10. Colomina, "Excerpts," 314–20.

11. Reynolds, *Geographies of Writing,* 3.

12. Giroux, *Border Crossings,* 4–5.

13. Bell, *Contemporary African American Novel,* 167.

14. Ibid., 168.

15. Wright, *Native Son,* 407.

16. Ibid., 406.

17. Deleuze and Guattari, *A Thousand Plateaus,* 79–85.

18. Alexander, *Black Interior,* x.

19. Wright, *Native Son* 382–406.

20. Giroux, *Public Spaces, Private Lives,* 129.

21. West, *Democracy Matters,* 68.

CHAPTER 8

1. Miller, *Cultural Citizenship,* 138.

2. Kanye West, *Graduation,* track 6.

3. Ibid.

4. Hendricks, "A More Perfect (High-Tech) Lynching," 160; and Van Vector, "Tiger Woods."

5. Hendricks, "A More Perfect (High-Tech) Lynching," 160.

6. Joy James, personal communication.

7. Obama, "A More Perfect Union," 238.

8. Hendricks, "A More Perfect (High-Tech) Lynching: Obama, the Press, and Jeremiah Wright." 132–41.

9. Howard-Pitney, *Afro-American Jeremiad,* 8.

10. Ibid.

11. Ibid.

12. Obama, "A More Perfect Union," 242.

13. Ibid., 240.

14. Ibid., 244–45.

Bibliography

Airriess, Christopher A. "Creating Vietnamese Landscapes and Place in New Orleans." In *Geographical Identities of Ethnic America: Race, Space, and Place*, ed. Kate A. Berry and Martha L. Henderson, 228–54. Reno: University of Nevada Press, 2002.

Alexander, Elizabeth. *The Black Interior*. Minneapolis: Grawolf Press, 2004.

Alkebulan, Adisa A, "The Spiritual Essence of African American Rhetoric." In *Understanding African American Rhetoric: Classical Origins to Contemporary Innovations*, ed. Ronald L. Jackson II and Elaine B. Richardson, 23–40. New York: Routledge, 2003.

Aristotle. *Nicomachean Ethics*, ed. Roger Crisp. Cambridge: Cambridge University Press, 2000.

Asante, Molefi K. *The Afrocentric Idea*. Rev. and expanded ed. Philadelphia: Temple University Press, 1997.

Barnes, S. Brandi. "Gentleman in the Barber Shop." In *Beyond the Frontier: African-American Poetry for the 21st Century*, ed. E. Ethelbert Miller, 87. Baltimore, MD: Black Classic, 2002.

Baugh, John. "Black Street Speech: Its History, Structure and Survival." In *African*

American Communication & Identities: Essential Readings, ed. Ronald L. Jackson II, 89–101. Thousand Oaks, CA: Sage, 2004.

Belafonte, Harry. "Harry Belafonte on Bush, Iraq, Hurricane Katrina and Having His Conversations with Martin Luther King Wiretapped by the FBI." Interview by Amy Goodman. *Democracy Now!* Daily TV/radio news program, January 30, 2006. http://www.democracynow.org/about/staff.

Bell, Bernard W. *The Contemporary African American Novel: Its Folks Roots and Modern Literary.* Amherst: University of Massachusetts Press, 2004.

Berlin, Ira, Marc Favreau, and Steven F. Miller, eds. *Remembering Slavery: African Americans Talk about Their Personal Experiences of Slavery and Emancipation.* New York: New Press, 1998.

Berlin, James. *Rhetoric and Reality: Writing Instruction in American Colleges, 1900–1985.* Studies in Writing and Rhetoric series. Carbondale: Southern Illinois University Press, 1987.

Berry, Kate A., and Martha L. Henderson, eds. *Geographical Identities of Ethnic America: Race, Space, and Place.* Reno: University of Nevada Press, 2001.

bomani, mawiyah kai el-jamah. "Roots." In *Beyond the Frontier: African-American Poetry for the 21st Century,* ed. E. Ethelbert Miller, 88. Baltimore, MD: Black Classic, 2002.

Bonner, Fred A., II. "Black Professors: On Track but Out of the Loop." *Chronicle of Higher Education Review* 50, no. 4 (2004): B11.

BrainyQuote. "Muhammad Ali." www.brainyquote.com/quotes/authors/m/muhammad_ali.html (accessed 10 March 2003).

Brown, Sterling. "Slim Hears 'The Call'" (ca. 1932). In *The Collected Poems of Sterling A. Brown,* ed. Michael S. Harper, 83–88. Evanston, IL: Northwestern University Press, 1980.

———. "Slim in Hell" (ca. 1930–33). In *The Collected Poems of Sterling A. Brown,* ed. Michael S. Harper, 89–92. Evanston: Northwestern University Press, 1980.

Brown, Wendy. "American Nightmare: Neoliberalism, Neoconservatism, and De-democratization." *Political Theory* 34, no. 6 (2006): 690–714.

Brummett, Barry, and Detine L. Bower. "Subject Positions as a Site of Rhetorical Struggle: Representing African Americans." In *At the Intersection: Cultural Studies and Rhetorical Studies,* ed. Thomas Rosteck, 117–36. Revisioning Rhetoric series. New York: Guilford, 1999.

Burke, Kenneth. *Language as Symbolic Action: Essays on Life, Literature, and Method.* Berkeley: University of California Press, 1966.

Butler, Judith. *Frames of War: When Is Life Grievable?* London: Verso, 2009.

Byrd, Ayana D., and Lori L. Tharps. *Hair Story: Untangling the Roots of Black Hair in America.* New York: St. Martin's, 2001.

Calmore, John O. "Reasonable and Unreasonable Suspects: The Cultural Construction of the Anonymous Black Man in Public Space (Here Be Dragons)." In *Progressive Black Masculinities,* ed. Athena D. Mutua, 137–53. New York: Routledge, 2006.

Childers, Joseph, and Gary Henzti, eds. *The Columbia Dictionary of Modern Literary and Cultural Criticism.* New York: Columbia University Press, 1995.

Christian, Barbara. "The Race for Theory" (1987). In *The Nature and Context of Minority Discourse,* ed. Abdul R. JanMohamed and David Lloyd, 37–49. New York: Oxford University Press, 1991.

Coleman, Willie M. "Among the Things That Use to Be" (1979). In *Home Girls: A Black Feminist Anthology,* ed. Barbara Smith, 221–22. Latham, NY: Kitchen Table--Women of Color Press, 1983.

Colomina, Beatriz, "Excerpts from 'The Split Wall: Domestic Voyeurism.'" In *Gender Space Architecture: An Interdisciplinary Introduction,* ed. Jane Rendell, Barbara Penner, and Iain Borden, 314–20. New York: Routledge, 2000.

Cummings, Melbourne S., and Abhik Roy. "Manifestations of Afrocentricity in Rap Music." *Howard Journal of Communications* 13, no. 1 (2002): 59–76.

Cruz, Jon. *Culture on the Margins: The Black Spiritual and the Rise of American Cultural Interpretation.* Princeton, NJ: Princeton University Press, 1999.

Dawson, Michael C. "A Black Counterpublic? Economic Earthquakes, Racial Agenda(s), and Black Politics." In *The Black Public Sphere: A Public Culture Book,* ed. Black Public Sphere Collective, 199–228. Chicago: University of Chicago Press, 1995.

Delaney, David. *Race, Place, and the Law: 1836–1948.* Austin: University of Texas Press, 1998.

Deleuze, Gilles, and Felix Guattari. *A Thousand Plateaus: Capitalism and Schizophrenia,* trans. and foreword by Brian Massumi. Minneapolis: University of Minnesota Press, 1987.

de Moraes, Lisa. "Kanye West's Torrent of Criticism, Live on NBC." TV Column. *Washington Post,* September 3, 2005. www.washingtonpost.com/wp-dyn/content/article/2005/09/03/AR2005090300165.html.

Douglas, Mary. *Purity and Danger: An Analysis of the Concepts of Pollution and Taboo.* New York: Praeger, 1966.

Dunbar, Paul Laurence. "An Ante-Bellum Sermon" (1896). In *The Vintage Book of African American Poetry: 200 Years of Vision, Struggle, Power, Beauty, and Triumph from 50 Outstanding Poets,* ed. Michael S. Harper and Anthony Walton, 81–82. New York: Vintage, 2000.

Ede, Lisa, and Andrea Lunsford. "Audience Addressed/Audience Invoked: The Role of Audience in Composition Theory and Pedagogy." *College Composition and Communication* 35, no. 2 (1984): 155–72.

Elder, Lonne, III. *Ceremonies in Dark Old Men: A Play.* New York: Farrar, Straus and Giroux, 1969.

Ellison, Ralph. *Invisible Man,* volume 1952, part 2. 2nd ed. 1952; repr., New York: Random House, 1995.

Everett, Percival. *Erasure.* New York: Hyperion, 2001.

Fields, Darell Wayne. *Architecture in Black.* New York: Continuum International, 2000.

Flyvberg, Brent. *Making Social Science Matter: Why Social Inquiry Fails and How It Can Succeed Again.* Cambridge: Cambridge University Press, 2001.

Forman, Murray. *The Hood Comes First: Race, Space, and Place in Rap and Hip-hop.* Middletown, CT: Wesleyan University Press, 2002.

Forrest, Leon. *Divine Days.* New York: W. W. Norton, 1993.

Foucault, Michel. *Fearless Speech,* ed. Joseph Pearson. New York: Semiotext(e), 2001.

Fraser, Nancy. "Rethinking the Public Sphere: A Contribution to the Critique of Actually Existing Democracy." *Social Text* 25–26 (1990): 56–90.

Garrow, David J. *Bearing the Cross: Martin Luther King, Jr., and the Southern Christian Leadership Conference.* New York: William Morrow, 1986.

Gilbert, Derrick. 1994. "Shaping Identity at Cooke's Barbershop." Unpublished master's thesis, University of California–Los Angeles.

Gilmore, Ruthie W. *Golden Gulag: Prisons, Surplus, Crisis, and Opposition in Globalizing California.* Berkeley: University of California Press, 2007.

Gilyard, Keith. "Barbershops and Afros." In *American 40: Poems,* 24–25. New York: Eclipse III, 1993.

———. "Cultural Heroes." In *Liberation Memories: The Rhetoric and Poetics of John Oliver Killens,* 79–94. African American Life Series. Detroit: Wayne State University Press, 2003.

———. *Liberation Memories: The Rhetoric and Poetics of John Oliver Killens.* African American Life Series. Detroit: Wayne State University Press, 2003.

———. *Voices of the Self: A Study of Language Competence.* Detroit: Wayne State University Press, 1991.

Giroux, Henry A. *Border Crossings: Cultural Workers and the Politics of Education.* New York: Routledge, 1991.

———. "Critical Theory and Rationality in Citizenship Education." *Curriculum Inquiry* 10, no. 4 (1980): 329–66.

———. *Public Spaces, Private Lives: Democracy Beyond 9/11.* Lanham, MD: Rowman and Littlefield, 2002

Goldberg, David Theo. *The Threat of Race: Reflections on Racial Neoliberalism.* Blackwell Manifestos series. Ames, IA: Wiley-Blackwell, 2008.

Graham, Lawrence Otis. *Our Kind of People: Inside America's Black Upper Class.* Harper Perennial series. New York: HarperCollins, 1999.

Hall, Stuart. "What Is This 'Black' in Black Popular Culture?" In *Black Popular Culture: A Project by Michelle Wallace,* ed. Gina Dent, 21–33. Discussions in Contemporary Culture series. Seattle: Bay, 1992.

Hanchard, Michael. *Party/Politics: Culture, Community and Agency in Black Political Thought.* Transgressing Boundaries: Studies in Black Politics and Black Communities series. New York: Oxford University Press, 2006.

Hardt, Michael, and Antonio Negri. *commonWealth.* Cambridge, MA: Belknap Press of Harvard University Press, 2009.

Harris, Trudier. "Beautician." In *The Oxford Companion to African American Literature,* ed. William L. Andrews, Francis Smith Foster, and Trudier Harris, 54–55. New York: Oxford University Press, 1997.

———. *Summer Snow: Reflections from a Daughter of the South.* New York: Beacon, 2003.

Harris-Lacewell, Melissa Victoria. *Barbershops, Bibles, and BET: Everyday Talk and Black Political Thought.* Princeton, NJ: Princeton University Press, 2004.

Hartman, Saidiya V. *Scenes of Subjection: Terror, Slavery, and Self-Making in Nineteenth-Century America.* New York: Oxford University Press, 1997.

Harvey, David. *Cosmopolitanism and the Geographics of Freedom.* New York: Columbia University Press, 2009.

Hayden, Dolores. *The Power of Place: Urban Landscapes as Public History.* Cambridge,

MA: MIT Press, 1997.

Hendricks, Obery M., Jr. "A More Perfect (High-Tech) Lynching: Obama, the Press, and Jeremiah Wright." In *The Speech: Race and Barack Obama's "A More Perfect Union,"* ed. T. Denean Sharpley-Whiting, 155–83. New York: Bloomsbury USA, 2009.

hooks, bell. "Straightening Our Hair." In *Tenderheaded: A Comb-Bending Collection of Hair Stories,* ed. Pamela Johnson and Juliette Harris, 111–15. New York: Pocket, 2001.

Howard-Pitney, David. *The Afro-American Jeremiad: Appeals for Justice in America.* Philadelphia: Temple University Press, 1990.

Hughes, Gerard J. *Routledge Philosophy Guidebook to Aristotle on Ethics.* Routledge Philosophy Guide Books series. New York: Routledge, 2001.

Hurston, Zora Neale. "Characteristics of Negro Expression." In *Within the Circle: An Anthology of African American Literary Criticism from the Harlem Renaissance to the Present,* ed. Angelyn Mitchell, 79–96. Durham, NC: Duke University Press, 1994.

Huxley, Margo. "Geographies of Governmentality." In *Space, Knowledge and Power: Foucault and Geography,* ed. Jeremy W. Crampton and Stuart Elden, 185–204. Aldershot, UK: Ashgate, 2007.

Iton, Richard. *In Search of the Black Fantastic: Politics and Popular Culture in the Post–Civil Rights Era.* Transgressing Boundaries series. New York: Oxford University Press, 2008.

Jackson, Major. "Mr. Pate's Barbershop." In *Leaving Saturn,* 20–21. Cave Canem Poetry Prize series. Athens: University of Georgia Press, 2002.

Jackson, Ronald L., and Elaine B. Richardson. *Understanding African American Rhetoric: Classical Origins to Contemporary Innovations.* New York: Routledge, 2003.

Jarratt, Susan. *Rereading the Sophists: Classical Rhetoric Refigured.* Carbondale: Southern Illinois University Press, 1991.

Kelley, Norman. *The Head Negro in Charge Syndrome: The Dead End of Black Politics.* New York: Nation, 2004.

Killens, John O. *The Cotillion (or One Good Bull Is Half the Herd).* New York: Trident, 1971.

———. *Youngblood.* Foreword by Addison Gayle. Athens: University of Georgia Press, 1982.

Le Batard, Dan. "Open Look." *ESPN the Magazine,* June 23, 2003.

Lefebvre, Henri. *The Production of Space,* trans. Donald Nicholson-Smith. Hoboken, NJ: Wiley-Blackwell, 1992.

Lee, Spike, dir. *Bamboozled.* DVD. Burbank, CA: New Line Cinema, 2000; 1 hr., 16 min.

———. *Joe's Bed-Stuy Barbershop.* VHS. Brooklyn, NY: Icarus Films, 1983; 1 hr.

———. *Malcolm X.* DVD. Burbank, CA: Warner Home Video, 1992; 4 hr., 54 min.

Levine, Lawrence W. *Black Culture and Black Consciousness: Afro-American Folk Thought from Slavery to Freedom.* London: Oxford University Press, 1997.

Loos, Adolf. "Ornament and Crime" (1908). In *Crime and Ornament: The Arts and Popular Culture in the Shadow of Adolf Loos,* ed. Bernie Miller and Melony Ward, 29–39. Toronto: YYZ, 2002.

Mackey, Nathaniel. *Discrepant Engagement: Dissonance, Cross-culturality and Experimental Writing.* Cambridge Studies in American Literature and Culture Series 71. Tuscaloosa: University of Alabama Press, 1993.

Mailloux, Steven. *Rhetorical Power.* Ithaca, NY: Cornell University Press, 1989.

Marberry, Craig. *Cuttin' Up: Wit and Wisdom from Black Barber Shops.* New York: Doubleday, 2005, 3.

Massey, Doreen B. *Space and Gender.* Minneapolis: University of Minnesota Press, 1994.

McCall, Nathan, with Lourdes March. *Makes Me Wanna Holler: A Young Black Man in America.* New York: Random House, 1995.

Miller, Toby. *Cultural Citizenship: Cosmopolitanism, Consumerism, and Television in a Neoliberal Age.* Philadelphia: Temple University Press, 2006.

Morrison, Toni. *Beloved.* New York: Penguin, 1987, 87–88.

Muhammad, Askia, with Debra Morris, prod. "Conversations in a Black Barbershop." Broadcast live from King Library, Miami University, Oxford, Ohio, April 11, 2003. Phoenix, AZ: Soundprint.

Murphy, Melvin. *Barbershop Talk: The Other Side of Black Men.* Merrifield, VA: Melvin Murphy, 1998.

Neal, Mark Anthony. *What the Music Said: Black Popular Music and Black Public Culture.* London: Routledge, 1998.

Obama, Barack. "A More Perfect Union." In *The Speech: Race and Barack Obama's "A More Perfect Union,"* ed. T. Denean Sharpley-Whiting, 237–52. New York: Bloomsbury, 2009.

Pate, Alexs D. Foreword to *The Cotillion; or, One Good Bull Is Half the Herd,* by John

Oliver Killens, x–xxi. Black Arts Movement Series. Minneapolis, MN: Coffee House, 2002.

Pough, Gwendolyn D. *Check It while I Wreck It: Black Womanhood, Hip-hop Culture, and the Public Sphere.* Boston: Northeastern University Press, 2004.

Raboteau, Albert J. *A Fire in the Bones: Reflections on African-American Religious History.* Boston: Beacon, 1995.

Rank, Mark R., and Thomas A. Hirschl. "Estimating the Risk of Food Stamp Use and Impoverishment during Childhood." *Archives of Pediatrics & Adolescent Medicine* 163 (2009): 994–99.

Rediker, Marcus. *The Slave Ship: A Human History.* New York: Viking, 2007.

Reynolds, Nedra. *Geographies of Writing: Inhabiting Places and Encountering Difference.* Carbondale: Southern Illinois University Press, 2003.

Ross, Brian, and Rehab El-Buri. "Obama's Pastor: God Damn America, U.S. to Blame for 9/11—Obama's Pastor, Rev. Jeremiah Wright, Has a History of What Even Obama's Campaign Aides Say Is 'Inflammatory Rhetoric.'" *Blotter from Brian Ross,* ABC News, March 13, 2008. abcnews.go.com/blotter/story?id=4443788.

Samuels, Robert. "Re-inventing the Modern University with WAC: Postmodern Composition as Cultural and Intellectual History." *Across the Disciplines* 1 (2004). http://wac.colostate.edu/atd/articles/samuels2004.cfm.

Sanders, Mark A. *Afro-Modernist Aesthetics and the Poetry of Sterling A. Brown.* Athens: University of Chicago Press, 1999.

Scott, James C. *Domination and the Arts of Resistance: Hidden Transcripts.* New Haven, CT: Yale University Press, 1990.

Sharpley-Whiting, T. Denean, ed. *The Speech: Race and Barack Obama's "A More Perfect Union."* New York: Bloomsbury, 2009.

Smitherman, Geneva. *Talking and Testifyin: The Language of Black America.* Detroit: Wayne State University Press, 1977.

Spillers, Hortense J. "Mama's Baby, Papa's Maybe: An American Grammar Book." In *Black, White, and in Color: Essays on American Literature and Culture,* 203–29. Chicago: University of Chicago Press, 2003.

Story, Tim, dir. *Barbershop.* DVD. Santa Monica, CA: MGM, 2002; 1 hr., 42 min.

Strange, Sharan. "Barbershop Ritual." In *In the Tradition: An Anthology of Young Black Writers,* ed. Kevin Powell and Ras Baraka, 286. New York: Harlem River, 1992.

Summers, David. *Real Spaces: World Art History and the Rise of Western Modernism.*

New York: Phaidon, 2003.

Thompson, Robert Farris. *Flash of the Spirit: African & Afro-American Art & Philosophy.* 1884; repr., New York: Random House, 2010. Kindle edition.

Van Vector, Dick. "Tiger Woods and Political Neutrality: Does the Financial Advantage of Remaining Politically Uncontroversial Justify Tiger's Silence?" *Associated Content,* May 31, 2007. www.associatedcontent.com/article/257276/tiger_woods_and_political_neutrality.html?cat=49.

Wallace, Maurice O. *Constructing the Black Masculine: Identity and Ideality in African American Men's Literature and Culture, 1775–1995.* John Hope Franklin Center Book series. Durham, NC: Duke University Press, 2002.

Wallace, Michelle. *Dark Designs and Visual Culture.* Durham, NC: Duke University Press, 2004.

West, Cornel. *Democracy Matters: Winning the Fight against Imperialism.* New York: Penguin, 2004.

———. *Hope on a Tightrope: Words and Wisdom.* Carlsbad, CA: Hay House, 2008.

———. *Street Knowledge.* 2 Audio CDs. Rancho Murietta, CA: Roc Diamond Records, 2004. ASIN: B000093NQD.

West, Kanye. *The College Dropout.* New York: Roc-A-Fella Records, 2004. ASIN: B0001AP12G.

———. *Graduation.* New York: Roc-A-Fella Records, 1997. ASIN: B000FUF80M.

Wiley, Ralph. *Why Black People Tend to Shout: Cold Facts and Wry Views from a Black Man's World.* New York: Penguin, 1992.

Williams, Heather Andrea. *Self-Taught: African American Education in Slavery and Freedom.* John Hope Franklin Series in African American History and Culture. Chapel Hill, NC: University of North Carolina Press, 2005.

Woodruff, Billie, dir. *Beauty Shop.* DVD. Santa Monica, CA: MGM Studios, 2005; 1 hr., 45 min.

Wright, Richard. "Barbershop" (1960). In *Haiku: This Other World,* ed. Richard Wright, Y. Hakintani, and Robert Tenner, 113 (haiku 450). Introduction by Julia Wright. New York: Knopf, 1998.

———. *Native Son.* Perennial Classics series. 1940; repr., New York: Harper Perennial, 1998.

Wright, Richard L. "The Word at Work: Ideological and Epistemological Dynamics in African American Rhetoric." In *Understanding African American Rhetoric:*

Classical Origins to Contemporary Innovations, 85–98. New York: Routledge, 2003.

Young, Kevin. "Eddie Priest's Barbershop & Notary: Closed Mondays" (1995). In *Spirit and Flame: An Anthology of Contemporary African American Poetry*, ed. Keith Gilyard, 303–4. Syracuse: Syracuse University Press, 1997.

Zwick, Edward, dir. *My Big Fat Greek Wedding*. DVD. Mew York: HBO Video, 2003; 2 hr., 10 min.

FURTHER READING

Barkley, Charles. *Who's Afraid of a Large Black Man?* New York: Penguin, 2005.

Berlin, Ira. *Many Thousands Gone: The First Two Centuries of Slavery in North America.* Cambridge, MA: Belknap, 1998.

Bernard-Donals, Michael, and Richard R. Glejzer, eds. *Rhetoric in an Antifoundational World: Language, Culture, and Pedagogy.* New Haven, CT: Yale University Press, 1998.

Brenner, Frederick. "The Jewish Journey: Frederic Brenner's Photographic Odyssey." Exhibition, Brooklyn Museum of Art, October 3, 2003–January 11, 2004.

Brooks, Sonya. "Middle Passage," "Untitled," and "Grandma Talk." In *In the Tradition: An Anthology of Young Black Writers*, ed. Kevin Powell and Ras Baraka, 118, 119, 120. New York: Harlem River, 1992.

Bruns, Gerald. "The Hermeneutical Anarchist: *Phronesis*, Rhetoric, and the Experience of Art." In *Gadamer's Century: Essays in Honor of Hans-Georg Gadamer*, ed. Jeff Malpas, Ulrich Arnswald, and Jens Kertscher, 45–76. Cambridge, MA: MIT Press, 2002.

Cowan, Tynes. "The Slave in the Swamp: Affects of Uncultivated Regions on Plantation Life." In *Keep Your Head to the Sky: Interpreting African American Home Ground*, ed. Grey Gundaker, 193–208. Charlottesville: University Press of Virginia, 1998.

Ellison, Ralph. *Shadow and Act*. New York: Random House, 1964.

Foner, Phillip S., and Robert James Branham, eds. *Lift Every Voice: African American Oratory—1767–1900*. Montgomery: University of Alabama Press, 1998.

Foucault, Michel. *The Essential Works of Foucault, 1954–1984*. Vol. 3, *Power*, ed. James D. Faubion. New York: New Press, 2001.

Gates, Henry L. *The Signifying Monkey: A Theory of African-American Literary Criticism.* New York: Oxford University Press, 1989.

Gatewood, Willard B. *Aristocrats of Color: The Black Elite, 1880–1920*. Bloomington: Indiana University Press, 1993.

Gilyard, Keith, and Vorris Nunley, eds. *Rhetoric and Ethnicity*. CrossCurrents Series. Portsmouth, NH: Boynton/Cook, 2004.

Glenn, Cheryl. *Unspoken: A Rhetoric of Silence*. Carbondale: Southern Illinois University Press, 2004.

Gordon-Hazzard, Katrina. *Jookin': The Rise of Social Dance Formations in African-American Culture*. Philadelphia: Temple University Press, 1990.

Harris, Juliette, and Pamela Johnson. "Ms. Strand Calls a Press Conference." In *Tenderheaded: A Comb-Bending Collection of Hair Stories*, ed. Juliette Harris and Pamela Johnson, xv–xi. New York: Pocket, 2001.

Harris, Trudier. "Barbers." In *The Oxford Companion to African American Literature*, ed. William L. Andrews, Francis Smith Foster, and Trudier Harris, 51–52. New York: Oxford University Press, 1997.

———. "The Barbershop in African American Literature." *Black American Literature Forum* 13, no. 3 (1979): 112–18.

Henderson, Stephen. *Understanding the New Black Poetry: Black Music and Black Speech as Poetic References*. New York: William Morrow, 1973.

Higginbotham, Evelyn B. *Righteous Discontent: The Women's Movement in the Black Baptist Church, 1880–1920*. Cambridge, MA: Harvard University Press, 1993.

Hughes Wright, Roberta, and Wilbur B. Hughes III. *Lay Down Body: Living History in African American Cemeteries*. Detroit: Visible Ink, 1996.

Hurston, Zora Neale. *Mules and Men*. New York: HarperCollins, 1990.

Kelley, Robin D. G. *Race Rebels: Culture, Politics, and the Black Working Class*. New York: Free Press, 1996.

Lyons, Scott R. "Rhetorical Sovereignty: What Do American Indians Want from Writing." *Composition and Communication* 51, no. 3 (2000): 447–68.

Ramsey, Guthrie P., Jr. *Race Music: Black Cultures from Bebop to Hip-hop*. Music of the African Diaspora series. Berkeley: University of California Press, 2003.

Rothstein, Edward, Herbert Muschamp, and Martin E. Marty. *Visions of Utopia*. New York: Oxford University Press, 2004.

Smitherman, Geneva. "Testifyin, Sermonizin, and Signifyin: Anita Hill, Clarence Thomas, and the African American Verbal Tradition." In *Talkin That Talk: Language, Culture and Education in African America*, 251–67. London: Routledge, 2000.

Stern, Richard. "That Same Pain, That Same Pleasure: An Interview with Ralph Ellison." In *Black Voices: An Anthology of African-American Literature,* ed. Abraham Chapman, 645–59. Chicago: Signet Classics, 2001.

Sundquist, Eric J. *To Wake the Nations: Race in the Making of American Literature.* Cambridge, MA: Belknap, 1993.

Walker, Daniel E. *No More: No More: Slavery and Cultural Resistance in Havana and New Orleans.* Minneapolis: University of Minnesota Press, 2004.

West, Cornel. *Restoring Hope: Conversations on the Future of Black America,* ed. Kelvin S. Sealey. Boston: Beacon, 1997.

Wilbon, Michael. *Pardon the Interruption.* ESPN, 23 October 2003.

Williams, Juan, and Quinton Dixie. *This Far by Faith: Stories from the African American Religious Experience.* New York: William Morrow, 2003.

Winant, Howard. *The New Politics of Race: Globalism, Difference, Justice.* Minnesota: University of Minneapolis, 2004.

Index

African American hush harbor rhetoric (AAHHR): public podium–auction block rhetoric, contrasted to, 5–6, 27, 169–70, 171–73; Black dissonance in, 153; and Black neoliberalism, 168; commodification of, 14, 170; consumption of, 14; as cultural rhetoric, 37; as dangerous, 13, 46, 70; defined, 3–4, 23–25, 26, 37; entry into public sphere of, 11, 13, 46, 66, 163–65; and epistemology, 9, 10, 28, 72, 84, 151, 153; exclusion of, 13; as field of intelligibility, 18; in Gilyard, 112; and globalization, 105; hermeneutics of, 71, 146; hidden transcripts of, 2, 7, 26, 94, 111, 115; improvisation in, 62; and *kairos*, 81; and knowledge, African American, 6, 30, 79, 114, 130, 152, 153, 165; limits of, 103; mascons of 126, 131; and nappy rhetoric, 94, 95, 149, 184n. 33; *nommo* in, 62, 64, 72–73, 147; and Obama, 2–3; and ontology, 7, 162; and *parrhesia* 46, 65, 121, 171; as pedagogy, 113, 152; and performativity, 140–42; as philosophy, 108, 117, 129; *phronesis* in, 81, 102, 103; *phronimos* in, 118, 129; as practical art, 162–63; as profane, 72, 84, 121; and public sphere, 8, 68; racism in, 71; and rationalities, African American, 14,

173; and *parrhesia*, 121; pedagogy of, 163; pool halls as, 5, 55, 99, 163; as practiced spatialities, 43; as refuge, 78; rationalities of, 13; rhetorical freedom in, 72, 116, 138; and slavery, 2–3, 18–19, 23–24, 25–29, 62; violence in, 55. *See also*, AAHH; AAHHR; barbershops; slavery

Huxley, Margo, 11–12

identity politics, 48, 110

improvisation: African American, 4; and AAHHR, 62; in *Divine Days*, 61; and jazz, 59, 60, 112, 126; and subjectivity, African American, 59

In Search of the Black Fantastic (Iton), 16

Invisible Man (Ellison), 3, 42, 117, 124

Iton, Richard, 16

Jackson, Major, 86–88, 130

James, Joy, 171

jazz: and auction block–public podium, rhetoric, 3; epistemology, 126; and *game*, 112–13; and improvisation, 59, 60, 112, 126; and *nommo*, 55; rhetoric of, 135

jeremiads, American, 170, 171, 174

Jet, 90–91, 141; and Blackness, 91

Joe's Bed-Stuy Barbershop, 147

Johnson, Robert (BET founder), 11

Jolson, Al, 142

jook joints (juke joints): as Black space, 3; as hush harbors, 55, 99

Jordan, Michael, 11, 167, 168, 169–70

kairos, 4, 81, 99

Killens, John Oliver, 4, 27, 48, 51, 62–63

King, Coretta Scott, 15

King, Martin Luther, Jr., 4, 15, 134, 135, 145; and public sphere rhetoric, 73

King, Rodney, 146

knowledge, African American, 4–6, 9, 15–16, 30, 31, 34, 47, 71; and AAHHR, 6, 30, 79, 114, 130, 152, 153, 165; domestication of, 164. *See also* AAHH; AAHHR; barbershops

Lee, Spike, 142, 147

Lefebvre, Henri, 40

Leff, Michael, 6

Levine, Lawrence, 25, 27

lifeworlds: Black, 54; Hanchard on, 37–38; as term, 38

Loos, Adolf, 41–42

Lubiano, Wahneema, 118

Mackey, Nathaniel, 116

Mailloux, Steven, 37

Malcolm X, 73–74, 134, 146–50, 170–71

Malcolm X (film), 146–50; barbershops in, 146; *phronesis* in, 149; White privilege in, 150

Marberry, Craig, 66

Marx, Karl, 117

mascons, 56, 57, 60–62; of AAHHR, 126, 131; as Black commonplaces, 47; and *nommo*, 61

spaces of, 39, 42. *See also* AAHH
slave ships, 19, 24, 39; hush harbors, precursor to, 24
Slave Ship, The: A Human History (Rediker), 24
Slim cycle, the (Brown), 58, 77, 98, 99–105
"Slim Hears 'The Call'" (Brown), 77, 98
Smith, Arthur (later Molefi Kete Asante), 44–45
Smitherman, Geneva, 8, 56, 121; on narrative sequencing, 119; on *parrhesia*, 121
social death, 24; resistance to, 26
soul talk, 67–68
space: and African Americans, 2–3, 19, 43, 112; and Blackness, 19–20, 43; construction of, 156; and hegemony, 41, 45; as ideological, 157; and history, African American, 39; and literary analysis, 157; place, distinct from, 43; and race, 39, 42–43; and rhetoric, African American, 38, 42–43; and subjectivity, 157; and Whiteness, 65. *See also* AAHH; barbershops; public sphere; spatiality; spatiality, Black
spatiality: and subjectivity, 43; as social product, 40; as term, 40, 181n. 19. *See also* AAHH; public sphere; space; spatiality, Black
spatiality, Black, 34–44, 42, 108, 112, 155–56, 181n. 19; as extra-rational, 42; practiced, 43; and rhetoric, 108,

155–56; and subjectivity, 155. *See also* AAHH; barbershops; public sphere; space; spatiality
Spillers, Hortense, 19
Stewart, Maria W., 3–4
Strange, Sharan, 75, 76
subjectivity, 11–12, 43; and space, 157. *See also* subjectivity, African American
subjectivity, African American, 1, 2, 7, 9, 36–37, 76, 66, 83, 115, 146; and AAHH, 12, 13, 66; and AAHHR, 15, 30, 69, 95; and barbershops, 78, 115; and Black hair, 92–96; as challenge to hegemony, 24; and improvisation, 59; and *parrhesia*, 69; "undomesticated," 93; in *Voices of the Self*, 111. *See also* subjectivity
Summers, David, 90

terministic screens, 30–31, 34, 36, 46–47, 162, 170; and *nommo*, 52; and *nomos*, 68
tricksters, African American, 52, 56, 57, 61–62, 99

Uncle Tom, 69–70

Voices of the Self (Gilyard), 107, 110–23, 128, 130–31, 186n. 37; as bildungsroman, 111; Black male subjectivity in, 111; pedagogy in, 111, 130; *phronesis* in, 111, 122; *phronimos* in, 117, 122